The French in Germany
1945-1949

STANFORD STUDIES IN HISTORY, ECONOMICS,
AND POLITICAL SCIENCE, XXIII

The French in Germany
1945-1949

F. ROY WILLIS

STANFORD UNIVERSITY PRESS
STANFORD, CALIFORNIA
1962

STANFORD UNIVERSITY PRESS
STANFORD, CALIFORNIA

© 1962 BY THE BOARD OF TRUSTEES OF THE
LELAND STANFORD JUNIOR UNIVERSITY

Library of Congress Catalog Card Number: 61-16886

PRINTED IN THE UNITED STATES OF AMERICA

PUBLISHED WITH THE ASSISTANCE OF THE
FORD FOUNDATION

TO

MY MOTHER AND FATHER

Preface

THE history of the French zone has, for the most part, been written by its critics. Any nation that undergoes occupation by the military forces of an alien power is bound to feel that it is being exploited for the benefit of that power, and the natural resentment of the Germans at finding themselves at the mercy of their conquerors was magnified by the economic hardship produced by the unparalleled destruction of the Second World War. All the criticism was not, however, restricted to the occupied. The military government of the French zone was, indeed, more sharply criticized by groups in France than by the Germans themselves. Occupation policy in the French zone was in many ways dominated by France's own internal conflicts. France, which had received a moral as well as a physical wound in the defeat of 1940 and the years of German occupation, was split many ways—between the Vichy collaborators and the Resistance fighters, between the conservatives of the regular army and the radicals of the underground groups, between the supporters of the capitalist structure of the French economy and those who wished to renovate it along collectivist lines. These internal divisions which plagued French society were also present in the government of the zone—and they have done much to hinder the establishment of an unimpassioned judgment of French policy in Germany.

It is particularly useful at this time to consider the effect of French policy on its zone of Germany, in view of the growing *rapprochement* of these two traditional enemies. One ironic conclusion emerging from this study is that the occupation, which seemed to many critics to be hopelessly embittering relations between France and Germany, did in fact prepare the way for the closer understanding that followed in the nineteen-fifties.

This study attempts not only to assess the truth in the negative criticisms but also to find those positive aspects of occupation policy which made possible better relations between the two countries. People in both countries spoke freely with me about the occupation. I am deeply grateful to the many busy men and women, whose names are listed in the Bibliographical Note, who took time out from important duties to answer my questions and to lead me to better documentation. I have acknowledged in the notes the specific facts that I learned from them. In a more general way, however, the final conclusions of this study were greatly influenced by the considered opinions of these persons who had been major actors in the occupation drama. For these conclusions, however, I alone am responsible.

I owe thanks to the publishers for permission to cite from: Charles de Gaulle, *Mémoires de guerre* (Paris: Librairie Plon, 1954–59); Jean de Lattre de Tassigny, *The History of the French First Army*, translated by Malcolm Barnes (London: George Allen and Unwin Ltd., 1952); Institut für Besatzungsfragen, *Sechs Jahre Besatzungslasten* (Tübingen: J. C. B. Mohr [Paul Siebeck], 1951); Elisabeth Noelle and Erich Peter Neumann, *Jahrbuch der öffentlichen Meinung, 1947–1955* (Allensbach am Bodensee: Verlag für Demoskopie, 1956); and to the Institut Français d'Opinion Publique, for permission to cite from their publication *Sondages*.

The major part of the work for this book was done in the extremely rich collections of the Hoover Institution on War, Revolution, and Peace at Stanford University, supplemented especially by work in Europe in the Library of Contemporary Documentation of the University of Paris, in the library of the West German Parliament in Bonn, and in the collections of the Institute for Occupation Questions in Tübingen. From these institutions I received both aid and encouragement in my work. In preparing this manuscript, first as a dissertation and later in its expanded, revised form, I received financial assistance from the School of Humanities and Sciences at Stanford University, the University of Tübingen, and the Hoover Institution on War, Revolution, and Peace. Many people have helped me write this book. My wife has aided in the research and final preparation of the manuscript. Dr. Karl Schmidt-Lüders read the manuscript and gave me the insights of an historian turned businessman who lived in the zone throughout the occupation. Professors David Harris and Philip Buck of Stanford University read the manuscript as a dissertation, and their valuable suggestions have been incorporated into the text. Perhaps most of all, I owe a debt of gratitude to Professor Gordon Wright, also of Stanford University, under whose guidance this work took shape, who gave unstintingly of his time, wisdom, and friendship.   F. R. W.

Contents

The French in Germany
1945-1949

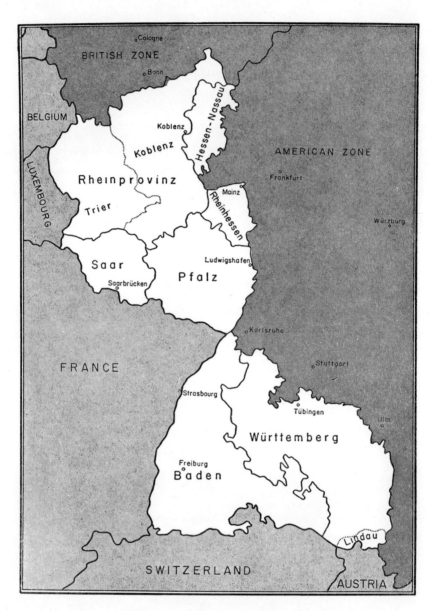

THE FRENCH ZONE OF OCCUPATION IN GERMANY, 1945

CHAPTER I

The Long Road to Greatness

IN the summer of 1940, when General Charles de Gaulle flew from Bordeaux to London to found the Free French movement, he left his country in the depths of misfortune. The vaunted French army had crumpled like a Chinese lantern before the armor of Germany. The French premier, Paul Reynaud, had appealed in vain to the American government that "clouds of war planes from across the Atlantic come to crush the evil force that dominates Europe."[1] On June 22 the government of Marshal Pétain, which had replaced the Reynaud government on June 16, signed an armistice with Germany, an action that seemed to win France a modicum of safety only at the expense of its ally, Britain. Moreover, the Marshal's cease-fire order was obeyed by the major part of the French army and navy, giving plausibility to Stalin's later charge that "France opened the gates to the enemy" and to his remark at Teheran that it was Pétain rather than de Gaulle who represented "the real physical France."[2]

For France to return to a position of greatness after the war, it was necessary for it to give up the tawdry benefits of collaboration and to re-establish its national independence by its own efforts. At that time of bewilderment, France's hope of regeneration lay with a somewhat cantankerous general, who had shown his foresight years earlier by predicting the importance of the striking power of the armored division.[3] Charles de Gaulle displayed his greatness at this moment by breaking the strong ties of loyalty to the established authority of the army in which he had been educated and by perceiving that France's

---

[1] Numbered notes will be found at the back of the book, pp. 251–89.

need was for a symbol of its own invincible spirit. That symbol was to be the Fighting France movement (*France Combattante*).

De Gaulle rendered his country great services throughout the war years by maintaining a symbolic force which could stand as proof that France had not entirely lost its self-respect or its claim to a voice in the councils of Europe. The liberation of France would have come, with or without French participation; France's army would have been re-created without him, by a Giraud or a Leclerc. But de Gaulle set out to restore France's pride in itself as a great nation, its position as an independent political force, and finally its right to be considered as a great power. Only when it had achieved this position again could France demand a share in the occupation of Germany.

In 1940 Britain and the United States had two possible candidates for recognition as the representative of France. There was, first, the government of unoccupied France, the Vichy government of Marshal Pétain, which controlled the principal sections of the French empire as well as the army and the navy. Then there was de Gaulle's Free French movement, with headquarters in London. De Gaulle decided upon arriving in London to appeal directly to French soldiers and civilians to join him in England. Using the facilities of the British Broadcasting Corporation, which had been put at his disposal by the British government, he appealed "to all French officers and men who are now, or may be in the future, on British soil, . . . all engineers and skilled workers who are now, or may be in the future, on British soil, to get in contact with me. Whatever happens," he concluded, "the flame of French resistance must not go out, and shall not go out."[4]

By the end of June 1940, de Gaulle had rallied some three thousand men, and his strength increased considerably during the following months. By September 1941 several of the French colonies had put themselves under Free French control, including Chad, Cameroon, Ubangi, Middle Congo, and Oceania. At this point, de Gaulle placed his movement on a political footing by organizing the French National Committee (*Conseil National Français* or CNF).[5]

From the start, the British government looked with favor on the Gaullist movement. Churchill, on visiting France before the armistice, had felt instinctively that de Gaulle was the one man with the will to lead France to victory. There, he had once said, is *"l'homme du destin,"* the "Constable of France."[6] By an agreement on August 7,

1940, the British government regularized its relations with the Free French movement, recognized that an exclusively French force under the command of General de Gaulle was being recruited on British soil, and announced that the costs of maintaining this force would be borne by the British government.[7] Meanwhile, the British government, while not wishing to declare war against Vichy France, had made its unfriendliness evident by an economic blockade of France and the colonies that had rallied to Pétain. It did not, however, wish to push Vichy France into hostilities; in fact, Britain went so far as to encourage Canada to keep its ambassador in Vichy and agreed that the United States should maintain fairly close relations with the Pétain government.[8]

The attitude of the United States was of great importance. Though not yet at war, the United States government was steadily moving into a strong anti-German position, as reflected in the Atlantic Charter and the grant of over-age destroyers to Britain. However, in 1941 both President Roosevelt and his Secretary of State, Cordell Hull, believed that the United States would gain by keeping up diplomatic relations with Vichy, thereby strengthening Pétain's will to resist Hitler's demands and maintaining a listening-post in the heart of Nazi-controlled Europe. For these reasons Roosevelt sent his old friend, Admiral William D. Leahy, as ambassador to Vichy, and Robert Murphy, former counselor of the United States embassy in Paris, was sent to North Africa to reach an agreement with General Maxime Weygand, the French delegate-general. This policy was obviously incompatible with support of de Gaulle's Free French movement.[9]

This American policy was fully supported by Churchill.[10] It remained quite unintelligible to de Gaulle, however, since it involved a refusal to recognize his movement as the one representative of France. "For the State Department," he wrote to René Pleven, his emissary in Washington, "the whole French question consists in ensuring that Vichy does not collaborate actively with Germany. Cordell Hull believes he can bring this about by appeasing Vichy at any price." Pleven replied, with some bitterness, "It is astonishing how little the Free France movement is known to the American public and that what is known of it is, very often, in its disfavor. Powerful propaganda has undoubtedly been carried on by Vichy to throw a false light on the movement and on the intentions of its head. . . . The movement is no better known to the French element in the United States."[11]

The attitude of President Roosevelt and Secretary Hull toward de Gaulle was based on a determination to carry through what was later called "our Vichy gamble."[12] Other factors also militated against de Gaulle. Reports reaching Washington from sources inside France did not indicate that de Gaulle was supported by large numbers of French people. In the summer of 1944 Roosevelt was still convinced that de Gaulle was only a minor figure in the French resistance movement. Henry L. Stimson, the Secretary of War, reported even after the liberation of France that Roosevelt "believes that De Gaulle will crumple and that the British supporters of De Gaulle will be confounded. . . . The President thinks that other parties will spring up as the liberation goes on and that De Gaulle will become a very little figure. He said that he knew of some such parties."[13]

Moreover, considerable personal animosity disturbed the relationship of Roosevelt and Hull with de Gaulle. The growing dislike of the two American statesmen for de Gaulle probably received its greatest impetus from the famous incident of the Free French seizure of the islands of St. Pierre and Miquelon on Christmas Eve, 1941. De Gaulle's action was contrary to assurances he had given only a week before, and it placed the United States government in the awkward position of seeing broken, with the vociferous support of the American public, an agreement it had made with the Vichy governor of Martinique to maintain the *status quo* in the Western Hemisphere. Hull was so outraged at the incident, and especially at Churchill's support of de Gaulle, that he seriously considered resigning.[14] This incident set the tone for the whole relationship of de Gaulle with Roosevelt and Hull. It was only as the war progressed that the three men came to see that their disagreements arose from differences of principle as well as from clashes of personality.

De Gaulle and Roosevelt met only twice. Their first meeting was at Casablanca in January 1943. The purpose of the meeting was to enable Britain and the United States to come to some agreement on their attitude toward the French *émigré* groups. The situation had changed greatly since 1940. After the United States had entered the war, relations with Vichy had deteriorated. In April 1942 Leahy had been recalled to the United States for "consultations" and had not returned to Vichy. In November 1942 British and American forces had invaded French North Africa, and on November 13 General Dwight D. Eisenhower, commander of the operation, had signed a pact with Admiral Jean Darlan, the Vichy minister of the interior, who was in North Africa at the time. The pact placed administrative control of the French interests in North Africa in Darlan's hands. De Gaulle was outraged, not only because he had been left in ignorance of the invasion plans, but also because the government had been turned over to a high official of the Vichy regime. At this time, it seemed to the Free French leaders that this was an American plan "aimed at excluding us [the Free French] from North Africa for the benefit of a new Vichy."[15]

However, the assassination of Darlan on December 24, 1942, and the choice of General Henri Giraud as his successor, made it clear that American policy was intended not to create a new Vichy but rather to avoid making political commitments to any group until the French people could make its will felt through free elections. Roosevelt was willing to support the Free French as a military force but not as a future government of France. Giraud was much more welcome to him than de Gaulle, since Giraud took every opportunity to point out that he had no political aims. Giraud told de Gaulle at Casablanca that "he did not wish to get involved in politics . . . that he never listened to anyone who wanted to explain to him a theory or a program."[16] Churchill, on the other hand, continued to support de Gaulle in preference to Giraud. As Churchill pointed out to Roosevelt, they were in the curious position of each supporting a different *émigré* government, Roosevelt backing Giraud, who controlled French North Africa, and Churchill backing de Gaulle, who controlled French Equatorial Africa and Oceania.[17] At Casablanca, the matchmakers intended to bring about a union of the two French groups.

It was at this conference that de Gaulle met Roosevelt for the first time. In the musical-comedy atmosphere of Roosevelt's villa, where secret service men lurked in the shadows of the balconies, Roosevelt and de Gaulle exchanged their views on the future of Europe. De Gaulle saw in Roosevelt only "the greatest ambitions." The American president, he felt, intended to see that the United States would dominate the world. "Roosevelt intended that the peace be an American peace . . . that, in particular, France have him for her savior and arbiter."[18]

During the next year, de Gaulle was able to gain ascendancy over the Giraud group in the French Committee of National Liberation, which had been formed in May 1943 as a joint committee controlling all territories that recognized either Giraud or de Gaulle. On November 8, 1943, Giraud resigned from the committee, leaving de Gaulle as sole president. Thus by the end of 1943 de Gaulle was in undisputed control of a committee that was being formed as a future government of France. Moreover, a French army and navy had been created, and they would be a major asset in the power struggle ahead. As General de Lattre de Tassigny wrote, "The French army of 256,000 men, which was feverishly preparing for the liberation, was not therefore a symbolic force, but a solid and powerful reality, forming an appreciable part of the total allied strength."[19]

The increasing strength of de Gaulle's position was not at all pleasing to Roosevelt. Stimson was "disappointed by the degree of feeling which seemed to enter into the thinking of Mr. Roosevelt and Mr. Hull, both of whom had been sorely tried, over a long period, by the personal peculiarities of the Free French leader."[20] Despite growing pressure from such men as Stimson, John McCloy (Assistant Secretary of War), and General Eisenhower, Roosevelt refused to consider adopting closer relations with de Gaulle, and at a cabinet meeting on May 20, 1944, he added, according to Hull, "that he had told Winant that if anyone could give him a certificate proving that De Gaulle was a representative of the French people he would deal with him, but that otherwise he had no idea of changing his mind."[21] As the Liberation progressed, however, it became obvious that de Gaulle was recognized as the head of the legal French government by the majority of Frenchmen in the liberated areas. De Gaulle, moreover, paid a most successful visit to the United States in July, where he won over such hardened opponents as Leahy and Hull.[22] As a result the United States government accorded *de facto* recognition to de Gaulle's committee, which had been reorganized in August 1944 as the Provisional Government of the French Republic; this act was followed by *de jure* recognition by Britain, the Soviet Union, and finally the United States, on October 24, 1944. France's return to a position of importance in Europe was further recognized on November 11, 1944, when it was invited to become the fourth member of the European Advisory Commission, which was deliberating on the problems of postwar Europe.

These two steps were not taken without French prompting. In a major speech in the Palais de Chaillot in Paris on September 12, 1944, de Gaulle had demanded greater participation in the current Allied offensive and a major French share in the future negotiations over a German settlement. "We believe," he said, "that it is in the superior interest of mankind that the decisions which tomorrow will lay down the fate of Germany should not be discussed and adopted without France." Two days later, the French government sent a note to the British, Russian, and American governments asking that France be given a seat on the European Advisory Commission. On October 14 Churchill pressed Roosevelt "to recognize de Gaulle's administration as the Provisional Government of France." De Gaulle himself later stated that he believed the *de jure* recognition of his government was due to Roosevelt's desire to conciliate the American public before the coming election.[23]

De Gaulle's Washington trip in July 1944, however, had convinced him even further that Roosevelt's aims for France were quite unacceptable, if not actually dangerous. As de Gaulle wrote later, "His conception seemed to me grandiose, as well as disquieting for Europe and for France. . . . He intended to institute a permanent system of intervention. In his view, a directorate of four—America, Soviet Russia, China, Great Britain—would regulate the problems of the universe."[24] De Gaulle returned to Paris convinced that if Roosevelt had his way, France would be relegated to the position of a minor power, and that in this critical time France could count only on itself.[25] In taking this attitude, however, de Gaulle was forgetting the aid he had received from Great Britain. Churchill had supported him throughout the war, from the moment of his first landing in England until the Liberation itself, since he had seen that postwar Europe would need, above all, a strong France.[26]

In the winter of 1944 the status of France was still undecided. The French army had increased in size to almost half a million men as a result of the amalgamation of the French forces that had taken part in the invasion of France with the Resistance forces inside France.[27] The French government was firmly established, with popular support, and the specter of revolution, which had obsessed Roosevelt, seemed exorcised.[28] De Gaulle therefore felt that he had a right to seek for France its position among the great powers. He demanded a share in

the military operations in Germany, the right to be consulted on measures involving the future of Europe or of the French empire, and,
above all, occupation of an area of Germany by French forces after
the war. De Gaulle quickly made clear what he envisaged as France's
area of occupation in Germany. On his visit to Washington, he asked
for French occupation of the Rhine.[29] And on August 12, 1944, in the
National Defense Committee in Algiers, he demanded for France a
zone of occupation that would run from Cologne to Konstanz, giving
France not only the left but also the right bank of the Rhine.[30]

In the winter of 1944 it seemed that at least some of de Gaulle's
claims for France were being met. France had been invited to join
the European Advisory Commission. According to plans for the future
United Nations Organization, France was to be one of the five permanent members of the Security Council. The French army was preparing for the invasion of Germany. Nevertheless, opposition from
both Stalin and Roosevelt prevented France from participating in the
most important wartime conference of all; Yalta was to remain a
meeting of the Big Three.

YALTA AND THE DIVISION OF GERMANY

A conference of Roosevelt, Stalin, and Churchill was being considered as early as September 1944. Although military plans were
well coordinated for the final Allied assault, political plans had to be
made for the future, and particularly for the postwar treatment of
Germany. Harry Hopkins, Roosevelt's personal adviser, later recalled
that the Yalta Conference was necessary in part to deal with the problem of the future status of France. "The place of France in European
and world affairs was in an irritating state. France wanted a Zone of
Occupation. She had not been given one. France wanted to be on any
Control Commission governing Germany. The Allies had given her
no security on this point. . . . France wanted to have a full part in
world affairs, and the decision on this point, if not made at an early
date, would cause endless troubles."[31] France, it was thought, could
not be invited to a conference that was to pass judgment on her own
status.

There were other reasons for not having France represented at
Yalta. Although France's army was now half a million and growing
daily, the Big Three was still an "exclusive club," as Stalin said, "re-

stricted to a membership of nations with five million soldiers," or rather three million, as Churchill quickly pointed out. Stalin, moreover, was still opposed to any form of French participation in control of the occupation of Germany, in spite of de Gaulle's visit to Moscow in December 1944. "It was unrealistic," he told Roosevelt at Yalta, "for De Gaulle to insist upon full rights with the Big Three, in view of the fact that France had not done much fighting in the war." Roosevelt, too, still felt that to invite de Gaulle to an international conference of this nature would be "to introduce a complicating and undesirable factor." Churchill, on the other hand, after visiting de Gaulle in November, had envisaged "a triple meeting if U. J. ["Uncle Joe" Stalin] will not come, or a quadruple meeting if he will. In the latter case the French will be in on some subjects and out on others. One must always realize that before five years are out a French army must be made to take on the main task of holding down Germany." Roosevelt did, however, concede a little to French demands for status by noting in his State of the Union message on January 6, 1945, that the liberation of France "means that her great influence will again be available in meeting the problems of peace. We fully recognize France's vital interest in a lasting solution of the German problem and the contribution which she can make to achieving international security." He did not, however, go so far as to think France should participate in the Yalta Conference.[32]

It was left to Britain to act as the champion of France's interests at Yalta. In November 1944 Churchill had already broached the question of what would happen when the American troops went home from Europe, and he had expressed sympathy with de Gaulle's wish for a French zone of occupation in Germany; as he said in a telegram to Roosevelt, "there will be a time not many years distant when the American armies will go home and when the British will have great difficulty in maintaining large forces overseas."[33] This fear that the United States would abandon Europe shortly after the war was won, as it had done after the First World War, played a large part in Churchill's thinking. For this reason he wanted to build up France as a strong political and military force. Even before his visit to France in November 1944, Churchill had proposed that the American government agree to arm between eight and twelve French divisions, which would be ready to replace the French colonial troops in the occupation of Germany; and on November 26, Roosevelt agreed to the equipping of a "French occupation force" with captured German equipment.[34] During his November visit to France Churchill had offered to give up part of the British zone to the French. It therefore remained for him to persuade Roosevelt to give up part of the American zone to France and to get Stalin to agree to this change. This was to be one of Churchill's main tasks at the Yalta Conference.

Several important decisions on the future of Germany had already been taken before the Yalta Conference convened. At the Foreign Ministers' conference in Moscow in October 1943, it had been decided to set up a European Advisory Commission which would be given, among other duties connected with the details of surrender terms to be imposed on Germany, the task of dividing Germany into zones of occupation to be taken over by the armies of the three major allies. Since the American delegation received no detailed instructions from Washington, a British proposal, presented on January 15, 1944, was accepted as laying down the boundaries of the three future zones. The eastern zone was to be taken by Russia, the Soviet delegate accepting for his government on February 18. The rest of Germany was to be divided between a northwestern zone, which was highly industrialized, and a southwestern zone, which was largely agricultural. The American delegation refused to take the southwestern zone, as the British had proposed it should, partly because it wished some control of Germany's industry but largely because Roosevelt did not wish to be dependent upon the transportation lines through France, especially at a time when American troops would be redeployed to the Far East.[35]

Roosevelt finally agreed, when he met Churchill at Quebec in September 1944, that the United States would take the southwestern zone. In return, Churchill drafted a statement based on the recommendations of the Morgenthau plan, to which both he and Roosevelt put their initials, and further agreed that the United States should be given an enclave around Bremen to solve its redeployment problems.[36] Following the decisions to recognize the Provisional Government of de Gaulle (made on October 24, 1944) and to invite France to become a member of the European Advisory Commission (made on November 11, 1944), the State Department became gradually more favorable to the idea of developing the power of France.

Secretary Hull suggested in a memorandum to Roosevelt on January 4, 1945, that "it is in the interest of the United States to assist France to regain her former position in world affairs in order that she may increase her contribution in the war effort and play an appropriate part in the maintenance of peace."[37] He advised that the proposals circulated by René Massigli in the European Advisory Commission—which suggested that France be given a share in the control of Germany, a role in the signing of the surrender, and a zone of occupation in Germany—should be accepted by the American government. Roosevelt approved these proposals in principle. Hence, when the British and American delegations met in Malta before going on to Yalta, they were already in agreement that France should be given a zone of occupation, and Stettinius was able to tell Anthony Eden, the British Foreign Secretary, that "the President attached great importance" to this provision.[38]

It became clear in Roosevelt's first conversation with Stalin at Yalta that Stettinius had somewhat exaggerated Roosevelt's desire to have the French given a zone. Stettinius later reported the conversation. Roosevelt, he said, remarked that he thought "it is not a bad idea that the French should have a zone. When Marshal Stalin asked the President why he favored a zone for France, Roosevelt replied that he favored it only out of kindness. Both the Marshal and Molotov, in vigorous tones, said that this was the only reason to give the French a zone."[39] Roosevelt also took the occasion, according to the minutes of Charles E. Bohlen, the assistant to the Secretary of State, "to tell the Marshal something indiscreet, since he would not wish to say it in front of Prime Minister Churchill, namely, that the British for two years have had the idea of artificially building up France into a strong power which would have 200,000 troops on the eastern border of France to hold the line for the period required to assemble a strong British army. He said that the British were a peculiar people and wished to have their cake and eat it."[40]

While Roosevelt did not seem particularly concerned over the effect of an early postwar evacuation of American troops from Europe, and since he quite casually dropped the bombshell news that he could keep American troops in Europe for only two years, his advisers were well aware of the problem.[41] Byrnes stated in the preliminary discussions at Yalta that "most important of all . . . was that the United States would be loath to accept the responsibility for the internal affairs of Europe"; Leahy, in a pointed joke, "suggested that we give the French our zone, saying that our troops wanted to return home promptly."[42] For Churchill the possibility of the American troops leaving within two years was vitally important. As he later noted, this was "a momentous statement. . . . Formidable questions arose in my mind. If the Americans left Europe, Britain would have to occupy singlehanded the entire western portion of Germany. Such a task would be far beyond our strength."[43] At the meeting when Roosevelt had made this statement, on February 5, 1945, Churchill had outlined the reasons for giving France a zone. He said that "the French had had long experience in occupying Germany and they would not be lenient. France must become strong again to help check a revived Germany; . . . France was the most important neighbor of Germany. . . . Should Germany once more get near to the channel coast we would suffer again."[44] When Stalin asked Roosevelt how long the American troops would remain in Europe, Roosevelt's reply of two years clinched the whole argument; it was agreed with little further discussion that France should be given a zone formed out of the British and American zones.

On the other hand, both Stalin and Roosevelt remained opposed to French participation in the Control Council. Churchill had the matter referred to the foreign ministers for further discussion, although in the thinking of Stalin and Roosevelt the grant of a zone seemed linked to the decision that France should not be represented on the Control Council.[45] The next day the foreign ministers argued the question of French participation on the Control Council, and Churchill took up the matter again on February 7, saying that "the French would cause endless trouble if such a procedure [no seat on the Control Council] were followed . . . , that French participation in the Control Commission would be necessary to secure uniformity in the zones."[46] On Roosevelt's suggestion, the matter was dropped at that point. During the next two days, Hopkins worked hard to persuade Roosevelt to accept Churchill's position, and this pressure, combined with Roosevelt's own knowledge of de Gaulle's touchy pride, brought the President to change his mind. He sent Averell Harriman to inform Stalin of his changed opinion, and Stalin concurred without protest.[47]

At the meeting on February 10, Roosevelt announced "that he

had changed his mind in regard to the question of the French participation in the Control Commission. He now agreed with the views of the Prime Minister that it would be impossible to give France an area to administer in Germany unless they were members of the Control Commission. He said he thought it would be easier to deal with the French if they were on the Commission than if they were not." Stalin at once agreed, and on Churchill's suggestion a telegram was dispatched the next day to de Gaulle. The telegram informed de Gaulle that the three powers meeting in Yalta had decided that it would be "highly desirable for the Provisional Government of the French Republic, if they will, to accept responsibility for a zone of occupation and to be represented on the Central Machinery of Control."[48]

The next day the conference broke up. Roosevelt now prepared to meet neighboring heads of state on his return journey. He received the rulers of Saudi Arabia, Ethiopia, and Egypt on his cruiser, and was prepared to call at Algiers to meet de Gaulle. De Gaulle, however, had no intention of flying down to Algeria, the invitation reminding him too closely of the humiliating summons to Casablanca in 1943. The American Ambassador in Paris, Jefferson Caffery, reported that "de Gaulle was in a sulky mood because the public statement issued at the end of the Yalta conference had not paid enough attention to him personally."[49] De Gaulle himself issued an official communiqué in which he regretted that the President could not visit Paris. As for himself, he said, the invitation to Algiers "caught him unprepared, at a time when many matters required his presence in Paris, and immediately after a conference between three Allied heads of state, their advisers and experts, a conference in which France had not taken part and the results of which it still did not know."[50]

This refusal, made almost solely for reasons of prestige, was probably a mistake on de Gaulle's part. Although France had not been invited to Yalta, its interests had been well served there. Moreover, de Gaulle needed at this time to come to a firm agreement with Roosevelt on the role to be taken by France in the invasion of Germany and on the boundaries of the zone of occupation to be assigned to France. The European Advisory Commission had foreseen the grave dangers that would result if the zonal boundaries were not settled before the armies entered Germany: "in the closing phases of the war, strategy and tactics might be determined by the desire to occupy the largest possible area of Germany rather than by the aim to defeat Germany as quickly as possible."[51]

De Gaulle and Roosevelt might have been able to come to some agreement about the French claims. As it was, negotiations on the boundaries of the French zone were turned over to the European Advisory Commission, and were not finally agreed upon until over a month after the capitulation. As a result there occurred a competition for territory between the invading armies of the United States and France. The actions of the French army in the last months of the war can be understood only in relation to this diplomatic uncertainty. The failure to invite France to Yalta, the refusal of de Gaulle to meet Roosevelt, and the protracted boundary negotiations explain the confusion existing when France came into possession of its zone.

MILITARY AND DIPLOMATIC CONQUEST OF A ZONE

General de Gaulle made his first formal statement concerning the zone of occupation he envisaged for France in a meeting of the National Defense Committee in Algiers on August 12, 1944. At that time, he desired for France not only the "watch on the Rhine" but also bridgeheads on the right bank of the river. The whole of western Germany, including Westphalia, the Ruhr, Frankfurt, Mannheim, and the Black Forest, was to be placed under permanent military occupation. This occupation, according to de Gaulle, should be British as far south as Cologne and French from Cologne to the Swiss border. The French zone would thus have included almost the whole of the Prussian Rheinprovinz, Hessen-Nassau, most of Hessen, the Saar, the Pfalz, and Baden.[52] These demands, as outlined on August 12, 1944, were not changed throughout all the boundary negotiations that followed the Yalta Conference.

De Gaulle had made no secret of what he considered France's proper share in the occupation. On his visit to Washington in August 1944, he said that "France did not want to annex the Rhine but did want to occupy the left bank."[53] When Churchill visited him in November, de Gaulle pressed strongly for a "share in the occupation of Germany not merely as subparticipation under British or American command but as a French command," and also for a larger share in the fighting, so that France would "not have to go into Germany as a so-called conqueror who has not fought." In December, in Moscow, he made it clear to Marshal Stalin that he desired the Rhineland for France; Stalin noted in a message to Roosevelt that de Gaulle had touched on the question of "the frontier of France on the Rhine."[54] De Gaulle himself later summarized his proposals for the German settlement as follows: "on the left bank of the Rhine, no further sovereignty of the central German state; the territories thus detached preserving their German character but receiving autonomy and becoming part, from the economic point of view, of the western zone; the Ruhr basin placed under international control; the eastern frontier of Germany marked by the Oder and the Neisse."[55] At Yalta, Stalin told Roosevelt privately that de Gaulle had "said the Rhine was the natural boundary of France and he wished to have French troops placed there in permanency." In January the French representative in the European Advisory Commission, René Massigli, circulated a memorandum, which came to be known as the "Massigli Plan," proposing French participation in the Control Commission, in the signing of the capitulation and in the occupation, through the allocation of a French zone.[56] And on February 5, 1945, while the Yalta Conference itself was getting under way, de Gaulle made a radio speech to the French people. "I can state, yet again," he said, "that the assured presence of French forces from one end of the Rhine to the other, the separation of the territory on the left bank of the river and of the Ruhr basin from what will be the German State or States . . . are the conditions which France considers essential."[57]

Thus the French position was already clear when the actual demarcation of zonal boundaries was turned over to the European Advisory Commission, as decided at the Yalta Conference. The zone to be assigned to France was determined by direct negotiations between the French delegation and the British and American delegations separately. Although some haggling occurred, the British delegation soon agreed to turn over to France, from the British zone, the Saar, the Pfalz, and a large part of the Rheinprovinz. In the invasion of Germany, French troops were to enter only the southern corner of this territory, where the French swing into Germany had taken them as far north as Speyer.

The major French offensive in Germany was conducted in the southwestern corner of the proposed American zone, in the Länder of Baden and Württemberg. Agreement between the American and

French delegations was delayed for a long while, and for this reason the campaign in this area followed the very course that the European Advisory Commission had wished to avoid. Military policy, at least the French part in it, was very definitely influenced by the conviction that the amount of territory seized by the French First Army in the invasion of Germany would determine to an important degree the size of the French zone to be established by negotiations within the Commission. De Gaulle has stated in his memoirs that French participation in the German campaign was not only a question of French prestige. It was also "the only certain means of taking a share in the capitulation, in the occupation, and in the administration of the Reich. As soon as we should have in our hands a zone of Germanic territory, what was to become of Germany could not be decided without us. . . . In short, I intended that we should cross the Rhine and carry the French front as far as possible into the south German states." French troops, he added, "were to seize, on the right bank of the Rhine, a French zone of occupation."[58]

By early March, the French had still not entered Germany. The French army, feeling strongly the desire for revenge, was shocked when the invasion plan of February 1945 assigned to them the job of "maintaining a passive front on the upper Rhine." General de Lattre, the commander of the French army, has described his feelings at that time quite openly: "For a Frenchman the problem did not exist: to take part in the invasion of Germany was for our country a duty and a right. . . . It was for her the surest means of demonstrating her resurrection—and, even more, of making it a lasting resurrection by taking possession of some of the real symbols of her future security. This political aspect was assuredly that which most held General de Gaulle's attention. . . . In the eyes of the leader of the government it was a historical necessity, as much to raise our world prestige as to lay out the basis of our post-war position on the Rhine."[59] In March, however, the plan was modified to permit the French forces to follow behind the American troops into Württemberg and also to occupy the Rhine corridor between the Rhine and the Black Forest and to close the Swiss border. De Lattre, clutching at a straw, as he said, was able to transform this situation to make the French army lead the attack into Baden and south Württemberg. The straw was the chance to establish the French army on the Lauter, a tributary of the Rhine that marked the border of France and Germany, over a distance of some ten kilometers. He later wrote of his plans: "An embrasure on the Lauter, an embrasure on the Palatine Rhine. . . . To secure them I reckoned on the friendly understanding of General Devers [the American general in command of the American 7th Army and the French First Army] and on the easy-going cunning of General Guillaume [commander of the French 3rd Algerian Division]. The secret instructions which I gave the latter . . . were: 'Theoretically your front ends slantwise at the Lauter; do anything so that it ends squarely.' "[60]

The plan succeeded. In March the French army crossed the Lauter and broke through the Siegfried Line. On March 28, further instructions gave the French the duty of capturing Karlsruhe, Pforzheim, and Stuttgart, opening to them the whole of Baden and Württemberg. Their greatest fear after this was that the rush of the American forces would carry them into the sector assigned to the French army. On March 29, 1945, General de Gaulle sent de Lattre a personal telegram that stated, "My dear General, you must cross the Rhine even if the Americans are not agreeable and even if you have to cross it in boats. It is a matter of the greatest national interest. Karlsruhe and Stuttgart await you."[61] De Lattre later added the revealing note that "it was in no sense a question of crossing the Rhine without the Americans being agreeable, it was a question of crossing it before the Americans occupied the route of our later thrust." At the same time, de Lattre admitted that the French army lacked all adequate equipment for crossing the river. As French military circles later pointed out, "this decision was extremely daring: it seemed impossible to carry it out." On March 31, the day of the crossing, fifty-four of the ninety boatmen employed in taking the divisions across were killed or wounded, and three-quarters of the boats were lost.[62] Two days after the crossing, de Lattre ordered the attack on Stuttgart to begin. There followed in rapid order the fall of Leopoldshafen (April 3), Karlsruhe (April 4), Rastatt and Baden-Baden (April 12–13), and finally Stuttgart (April 18–21) and Freiburg (April 21). The French forces had taken the capital cities of both Baden and Württemberg, a feat that added considerably to French prestige.

De Lattre's next objective was to take Ulm, "for the pride of restoring ancient French glories and strongly demonstrating to the Germans the extent of our participation in the victory." In his letter of instruction to General Émile Béthouart, the commander of the First Army Corps, he ordered him to "rush to Ulm along all routes and with all means. The Americans will perhaps turn us out of it. But the French flag will have flown there."[63] By going full throttle and leaving behind various groups of Germans in the hills overlooking the highway, the French tanks reached Ulm just ten hours ahead of the American 44th Infantry Division.

A major crisis arose on April 22, when the boundary between the French army and the American 7th Army was laid down by General Devers.[64] This boundary was of exceptional importance. It gave the French their opening on the Austrian Alps and led to the later occupation of the Vorarlberg by the French troops. But by laying down the boundary along the *Autobahn* west and south of Stuttgart, it took away from the French the great city they had conquered only the previous day. Stuttgart, moreover, was a city of 400,000 people, the capital of Württemberg, and possessed great economic, political, and moral significance for the French. On April 26 General Devers asked General de Monsabert, commander of the French Second Army Corps, to hand over the city to his forces. De Lattre forbade him to do so, stating that the fighting in Stuttgart had ceased and that therefore the question of the occupation was a purely political one which he had to refer to his government in Paris. In fact, de Lattre had already received his orders from Paris, for on April 24, de Gaulle had sent him formal instructions: "I order you to keep a French garrison in Stuttgart and to establish a military government there at once. . . . To the eventual observations [of the Americans] you will reply that your orders are to hold and administer the territories occupied by our troops until the French zone of occupation has been settled between the interested governments, which so far as you know has not yet been done."[65] General Eisenhower later wrote that he was forced to intervene with the "threat of possible curtailment of equipment for the French forces."[66] This threat seemed to him to have made the French comply. But the French did not leave Stuttgart immediately; General de Gaulle considered Stuttgart too important to be surrendered so easily, and the French remained until the zonal boundaries were settled. They even organized a Joan of Arc festival in Stuttgart on May 13, which was attended not only by General de Gaulle but by General Devers as well.

Yet, as President Truman later pointed out in his memoirs, "De Gaulle gained nothing by this show of force."[67] The French zone of occupation was not to include Stuttgart.

Another incident took place when the American 15th Army requested the French to evacuate the Kreise of Landau, Bergzaben, Germersheim, and Speyer, where the French army had established its bridgehead on the Rhine. On May 1 de Lattre again referred this to de Gaulle, who refused to evacuate on the grounds that "since the left bank of the Rhine ought anyway to be occupied by French forces, it would be illogical and awkward to withdraw them now in order to take them back later."[68]

While French military operations were proceeding in this way, under the direct influence of political considerations, the French and American delegations had continued to discuss what section of the American zone should be handed over to France. At first the French had asked for Baden, Württemberg, Hessen-Nassau, and Hessen, which would have given them even more than de Gaulle had outlined in his demands of August 12, 1944.[69] This zone, moreover, would have included such important cities as Ulm, Stuttgart, Karlsruhe, Frankfurt, Wiesbaden, and Fulda. The American reply was based upon considerations of logistics only, notably on the desire of the War Department to keep the *Autobahn* from Karlsruhe to Stuttgart, Ulm and Munich, and the trunk railroad, in American hands. This boundary roughly followed the sector between the American and French armies as laid down on April 22, to which de Gaulle had already taken exception.

The American delegation to the European Advisory Commission objected strongly to their instructions. John G. Winant, the American delegate, Philip E. Mosely, his assistant, and Robert D. Murphy sent two telegrams to the Secretary of State in Washington, protesting the division of two of the historic Länder, which had "strong regional identity and a certain attachment to democratic self-government." They were ordered to insist on the War Department's demands, however, and in the final agreement in the European Advisory Commission, the only concession made was that the French zone should include Baden-Baden and that the French should have the right of access to Baden administrative records in Karlsruhe.[70]

An agreement on zonal boundaries was reached in the European

Advisory Commission on May 2.[71] The final agreement on zones was not, however, signed until June 22. The delay was due largely to General de Gaulle, for whom the boundaries proposed were unsatisfactory. De Gaulle had emphasized throughout the invasion of Germany that he saw a direct connection between the extent of German territory taken by the French army and the area of the zone of occupation. The proposals made by the American delegation to the EAC meant in fact that France would not only have to give up its ambitions for establishing itself on both banks of the Rhine but would also have to give up the sections of north Baden and north Württemberg which the French army had conquered.

On May 26, 1945, the *New York Times* noted that American proposals had been made three weeks earlier, but that de Gaulle was demanding Karlsruhe. On June 8 the London *Times* added the rumor that the French were being offered Württemberg as compensation for their failure to receive the Rhineland in its entirety. Finally, on June 14, the *New York Times* announced that de Gaulle had agreed to the zonal boundaries, largely owing to France's urgent need for coal, delivery of which was being held up pending the German settlement.[72] The boundaries were finally announced by the French Ministry of Information on June 23, the official agreement having been signed the previous day. Three days later an agreement was signed between the American and French governments, by which the transfer of control from the American forces holding parts of the French zone to the French army was decided.[73] A French government spokesman made a last appeal to the American government on July 28, when he expressed the view that the Americans should turn over Karlsruhe and Wiesbaden and perhaps Stuttgart to the French when the redeployment of American troops was completed, "so as to give certain homogeneity to the French zone, which at present does not possess historical, ethnical, political, or economic unity."[74] He was expressing a vain hope, however, for the zonal boundaries as laid down in the agreement of June 22 were not changed throughout the whole occupation.

In this agreement, France had gained part of the Prussian Rheinprovinz, parts of Hessen-Nassau and Hessen, the whole of the Saar and the Pfalz, the southern sections of Baden and Württemberg, the Bavarian Landkreis of Lindau, and the enclave of Hohenzollern.[75] French troops would hold the whole of the Rhineland as far north as

Remagen, including the whole of the section of Germany that bordered on France. De Gaulle had not succeeded in gaining the whole of the right bank, and he even had to withdraw French troops from territory they had conquered. On the other hand, the invasion of Germany had raised France's prestige, not only in Germany but among the other powers. By taking possession of its zone, France had seized a gage that could be used to ensure that France's voice would be heeded in future international policy-making, particularly with regard to Germany.

CHAPTER II

France and the German Problem
1945-1947

SPEAKING to a large audience in the Palais de Chaillot in Paris on September 12, 1944, General de Gaulle summed up his years of effort and frustration in working to restore France to its accustomed rank in the diplomacy of Europe. "We want to believe," he said, "that the right of France to take part in the future settlement of the conflict will finally no longer be contested. . . . We believe that it is in the superior interest of mankind that the decisions which tomorrow will lay down the fate of Germany will not be discussed and adopted without France, because there is no power more interested than France in what concerns its neighbor."[1] Yet France was to remain in "official relegation" until the end of the Potsdam Conference, in spite of the fact that France was then in possession of a zone of occupation in Germany. The results of this relegation might have been expected by the three great powers. France considered itself bound only by those Allied decisions on which it had been consulted; the others it felt free to accept or reject according to its own best interests.

The first Allied proposals for the postwar occupation of Germany were made as early as August 1941 in the Atlantic Charter, although the principles of the Charter were not applied to Germany when more specific plans were formulated.[2] At Teheran, in November 1943, Roosevelt put forward a plan for the division of Germany into five autonomous states, and the scheme was passed on to the European Advisory Commission for further consideration.[3] The Commission first met in December 1943, but made little progress, partly because of the American failure to supply Winant, the American representative to the EAC, with a policy directive. In July 1944, however, agreement was reached on the draft for Germany's unconditional surrender and in the same month the zonal boundaries for tripartite occupation were accepted. Although the Russians quickly accepted the eastern zone, neither the British nor the Americans were willing to allow the other to take the rich northwestern zone, which included the Ruhr valley.[4]

In September 1944 came the struggle over the Morgenthau plan.[5] The plan, drawn up by Secretary of the Treasury Morgenthau, aimed at enforcing a Draconian peace, which would include the cession of East Prussia and Upper Silesia to Poland, cession of the Saar and the Rhineland to France, internationalization of the Ruhr, partition of the remaining states, and the dismantling of Germany's industrial equipment. Both Churchill and Roosevelt initialed a draft embodying the economic clauses of this plan, drawn up by Churchill during the Quebec Conference of September 1944, but shortly after this Roosevelt disavowed the plan. Echoes of the territorial provisions were to be heard, however, as soon as France was admitted to a share in the consideration of the German question.

Up to this point France had played no direct part in the negotiations over the German problem, as was to be expected in view of the relationship that existed between de Gaulle and Hull and Roosevelt. During his visit to Moscow in October 1944, however, Churchill, with Roosevelt's agreement, persuaded Stalin that France should be offered a place as the fourth member of the European Advisory Commission. The Commission at once speeded up its work, in order to make a number of important decisions before the French delegate could join them. Thirteen days before the French delegate joined the Commission, the other three members signed the protocol accepting the tripartite division of Germany into zones of occupation. The French delegate, René Massigli, was a trained diplomat, and his presence eventually brought a more professional approach to the diplomatic work of the Commission.[6] French participation in the decisions of the European Advisory Commission was particularly important, since France was not to take part in the Yalta or Potsdam conferences and thus felt itself legally bound only by those decisions to which it had agreed in the EAC.

The EAC finally agreed to three major documents, which were

issued in Berlin by the four Allied commanders on June 5, 1945, in the form of three proclamations. These proclamations were of great importance, for they laid the basis for the organization of occupied Germany. The first proclamation stated that "unconditional surrender of Germany has . . . been effected"; that the governments of the four powers "hereby assume supreme authority with respect to Germany"; that all German armed forces were to be disarmed, all war equipment to be surrendered, all prisoners-of-war to be released, and all requested information, including facts concerning Nazi leaders, to be given; and finally, that "the four Allied governments will take such steps, including the complete disarmament and demilitarisation of Germany, as they deem requisite for future peace and security."[7]

The second proclamation divided Germany into four zones of occupation. The third announced that "supreme authority in Germany will be exercised, on instructions from their Governments, by the British, United States, Soviet and French Commanders-in-Chief, each in his own zone of occupation, and also jointly in matters affecting Germany as a whole. The four Commanders-in-Chief together will constitute the Control Council. . . . The Control Council, whose decisions shall be unanimous, will ensure appropriate uniformity of action by the Commanders-in-Chief in their respective zones of occupation and will reach agreed decisions on the chief questions affecting Germany as a whole."[8]

As a result of its participation in these agreements in the European Advisory Commission, France was bound to carry out two policies, disarmament and demilitarization, as well as to implement in its own zone all decisions reached in the Control Council. And in spite of French annoyance at the ignominy of not being invited to Yalta, there was little in the decisions reached at the Yalta Conference with which they could not agree. At Yalta, three main principles for the treatment of Germany were accepted—disarmament, demilitarization, denazification; dismemberment, although initially agreed upon, was soon dropped.[9] The three powers also agreed that reparations should be exacted from Germany, and that these should be in the form of confiscation of capital equipment, annual deliveries of goods from current German production, and the use of German labor. A reparations commission was to be set up in Moscow to consider the details of a plan for exacting reparations and fixing the total to be exacted.

An official of the Quai d'Orsay announced on February 22, 1945, that satisfactory replies had been received to the French government's questions concerning the Yalta agreements.[10] Only French exclusion from membership in the dismemberment and reparations commissions could be regarded as a further slight; it should be noted that de Gaulle's refusal to meet Roosevelt in Algiers did not receive a favorable notice in the Paris press, even from the MRP paper, *L'Aube*, which had long supported his policies.[11] The Communist paper, *L'Humanité*, declared itself well satisfied. "We think that France should congratulate itself highly on the results of the Big Three Conference," the paper pointed out. "It has been treated as a major ally. . . . It will take part in the occupation and administration of Germany. . . . We think that, after taking note of these obvious and indisputable advantages, certain circles would be ill advised to show displeasure and to formulate reservations."[12]

At Potsdam in July 1945, the Big Three proceeded to a much more detailed agreement on principles for the treatment of Germany, and with much of this France did not agree. The "Political Principles" were in part a reaffirmation of the Yalta agreement—supreme authority to the commanders-in-chief, disarmament and demilitarization, destruction of the Nazi party and arrest of its important members, a purge of the German administration, punishment of war criminals, control of education, a reorganization of the judicial system, and restoration of political life at the local level. With all this the French government was in agreement. There were two political principles that it did not accept. Clause 2 stated that "so far as is practicable, there shall be uniformity of treatment of the German population throughout Germany," and Clause 8(iv) stated that "certain essential German administrative departments, headed by State Secretaries, shall be established, particularly in the fields of finance, transport, communications, foreign trade and industry. Such departments will act under the direction of the Control Council." The French government objected strongly to the possible creation of centralized institutions foreseen in Clause 8(iv), and the commanders of the French zone, like the other zonal commanders, ignored Clause 2 whenever they found it necessary to do so for the implementation of directives from their own government.

Among the "Economic Principles" of the Potsdam agreement, the French were willing to carry out elimination of war potential, decentralization, and decartelization. But throughout the occupation they remained opposed to Clause 14, which stated: "During the period of occupation, Germany shall be treated as a single economic unit. To this end common policies shall be established in regard to (*a*) mining and industrial production and allocation; (*b*) agriculture, forestry and fishing; (*c*) wages, prices and rationing; (*d*) import and export programs for Germany as a whole; (*e*) currency and banking, central taxation and customs; (*f*) reparation and removal of war potential; (*g*) transportation and communications." And the French were especially opposed to Clause 15(c), which agreed upon "equitable distribution of essential commodities between the different zones so as to produce a balanced economy throughout Germany and reduce the need for imports."[13]

The French rejection of these aspects of the Allied solution to the German problem was due to a basic divergence of opinion about the measures to be applied to Germany. French opposition had the important effect of paralyzing implementation of the Potsdam decisions by the Allied Control Council. This paralysis brought about the virtual autonomy of each zonal commander and made possible a great differentiation of policy in the different zones. It also changed the very nature of the German problem by ensuring that the future trial of strength between Russia and the Western powers would have as its battlefield a divided rather than a unified Germany.

FRENCH OBSTRUCTION IN THE ALLIED CONTROL COUNCIL

The body which was to put into practice the principles laid down at Potsdam was the Allied Control Council, and it was in this body that French opposition to the above principles took effect. The Allied Control Council held its first formal meeting on July 30, 1945, with the French being represented by the deputy military governor, General Koeltz. At the second meeting on August 10, 1945, the Council approved a paper that established the machinery through which it would operate, providing in particular for a Coordinating Committee, where most legislation would be formulated, and for various directorates with specific functions in the government of Germany, such as transport and finances.[14]

Within the framework of the Potsdam declaration, a great number of laws were enacted in 1945. Uniform measures for all zones were agreed upon for liquidating Nazi laws and the Nazi organization, for raising the rate of taxation, for reorganizing the German judicial system, and for taking over German property abroad. Proclamations imposed additional duties on the Germans, the most important of which regulated such matters as demilitarization, the end of diplomatic relations, and property rights.[15]

The first signs of French obstruction appeared in the Finance Directorate on September 21 and 28, 1945, in the Transport Directorate on September 25, and in the Economy Directorate on October 2. This obstruction was accompanied by two important vetoes, on September 22 in the Coordinating Committee and on October 1 in the Control Council itself. On September 22 General Koeltz rejected the American proposal for a central German transport agency, although he added on October 12 that he was in agreement with the need for an Allied council, so long as the Germans had nothing to do with it.[16] On November 23 Koeltz vetoed the establishment of a central agency to control rail traffic. General Koenig, the French commander-in-chief, stated the official French point of view on October 1, when he pointed out that he would veto the creation of any central German administration until agreement was reached at an international level on the future western boundary of Germany.[17]

This decision was consistently maintained throughout the whole period during which the Control Council functioned. On October 26, 1945, the French rejected a measure which would have permitted the federation of trade-unions throughout Germany, Koeltz announcing that "trade-unions are political structures and will be decentralized."[18] On December 17, 1945, Koeltz turned down a proposal offered by the British and Americans to open the zonal boundaries to the passage of Germans. And on March 26, 1946, the French vetoed a proposal favored by the other three powers which would have permitted political parties to function on a national basis. Thus the French succeeded in preventing the creation of the central German administrative agencies and of the uniform economic planning for Germany as a whole which had been envisaged at Potsdam.

From this point on, growing disagreements between the Soviet and the Western representatives, rather than French obstruction, became the main obstacle to the creation of a common German economy. The first major break with the Russians occurred in April 1946, over reparations and in particular over the Russian view that the "import-export problem would have to be treated as a zonal problem until there was a favorable trade balance for Germany as a whole and reparations had been met in full."[19] The result of this deadlock was to throw the reparations question back to the Council of Foreign Ministers in Paris (April–July 1946). There, failure to obtain agreement caused Secretary of State Byrnes to make his offer to combine the American zone in economic unity with any or all of the other three zones. The British alone agreed, and the result was the creation of the Bizone in December 1946.

The formation of the Bizone was an admission that government of Germany by the Control Council had not proved effective. French opposition at first and disagreements with the Soviet representatives later had led to the establishment of zonal autonomy. After March 1946 the achievements of the Control Council were slight, consisting of measures for further denazification and demilitarization, a population census, and the establishment of administrative courts.[20] In anticipation of the Moscow conference in March–April 1947, the Control Council prepared a long report enumerating the differences that had prevented it from establishing a working government for Germany. After the failure of the Moscow conference, even less was achieved in the Control Council. A few more Nazi laws were repealed. Plants were listed for dismantling as reparations. The failure of the Paris conference of July 1947 and of the London conference of November 1947, accompanied by the offer of Marshall Plan aid in June 1947, led to the complete breakdown of the Control Council, which took place in 1948.

The Control Council meetings of January–March 1948 became increasingly vitriolic. On March 20, 1948, Marshal Sokolovsky walked out of the session, and the Council ceased to function. From that point onward, there was no semblance of government for the whole of Germany. There followed the decisions which led to the formation of separate states in West and East Germany. By the end of 1949 the division of Germany into two parts was both a practical and a constitutional fact.

Critics have argued that the French, by vetoing the proposals for economic unification in 1945, prevented the achievement of a form of centralization at the one time when Allied good will was at a peak, and that French opposition was maintained just long enough for the possibility of centralization to be lost in the power struggle between Russia and the West.[21] American displeasure was felt as early as October 1945. General Eisenhower received Koenig's veto on October 1 "coldly and even, it seems . . . with marked ill temper."[22] Howard K. Smith, in a broadcast on the American radio in November, stated that the other three powers had decided to create a central administration regardless of French objections. And President Truman went so far as to suggest at the end of November that the veto power in the Control Council be abolished. As the London *Times* commented, "the French objections to any central administrations or organizations in Germany were obviously in Mr. Truman's mind when he wished the unanimity rule to be altered."[23]

Why did the French government so stubbornly and so consistently prevent the taking of any positive measures which might have led to the formation of any type of centralized regime in Germany? France vetoed not only the setting up of an administration run by Germans but also the establishment of national organizations, such as an agency for control of rail traffic, which would have been under Allied management. As a result, all powers that were not exercised from the center were exercised by the zonal commanders, and, with few exceptions, each zone became autonomous. France desired this state of affairs for two reasons: first, its plans for dealing with its own zone were incompatible with the creation of a central economic administration or with political unification; and second, its plans for the reorganization of Germany as a whole, which were presented at the international level, would have been jeopardized by such changes.

FORMULATION OF THE "FRENCH THESIS"

The attitude of the French government toward the German problem, unlike that of the American government, did not change greatly in the period from the end of hostilities to the beginning of the Moscow conference in March 1947. In spite of several changes of government, the Ministry of Foreign Affairs was held throughout the period by Georges Bidault, with the sole exception of the four weeks of the all-Socialist government of Léon Blum (December 16, 1946, to January 16, 1947). Moreover, all the major political parties accepted, with differences of emphasis only, several basic principles which they believed should be observed in the treatment of Germany. Although signs of discontent appeared within the Socialist and Communist parties as early as the spring of 1946, an attempt to fuse Bidault's firm policy toward Germany with the slightly more liberal policy demanded by the Socialists was not successful, and the effect was merely to give the impression of a certain incoherence in French policy. In spite of this interlude, Bidault was able to make clear the so-called "French thesis" on Germany, which had been first stated before the end of the war and was upheld tenaciously until the setback of the Moscow conference.[24]

On September 9, 1944, the French provisional government was remodeled to include all individuals and groups in French political life who had not collaborated with the Vichy government. During the weeks following this reorganization, the efforts of the French government were concentrated on gaining the right to share in the deliberations on Germany, and it was uncertain what policy France intended to pursue. Even on November 11, 1944, when Secretary of State Edward Stettinius announced that France would be invited to be a member of the European Advisory Commission, he also added that General de Gaulle and his advisers were probably preparing to ask for the annexation of all territory on the left bank of the Rhine. The matter was still vague after the debate on foreign policy in the Consultative Assembly on November 22, 1944, when de Gaulle announced that any settlement of the German question must grant to France "the elementary security which nature itself put at the banks of the Rhine, for us as for Belgium, Holland and, to a large extent, England." At the same time, General de Gaulle served noticed to the great powers that "France cannot consider itself bound in any way, to any extent, by any decision concerning Europe, or by any important measure concerning any other part of the world, if it has not been invited to give its opinion on that matter in the same way as those who have taken the decisions."[25]

However, in his second press conference after the Liberation, held on January 25, 1945, de Gaulle became much more explicit. The Rhine was to be the key to French security, and although he did not demand the left bank of the Rhine, de Gaulle stated that "France wants to be assured that French forces will be stationed permanently from one end of the Rhine to the other. Its security, like that of western Europe and in a large degree that of the rest of the world, will be found on the Rhine. . . . As for the Rhenish-Westphalian basin which stretches on the right bank of the Rhine, the French government considers that this forms a unity within the limits of the strategic and economic security of western Europe. The political status of the Rhenish provinces will be regulated by those provinces themselves and to some extent by agreements concluded between the allies."[26]

Bidault, in an important press conference in San Francisco in May 1945, was able to state French aims somewhat more precisely, since on the same day the European Advisory Commission had agreed upon the new zonal agreement by which the French army would occupy the Rhine from the Swiss border at least as far as Remagen, sixteen miles south of Bonn. Bidault declared that although he could not support the formation of a Rhenish-Westphalian state, since he was not sure of the geographical justification of such a unit, the Ruhr must be detached from Germany and placed under international control; that France must have means to prevent the Rhineland from remaining an invasion route to France; and that the Saar mines should again become the property of France.[27]

The final communiqué of the Potsdam Conference, issued on August 2, 1945, came as something of a shock to France. Bidault immediately issued six letters to the ambassadors of Britain, the United States, and the Soviet Union. The letters formulated the French refusal to accept or to implement in their zone certain decisions taken at Potsdam. The French government refused to accept the possible reconstruction of a central German government and made certain reservations which were to be used as justification for its later use of the veto in the Control Council. In particular, the French government noted that "certain of the measures envisaged seem to lay down in advance the future political evolution of Germany, while at the present time it is impossible to see whether these measures are in the interests of peace in Europe or even in accordance with the wishes of the populations concerned. The French Government is concerned particularly, in this connection, with the reconstitution of political parties for the whole of Germany, and with the creation of central administrative Departments which would be controlled by Secretaries of State whose jurisdiction, it seems, would extend over the whole of German territory, the boundaries of which have not yet been determined."[28] French opposition to the creation of central German administrative agencies thus sprang from two fears: that such a centralization would lead to the recreation of German military power, and that such a measure would lead to the acceptance of the then-existing frontiers of Germany.

The latter fear was directly connected with French aims in the Saar, the Ruhr, and the Rhineland. It was especially feared that no frontier adjustment would take place in the west similar to that which had been "temporarily" accepted in the east. This fear was voiced by General de Gaulle in an important interview with the London *Times* published on September 10, 1945. By the Potsdam decisions, he said, "Germany was amputated in the east but not in the west. The current of German vitality is thus turned westwards. One day German aggressiveness might well face westwards too. There must therefore be in the west a settlement counter-balancing that in the east. The key areas are the Rhineland and the Ruhr."[29] The Rhineland, he said, was a "march" from which invasion had almost always come. The region from Cologne to the Swiss border was the French march, and should be controlled by France. The region to the north of Cologne was the natural gateway to Belgium, Holland, and even Great Britain, and should be under the control of those three powers. This area should be "cut off from the body of the German state in such a way that its inhabitants know that their future does not lie with Germany." The Ruhr must be put under an international regime of those powers whose economic security depends on Ruhr coal. The Rhine River must be internationalized.

In this way, the organization of Germany was to be linked to the military and territorial guarantees that France demanded for its security. But in the same interview de Gaulle introduced two vital new issues, and during the next four years these were to prove of deeper significance than the traditional French view of necessary guarantees. First, de Gaulle said that Western Europe was to be created as the new unit in which France would find her economic and military security. Second, French security was necessarily linked to the question of coal supplies. Coal supply was a major factor in every decision that France took regarding Germany in post-Liberation years. Coal shortages, disturbances of supply, annoyance at decreased Allied allotments, and the desire for greater zonal output—all derived from France's penury of coal—were at the basis of many of the demands France made during these years. Marcel Cachin, editor of the Communist paper *L'Humanité*, expressed this basic concern in an impassioned editorial on May 30, 1945. Under the title "We need coal," he wrote: "No problem is more urgent than that of coal. Without coal, there will be unemployment. Without coal, it is quite futile to make pompous speeches on 'French greatness.' . . . France needs 70 millions tons a year. And, today, we are producing less than 30 million. . . . There is coal in the Saar and the Ruhr, and the mines in those regions are intact. It seems to us totally just that we should receive our share of the products of those two basins."[30]

It was clear by September 1945 that France's demands were of two very different kinds. First, there were the traditional demands: that Germany should be disarmed and demilitarized, that it should lose the military potential of the Ruhr and the Saar; that the left bank of the Rhine should be placed under some form of non-German control; and that Germany itself should be split up into some kind of federation. But there was also a direct demand that the economy of Germany should be placed at the service of the other powers of Europe and, in particular, of France. This new demand, masked by such phrases as the "economic security" of France, revealed nothing less than a determination to exploit the German economy just as the Germans had exploited the French.

On his trip through the French zone of occupation from October 3 to 5, 1945, General de Gaulle made it abundantly clear that the economic advantages of occupation were foremost in his mind. At Baden-Baden, on October 5, in the major speech of the tour, he pointed toward final economic union of the French zone with France itself:

> To establish France here means giving it, first, disposal of those territories which, by their very nature, form a unity with it. . . . I mean by that those territories on the left bank of the Rhine, the Pfalz, Hessen, Rhenish Prussia and the Saar . . . , that Pfalz which is a continuation of our Alsace, that Hessen which is at the meeting point on the Rhine of those valleys which lead us along the Main to the Danube, those Eifel mountains which are, in fact, the continuation of our Ardennes. . . . This must be a moral and economic union, a permanent link and a lasting control.
>
> I am thinking of the Ruhr . . . , a guarantee, for, without it, Germany will not be able to rise again, and once more, threaten us, attack us and invade us. An instrument which will help France to become a great industrial power, a goal it cannot achieve without the contribution of that mining basin.[31]

Bidault, meanwhile, profited by the meeting of the Council of

Foreign Ministers in London in September 1945 to present the French
viewpoint. As this was the first time since the war that France had been
present at discussions on this level, the occasion was used for a full
presentation of the French case. In a memorandum dated September 14, Bidault stated at length the French objections to the creation
of a centralized German state and demanded the definitive separation
of the Rhenish-Westphalian region, including the Ruhr, from Germany. And he gave warning that the French representative on the
Control Council at Berlin "will not be authorized to agree to any
measure affecting the fate of the Rhenish-Westphalian region before
the question discussed above has been dealt with by the five ministers
and has been made the subject of a decision by the Council of Ministers."[32] Two weeks later, Koenig announced that he would veto the
proposed creation of central German administrative agencies.

During the early months of 1946 the French position was made
even clearer. French proposals for the Saar were presented formally
in a memorandum of February 12, 1946. This memorandum stated
that the mines of the Saar, which had been given to France by the
Treaty of Versailles and returned to Germany in 1935, should again
become the property of the French state. The territory of the Saar
should be included in the French customs system and in the French
currency area and should be removed from the jurisdiction of the Control Council. A French military force should be stationed permanently in the Saar, and France should take over permanent supervision
of the administration of the territory.[33]

The French proposals for the Ruhr were presented by Bidault in
the Constituent Assembly on January 17, 1946, and repeated in a
memorandum presented to the Paris meeting of the Council of Foreign
Ministers on April 25, 1946. According to these proposals, the Ruhr
should be separated from the rest of Germany and placed under international control, both political and economic. The local population
should be permitted to share in the administration. An international
force should be stationed permanently in the Ruhr. The most important mines and industrial enterprises should be taken over by an international consortium and run by international public enterprises. In
explaining these proposals on July 12, 1946, Bidault spoke much more
openly about French motives. Creating German economic unity must
not, he said, be used to justify an increase in the internal consumption

of coal in Germany. "This question of the export of coal is, I repeat, vital for the French economy," he said. "We ask for the assurance of receiving, for a great number of years, an important and definite quantity of German coal. Those guarantees should, in our opinion, result from the reintegration of the Saar into our customs area and from the internationalization of the Ruhr, as we proposed."[34]

As for the Rhineland, the French proposed that military forces should be stationed there permanently, that the area as far north as Cologne should be under French control with the possibility of participation by Belgium or Luxembourg, and that the Rhineland north of Cologne should be under Belgian, Dutch, and possibly British control. The area would be split up into two or three states, separated politically and economically from the rest of Germany. Germany itself would be reconstructed on a federal basis.[35]

Bidault presented these proposals at the meeting of the Council of Foreign Ministers in Paris in July 1946, with very unsatisfactory results. The French proposals on the Saar, which had been accepted by the United States and Britain, were rejected by Molotov. Two days earlier, on July 10, Molotov had also rejected the French proposals for the Ruhr, by refusing to acquiesce in the detachment of the Ruhr from the rest of Germany. What was worse, in French eyes, he had supported the political unification of Germany. Two important results followed from this setback. First, Secretary of State James F. Byrnes offered to unite the American zone economically with any or all of the other zones, and this offer was officially accepted by the British on July 29. Second, the unanimous support which Bidault had so far enjoyed in France was severely reduced by the Socialists' disagreements and by the Communists' uncertainty at finding their own proposals opposed by Molotov himself.

On August 10, 1946, General Koenig refused the American proposal for economic fusion of the zones because, he said, it would endanger coordinated action by the four occupying powers. In reply, reversing the position he had taken in 1945, he proposed the creation of allied bureaus which would lay the foundations of German economic unity under the supervision of the Control Council. This suggestion was rejected by the other three powers on the ground that it would simply create another, and unnecessary, piece of control machinery. On August 30 Koenig announced that the whole of the northern section of the French zone was to be united into a single political division, to be known as Rheinland-Pfalz. In short, with the coming economic union of the British and American zones and the strengthening of local political units in the French zone, the dismemberment of Germany was rapidly taking place.

FRENCH POLITICAL PARTIES AND THE GERMAN PROBLEM

From 1944 to 1947 cabinet government in France was based upon party coalitions, and, as a result, an attempt was made to formulate a policy toward Germany upon which all the major parties were agreed. This attempt was largely successful, since only the Socialist party developed views which differed from those of the French thesis as formulated by de Gaulle and Bidault, and the Socialist party's views were not implemented during this period. The French Provisional Government, as remodeled on September 9, 1944, was a government of "national unanimity" and was intended to include all groups which had not collaborated with the Vichy regime. After the elections of October 1945, de Gaulle re-formed his government, calling it this time a "government of national unity." The cabinet contained five Communists, five Socialists, five members of the MRP, three of the UDSR, and one Radical-Socialist.

The Communist party, which had played an important part in organizing the Resistance, seemed to be as concerned as any other party with the restoration of the national power of France. On August 22, 1944, *L'Humanité* called for a national insurrection. Day after day, the crimes of Buchenwald, Dachau, and Auschwitz were described, with demands for vengeance. Once Germany was defeated, permanent guarantees of security must be taken, the Communist party urged, and these guarantees would include the internationalization of the Ruhr and the detachment of the Rhineland from Germany. Two basic motives, beyond the desire for security, impelled this support of the French thesis. The first was ideologically inspired: the Communists demanded that the great German trusts should be destroyed. The Communists felt that Anglo-Saxon opposition to the French proposals on Germany was instigated by the international trusts. "The great international trusts," wrote the paper, "the great Anglo-American business firms, are not at all keenly in favor of any measure affecting their German counterparts. Ford, Du Pont de Nemours, General

Motors, Imperial Chemical Industries, and other cartels have maintained too close ties with the German trusts to allow radical measures to be taken without resisting."[36] Second, in the Communist view, the reconstruction of German society should be accompanied by the utmost rigor in demanding reparations. On October 20, 1945, Maurice Thorez, speaking on the radio, named as the first condition of French revival the need "to obtain from Germany compensation for the destruction France had suffered." France had the right, Thorez explained, to demand "in the greatest possible degree, legitimate reparations which are due to us, in material goods and in the use of German labor.... We have the right to demand the coal of the Saar, the wood of the Black Forest, and the agricultural products of Württemberg and the Pfalz."[37]

The most unequivocal support for Bidault's policy came from his own party, the Popular Republican Movement (MRP). In its program of November 8, 1945, the MRP announced: "Germany must not be permitted to become a menace. An allied occupation must enforce the punishment of war criminals and an effective reparations policy. It must bring about administrative and political decentralization of the Reich. The Rhenish-Westphalian basin must be withdrawn from the Reich's authority.... France, once again assaulted and laid waste by aggression, has the right to reparations, which it will find mainly in the German mines. The coal of the Saar must be granted to it. It must participate in the interallied administration of the Ruhr basin."[38]

Again and again, the MRP endorsed the position of de Gaulle and Bidault. On September 11, 1945, following de Gaulle's interview with the London *Times*, Maurice Schumann wrote in *L'Aube*: "What is our destiny? ... To place the Rhineland under the strategic and political control of France ... to guarantee by common exploitation of the Ruhr basin the economic security of the whole of western Europe, to internationalize the Rhine to make it a central feature of European cooperation: it is, quite simply, to give the French, the English, the Belgians, the Dutch, the assurance that Germanism has not succeeded in exterminating the elementary right of having and raising children. Who could oppose this?"[39] The final aim of the MRP was the restoration of French *grandeur*. Commenting on de Gaulle's ban on press comment about his failure to meet Roosevelt after the Yalta Conference, Schumann asked, "Why prevent us from saying that the reconquest of our rank and the reconquest of our greatness remain the obsession of France and should remain that of every Frenchman?"[40]

These views were echoed with even greater conviction by the parties of the Right. In particular, the Republican Federation welcomed the possible organization of a Western bloc, which would be the result of the application of de Gaulle's proposals of September 10, 1945. *La Nation* remarked that it was to be hoped that England would now rally to support the French thesis on Germany, but that it was still more important for France and England to form a Western bloc. "To maintain their common civilization, of which England and France are the guides, the countries which enjoy that civilization should play a role between the two enormous powers, American to the west and Slav to the east," the paper urged.[41] The key to the formation of this bloc would be the Rhine. On September 28, 1945, the Republican Federation summarized its attitude on the German question. Fearing that the Allies were falling into the same errors they had made in 1919, the party demanded "occupation, disarmament, removal of raw materials useful for war, supervision of war factories, moral disarmament, administrative and political break-up of the unity of Germany, alliance with England, the United States and Russia, . . . and *the definitive acceptance of the Rhine as the Franco-German military frontier*."[42]

All parties, with the exception of the Socialists, were therefore agreed on the ultimate aim to be achieved in Germany. All were in agreement that Germany must be so weakened, militarily and economically, as to cease to be a danger. All believed that certain territorial guarantees must be exacted—especially in the Rhineland, the Ruhr, and the Saar—and that Germany should be dismembered. All wanted the German economy to be put at the disposal of France in the largest measure possible.

The attitude of the Socialists was important because, from the outset, it differed basically from that of the other parties. Even though three Socialists were members of de Gaulle's "Government of National Unanimity," the Socialist organ, *Le Populaire,* took occasion to print, on September 11, 1945, its official declaration concerning Germany alongside the report of de Gaulle's interview with the London *Times.* This declaration insisted that Germany must experience a prolonged period of occupation, must be disarmed, must have its heavy industry socialized and operated by the nations of Europe, and must be thoroughly re-educated; but it opposed any dismemberment of Germany or the annexation of any territories specifically German.[43]

The Socialist cabinet members in the de Gaulle governments nevertheless endorsed the Bidault policy as it was presented before January 1946. After de Gaulle's resignation a new government was formed under the Socialist Félix Gouin, and it was based not on national unity but on a three-party coalition of Communists, Socialists, and the MRP. This government remained in power until June 1946. Bidault retained the Ministry of Foreign Affairs, however, and in the Paris Conference of Foreign Ministers he continued to advocate his thesis on Germany.

The Socialist party, however, became increasingly discontented with this formula. On March 14, 1946, an editorial in *Le Populaire* suggested that there was danger of losing the immediate possibilities of action in the Ruhr by linking the question of economic control with that of political control of the Ruhr and the Rhineland. What was needed in the Ruhr, it said, was an "international nationalization." Gouin himself, speaking at Strasbourg on March 25, 1946, demanded above all more coal from Germany and foresaw as a solution of the German problem a prolonged occupation followed by the establishment of an international consortium to direct and control the Ruhr. And on March 30, 1946, in a speech before the Socialist congress, Gouin made the most moderate demands yet made by a French statesman since the Liberation. Annexation, brutal or disguised, could not be a solution, he said. As for the Saar, the Rhineland, and the Ruhr, he went on, "we can only consider the administration and control of those territories, which constitute the vital heart of Germany, from the international point of view. . . . Hostile to any dismemberment or any annexation, and equally [hostile] to the division of Germany into four zones of occupation, the Party demands international occupation of this area, prolonged until total denazification has been carried out; economic internationalization, for the benefit of the war-torn countries, of that arsenal of war which is the Ruhr; and exploitation by France, as reparations, of the Saar mines."[44]

The London *Times* was quick to point out the essential novelty of Gouin's position—that he was willing to forgo the territorial separation of the Ruhr from Germany. The *Times* believed that this reflected a desire for British support in the neutralization of Germany, but added, somewhat wistfully, that Gouin could commit only the Socialists and that therefore little could be expected from this attitude.[45] Since Gouin had become so outspoken, conflict between him and Bidault was probably unavoidable. On April 6, 1946, the afternoon papers in Paris appeared with headlines announcing a "Gouin-Bidault quarrel." Pertinax, writing in *France-Soir*, noted that Bidault demanded both economic and political control of the Ruhr whereas Gouin wanted only economic control, and that Gouin wanted an English alliance before agreement on Germany whereas Bidault would have reversed the order.[46] This difference was quickly denied by the cabinet, which sensed the need to present a united front during the Paris conference. Hence, Bidault, on April 25, was able to put forward to the Council of Foreign Ministers the proposals already described, although they were in direct conflict with the Socialist point of view advanced by Gouin. On June 12, 1946, after the election of the second Constituent Assembly, Gouin resigned. A new government was formed on June 23, 1946, with Bidault as Premier and Minister of Foreign Affairs. Once again, it was a three-party government.

Léon Blum, the elder statesman of the Socialist party, intervened at this point to show that the appearance of unanimity in Gouin's government had been false. He asked, rather slyly, "Do I have to make my lantern even brighter? Although the divergence of opinions has been expressed with all suitable discretion, everyone in political circles knows . . . that, on the future political and territorial status of Germany, the cabinet of Félix Gouin was not unanimous. . . . If we are supporters of an 'international nationalization' of industry, we are not supporters of dismemberment, political or territorial. . . . Well, the thesis of the dismemberment of Germany, of amputation in the west symmetrical with that in the east, is the view that Georges Bidault, head of the MRP, has never stopped defending. . . . It is that which the Communists have never ceased to uphold."[47]

Paradoxically, the Socialists found themselves opposing the Communists by supporting Molotov's demand for a unified Germany, or, as Blum put it, "in agreement with Stalin against the French Communists and doubtless in league with the Holy See against the MRP."[48] With the setback of the Paris conference, discussion of the German problem was postponed until the London meeting in December 1946. At that meeting, and particularly in the discussions of December 7–12, Maurice Couve de Murville upheld the French position as formulated earlier by Bidault; the only result of the conference was the drawing up of a program for the discussions on the German peace treaty to be held in Moscow the following March.

On November 29, 1946, following the elections of the new National Assembly, Bidault resigned, and, after a long parliamentary crisis, an exclusively Socialist cabinet was formed under Léon Blum; this cabinet was to act for four weeks as a "caretaker" government. Although the London *Times* believed that "the French have abandoned their demand for political separation of the Ruhr and the Rhineland from the rest of Germany," the short-lived government was able to bring no fundamental change into French policy toward Germany.[49] In January Bidault was again back at the Ministry of Foreign Affairs, this time in the Cabinet headed by the Socialist Paul Ramadier, which was formed by a coalition of almost all parties. There was to be no change in the French point of view that was presented at the Moscow conference in March.

THE MOSCOW CONFERENCE REJECTS THE FRENCH THESIS

The French plan for the Moscow conference was elaborated before the conference met in two memoranda dated January 17, 1947, which were presented to the preliminary Lancaster House meetings in London on January 21. These meetings had the purpose of preparing a procedure to be followed by the Council of Foreign Ministers in March, and the French government was the sole member of the four major powers to present at this point a full, reasoned statement of its position.

The first of the two memoranda dealt with the proposed provisional organization of Germany. It foresaw a regional organization based on the German Länder, and specified the powers that each of these Länder should possess. Each Land would control its own education, fine arts, religion, justice, local administration, civil service, hygiene, and public health services. It would run its own finances and its national economy, as well as the various economic departments such as industrial production. These duties could be turned over immediately to German administrators. At the central level, it would be necessary to set up means of coordinating internal and foreign trade, food, postal services, and transport. Control of the economy and finances would for the moment remain under Allied direction.[50]

The second memorandum proposed a constitutional organization

for Germany whch would make possible a certain economic centralization accompanied by political decentralization. In considerable detail,
the memorandum described the possible division of authority between
the federal organisms and the Länder. The result would be a radically decentralized federation or *Bund*.[51] A third memorandum, presented on February 1, 1947, contained French proposals for the Ruhr.
The preoccupation with German coal was at the heart of this document,
which proposed to divide Ruhr property into two categories, mines
and metallurgical industry. Both would be placed under international
control and management, but coal production would be increased while
the industrial production would be severely restricted. The new arrangement would be written into the final treaty of peace.[52]

In short, the French delegation to Moscow had several clear aims.
It wished to obtain certain political and territorial changes: that the
Rhineland be separated from Germany and internationalized; that the
industrial potential of the Ruhr be put under international control and,
as later appeared at the conference, that the Ruhr itself be detached
from Germany; that the Saar mines be made the property of France
and that the territory be included in the French customs and financial
system; that Germany be organized on a federal basis, as a union of
the existing Länder; and especially that full economic advantage be
derived from the German economy, both by exacting reparations and
by providing the guarantee of a steady supply of German coal.

The French thought they had reason to hope that their propositions would be accepted, at least in some compromise form. Britain
and the United States had already indicated themselves moderately
favorable to all save the proposal for separating the Rhineland and
the Ruhr. Above all, France believed that it had certain claims on the
support of the Soviet Union. France had refused Byrnes's offer to fuse
all the zones into an economic unity on the ground that it would disturb
the working of four-power control in Germany. It had accepted the
frontier revisions which had taken place in the east. It had proposed
for the Ruhr an international control which would have given the
Soviet Union a right to share in the control of that area. Finally, the
French proposals were supported by the Communist party in France.
Yet Bidault found at Moscow that, on every issue other than reparations, his proposals were blocked by the opposition of Molotov. This
was the most important result of the Moscow conference for France;

from this point on, France gave up pretensions of remaining in the central mediating position between the two opposed blocs and threw in its lot with the Western powers.

On April 10, 1947, at Moscow, Bidault proposed the internationalization of the Ruhr and the political and economic separation of the Rhineland from Germany. The British and the Americans showed themselves unfavorable to the idea of permitting the Russians to participate in control of the Ruhr. Molotov refused to consider the separation of the Ruhr or the Rhineland from the rest of Germany. It seemed at first that in the Saar, at least, French demands would be granted, since both the British and the Americans had accepted the French proposals by April 10. But Molotov again prevented the acceptance of this proposal, this time by refusing to take a position on the question.

When the question of the future constitutional organization of Germany was discussed, great divergence of views again was voiced; a federal organization was desired in various forms by the Western powers, and a centralized form was favored by the Russians. Molotov's idea of putting the matter to the Germans for decision by plebiscite was, as Bidault pointed out, to ensure that the decision would be for a centralized government. Again, no agreement was reached. In fact, in Bidault's speech of March 22, it is possible to see the final break between the French and the Russians.

In the discussions on reparations, Molotov showed great sympathy for France's demands for more German coal, perhaps because the coal would come from the British and American zones. The French and the Russians were in agreement that reparations should be exacted from German industrial equipment and also from current production. Molotov would not, however, agree with the French demand that the level of steel production be severely restricted, and no decision was reached on this matter. In every one of its demands, France found itself checked. The only result of this month's negotiations was a coal agreement, worked out in London on April 14 by English, French, and American experts and signed in Moscow on April 21. By this agreement, the French share of the coal exports of the three western zones would be raised from 12 to 21 and later to 25 per cent. However, Hervé Alphand, the French representative at Moscow who had taken part in negotiating the agreement, stated that France would still lack sufficient coal until the Saar was incorporated in its economic system. For this shortage, as *Le Populaire* pointed out, Molotov was clearly to blame. His refusal to take a position on the Saar question had cost France 400,000 tons of coal a month.[53]

The Moscow conference thus brought to an end French efforts to have the French thesis on Germany adopted. The characteristics of this period had been the near-unanimity among French political parties as to the means for attaining their two major goals, security and coal; the attempt of France to maintain a central position between the two major power blocs; the refusal of France to accept any measure that would adversely affect the possibility of future acceptance of the French thesis on Germany; and the maintenance of virtual autonomy in the French zone itself, since any form of central control was blocked by the French veto in the Control Council. With the definitive rejection of the French thesis at the Moscow conference all this was changed. A new method of achieving security and economic benefit had to be found. The political unanimity inside France was decisively destroyed when the Communists left the government of Ramadier on May 4, 1947. A new plan for the future of Germany had to be conceived, a plan that would take into account the struggle for power between the Western and Eastern blocs. The rejection of the French thesis at Moscow was the necessary prelude to the creation of the West German Federal Republic.

CHAPTER III

France and the German Problem
1947-1949

WHEN Foreign Minister Bidault returned to Paris from the Moscow conference in April 1947, he announced, somewhat wryly, that his sole success had been to "bring back a little coal."[1] Beyond this meager achievement, he had been unable to secure the great powers' acceptance of any aspect of the French thesis on Germany which he had been advocating since 1945. The effects of this failure were not, however, immediately evident, since Bidault continued to press his demands until the dismal failure of the London conference in November 1947. But the months between the two conferences of 1947 saw certain changes in the international situation which forced France to develop a new orientation in its German policy and which finally brought an end to the separate existence of the French zone.

By April 1947 the French thesis on Germany included six major points. These were: (*a*) that the Rhineland should be demilitarized and detached from Germany; (*b*) that the Ruhr should be separated from the rest of Germany and placed under international control; (*c*) that the Saar should be joined in an economic union with France; (*d*) that Germany should be exploited economically for the benefit of its neighbors, by exacting reparations, controlling the distribution of its coal and steel, and maintaining a low ceiling on its industrial production; (*e*) that by a thorough process of demilitarization and denazification, Germany should be made incapable of menacing its neighbors; and (*f*) that Germany should be re-educated and reorganized as a democratic, federal state. These six aims, which were designed to provide military security and economic well-being for France, remained the basis of French policy up to the formation of the West German Federal Republic. The two years following the Moscow conference differed from the years that preceded it, not because France changed its aims, but because it was forced to accept a compromise.

Possession of a zone of occupation in Germany had great significance for France at this time. First, it ensured that in this section of Germany, at least, French aims could be carried out without prior international agreement. Second, the power to accept or reject trizonal fusion was a major point of bargaining strength in bringing the Anglo-Saxon powers to accept certain French proposals for Germany as a whole. The French were determined to hold on to their zone until they received specific guarantees that some of their aims in Germany would be achieved or until sufficient pressure should be applied to make it necessary for France to acquiesce in trizonal fusion. Between 1947 and 1949, both factors affected French diplomatic thinking.

The new guarantees of France's economic progress and military security were the Marshall Plan and the North Atlantic Pact, along with minor satisfaction on several of the points in the French thesis. What forced France's hand was the determination of Britain and the United States to act without France if necessary, as evidenced by the developments in the Bizone. The period between the Moscow conference of March 1947 and the entry into force of the Occupation Statute and of trizonal fusion on September 21, 1949, fell clearly into three parts. From April to December of 1947, France pursued its earlier aims, although major events took place which ensured that these aims would shortly be anachronistic. Between January and June of 1948 French policy was reoriented in a grudging change of approach. Between June 1948 and September 1949, the decisions of the previous six months were, very painfully, embodied in a practical form.

SWAN SONG OF THE FRENCH THESIS

In the months following the breakdown of the Moscow conference, the diplomats continued to go through the motions of seeking agreement. But the major events affecting Germany were the separate actions of the four occupying powers and, even more important in the long run, the development of a new orientation of American and European policy implied in the Truman Doctrine and the Marshall Plan.

During this time the French government continued to press its thesis within the limits of its power. The French zone's seclusion from the other zones was maintained, with the minor exception of an agreement on May 21, 1947, for an exchange of goods between the French zone and the Bizone. The French military government maintained its absolute ban on any form of centralization in Germany. For example, on June 4–6, 1947, at the Munich meeting of the German minister-presidents of all the zones, including the Soviet zone, the minister-presidents under French control announced that they were forbidden to discuss the formation of a central German government.[2] Plans were rapidly advanced for ensuring the economic fusion of the Saar with France. At Moscow in April, Bidault had received British and American approval of French aims in the Saar. On June 15, 1947, a separate Saar mark was created, thereby cutting off the Saar from the economy of the French zone. In the autumn, the Saar's own wishes were canvassed. The elections on October 5, 1947, gave an 87 per cent mandate for economic union with France, only the Communists opposing the fusion. On November 14, 1947, the whole Saar question was debated in the French National Assembly. Bidault proposed the introduction of the French franc into the Saar as a first step to economic union. Against vigorous Communist opposition, the Assembly voted a credit of 48 billion francs to make this currency change possible.[3]

Events in the Bizone, however, provided a serious challenge to any future implementation of the French thesis on several of its major points. The Bizone had been created to remedy the great economic drain on the occupying powers in both the British and American zones.[4] As the fusion agreement stated, "The aim of the two Governments is the achievement by the end of 1949 of a self-sustaining economy for the area."[5] Fusion would involve pooling of all resources of the area, transferring responsibility for foreign trade to the German Administrative Agency for Foreign Trade, and relaxing barriers to trade. The further effects became clearer in 1947.

The second stage of the development of the Bizone was a major attempt to associate Germans in the government, as could have been surmised from Secretary of State Byrnes's speech in Stuttgart on September 6, 1946.[6] It took practical form in the creation of an Economic Council for the Bizone on May 29, 1947. General Lucius Clay, the American military governor, admitted later that although it was intended to make this body an instrument of government, "we still wanted to avoid the impression of governmental authority."[7] This action was followed in July by the decision of the British and American commanders-in-chief to raise the bizonal level of production, especially in steel. This decision was considered further at an Anglo-American conference which met on August 12. It was decided that administration of coal production should be placed in German hands, under Allied control. Bidault objected strongly to these changes, and on August 7, demanded a tripartite conference, which took place in London on August 22–27, 1947. Ambassador Massigli and his deputy argued that the basic question in the level of industry discussions was coal. France's fundamental economic need was for coal. On July 17, in the sixteen-power conference on the Marshall Plan, the French delegate had declared, "German coal production must be expanded to the maximum: we all have need of it; and German agricultural production must be expanded to the maximum. . . . But as for the industrial revival of Germany, the French subordinate all measures of that kind to the needs of security."[8]

Massigli returned to this point on August 22, 1947, when he expressed sympathy for the British and American desire to alleviate their burden in Germany but noted that Germany ought to aid European recovery "by putting at the disposal of the countries of Europe the supplies of coal and of coke which are the key to this continent's production."[9] The French government insisted most of all on the importance of establishing a satisfactory system of international controls in the Ruhr. Very few concessions were made in the Anglo-American reply of August 28, 1947, which merely promised that a meeting of experts would study the problem of supplying France with greater quantities of coke and would review the sliding scale of coal exports.[10] The next day the revised Level of Industry plan for the Bizone was published, in which it was stated that the level of production would be raised to that prevailing in 1936, and that in particular production in the metal, machinery, and chemical industries would be raised.[11] Finally, on November 19, the British and American governments announced the creation of a German coal management board, with a German director assisted by German departmental directors and an advisory committee, in association with a bipartite Allied control group.

France was thus faced with a radically new situation in the Bizone. A centralized form of German government had been created in the

Economic Council. A higher level of industry had been planned, and this seemed to threaten both France's military security and its supply of German coal. And a German administration had been put in charge of the Ruhr mines. The first French reaction had been one of strong opposition. With the Anglo-American rejection of the French complaint, France was forced to consider other ways of making its wishes felt in the Bizone. The last resort was trizonal fusion; but every possible effort short of fusion was used for almost two years to influence events in the Bizone.

Meanwhile, Secretary of State Marshall's offer of economic aid on June 5, 1947, had revolutionized France's economic position. It was clear that France no longer depended on the exploitation of Germany for rebuilding its economic position. On signing the interim aid agreement on January 2, 1948, France was to receive $280 million in credits; and $337 million in credits was made available by a series of temporary arrangements in the crisis period of October through December of 1947. By June 30, 1954, France had received from Marshall Plan funds $3,104 million, a total of approximately $72 per person of France's population.[12]

One more event completed France's alignment with the Western powers. In May 1947 the Communist ministers were forced out of Paul Ramadier's cabinet, after which the Communist party remained permanently in opposition. Its stand was made clear in October 1947, when it refused to collaborate in the formation of a popular front with the Socialists and MRP. The swing to the Right was greatly accentuated by the successes of de Gaulle's new movement, the Rally of the French People (RPF), formed in April 1947, and by the failure of Léon Blum in November to form a "Third Force" of the Socialists and the MRP working in collaboration with the Radicals and conservatives.[13]

The London Foreign Ministers' Conference (November 25–December 16, 1947) was the last occasion when the French thesis was presented in its early, uncompromising form. As Bidault later reported to the Foreign Affairs Committee of the National Assembly, "As far as France is concerned, its representatives had set off, as they did to the Moscow conference, with the mission and the firm intention of defending, as much as circumstances permitted, the positions clearly stated by all governments since the Liberation."[14] From the start of the conference, Bidault opposed Molotov's demands for the creation of a central German government. When Molotov refused to discuss the question of frontiers, and thereby again excluded the question of the Saar, Bidault announced that France would not permit a central German government to extend its jurisdiction over the Saar. On December 5, he outlined the French economic proposals. Reparations, he argued, should be exacted by dismantling, by delivery of machine tools, and even by confiscations from current production. He again outlined the importance of the export of German coal. For the Ruhr, he demanded only a "special regime" of international control, which meant that France had at last abandoned its claims for the political detachment of the Ruhr from Germany.[15]

The sole decision made at the conference was that Germany should be permitted to double its steel production. It was clear to Bidault that his policy no longer had any chance of being imposed by quadripartite agreement; and he concluded in his report to the Foreign Affairs Committee: "For the moment, we must put up with this situation. We are responsible for our zone and, with the others, responsible as well for the general evolution of Germany. . . . We shall press on with our task, which is to achieve, with the means left to us, the permanent goals of French policy, for our own safety and for the peace of the world."[16]

A NEW ORIENTATION TO FRENCH POLICY, 1948

After the failure of the Foreign Ministers Conference in London, everything seemed to point the way to trizonal fusion. On December 7, 1947, Bidault, Marshall, and Bevin held a secret meeting which was thought to foreshadow fusion. Asked at a press conference in London about trizonal fusion, Bidault replied that it was not imperative but not impossible, either. Secretary Marshall told Clay before leaving London that, according to Bidault, the French government was now willing to consider trizonal fusion on condition that the Ruhr and the question of security be considered at the same time.[17]

Events in Germany, meanwhile, seemed to be making trizonal fusion necessary for France. A conference was held in Frankfurt on January 7–8, 1948, between the British and American military governors and the minister-presidents of the Bizone. By what became known as the Frankfurt Charter, a genuine form of German government was to be created in the Bizone.[18] As Clay pointed out at the time, these changes were only "the prelude to a government, at least of the British and American zones, to be made effective at an early date if quadripartite agreement for a unified Germany fails to materialize." Affairs were now at a critical point, he felt, where "we must either move forward to give the Germans increased responsibility in the bizonal area to insure their proper contribution to European recovery, or we must move backward to increase our own forces to run a more colonial type of government."[19]

The French government at once began a strong campaign against these proposals. On January 8, Massigli protested in London. On January 9, Bonnet did the same in Washington. The unexpected result was the announcement on January 21 that a tripartite conference would take place shortly in London to give France all possible information on plans for the Bizone, and to discuss trizonal fusion and the general problem of the organization of western Germany.[20] It was in this indirect way that the British, American, and French governments decided to hold what proved to be the most important conference on the future of Germany since the end of the war. Moreover, the exclusion of the Soviet government from this conference, and the later decision to associate the Benelux powers in this work, was of great significance, because it sanctioned not only the division of Germany but the division of Europe.

In spite of the arrangement for tripartite talks in London on February 23, the new bizonal statute was promulgated on February 9. A certain sop for French feelings was provided by the announcement on February 20 that a tripartite meeting of experts in Berlin had decided that the Saar coal should be progressively withdrawn from the German coal pool and assigned completely to France by April 1, 1949.[21]

The French government now adopted a very different approach. Bidault made the first clear statement of it in the National Assembly debate on foreign policy on February 13, 1948. The major turning-point in foreign relations since the war, he said, had come in the week of June 27 to July 3, 1947, when the Soviet Union refused to participate in the Marshall Plan. Since that time, France's field of action had been Europe as a whole. Marshall aid would help to create European unity, and only in European unity could the German problem be solved. For the German nation, he went on, "the solution—and there is no other—is the integration of a peaceful Germany in a united Europe, a Europe where the Germans, feeling secure in their position, will have been able to get rid of the idea of dominating Europe." For this reason he proposed reconstruction of Germany on a federal basis and further consideration of the problems of coal and control of the Ruhr. Finally, he returned to the two major demands of the French thesis. France wanted, he said, "concrete guarantees of which the main point would be, apart from a permanent occupation of the Rhenish provinces and the limitation or prohibition of certain particularly dangerous industries, an international regime for the Ruhr which would assure control of that essential region and an equitable distribution, by international decision, of the coal and coke it produces."[22] In short, France was at last prepared to admit Germany back into the European community, but she was determined to demand specific guarantees of her future economic and military security.

The London conference, which opened on February 23 as a tripartite conference of deputy foreign ministers, quickly expanded into a six-power meeting with the inclusion of Belgium, Holland, and Luxembourg. The sessions were to a large extent dominated by a rear-guard action fought by France against the propositions of the Anglo-American delegations. The major political demands of the latter, made as a result of their experiences in the Bizone, envisaged a federal form of government which, while guaranteeing the rights of the Länder, would still leave the central government adequate power. In economic matters, France asked for international control of both the production and distribution of the products of the Ruhr mines and industries. The first series of meetings ended on March 6, 1948.

Important changes were near. It had been agreed that Germany should have a federal constitution guaranteeing the rights of the Länder but giving sufficient power to the federal government. Germany was to be associated in the Marshall Plan. International control was to be exercised over the distribution of the products of the Ruhr, and it was tacitly understood that administration would remain in German hands. No agreement had been reached on trizonal fusion, and the conference recommended that political fusion should precede economic fusion.[23]

Events moved rapidly in the interval between the closing of the first session of the London talks on March 6, and the opening of the second session on April 20. In Germany, the differences of approach between the military governors of the Bizone and the French military governor, General Koenig, became even more pronounced when the three formed a working party to consider basic principles for a constitution. General Clay became convinced at this time that the French government was far more interested in obtaining agreement than was General Koenig. On April 6–8, Couve de Murville, the French representative at the London talks, visited Clay in Germany. As a result, a compromise memorandum was agreed upon and accepted by Koenig; it stated that it was impractical to establish trizonal fusion at once, but that individual measures of fusion, such as a common export-import policy, would be taken.[24]

The major event of this period was, however, the beginning of the Berlin Blockade. On March 20, General Sokolovsky, the Soviet military governor, declared in the Control Council that the London conference had broken the Potsdam agreement and that "by their actions these three delegations once again confirm that the Control Council virtually no longer exists as the supreme body of authority in Germany."[25] On March 30 the Soviet authorities imposed a blockade on road and rail traffic into Berlin. A trial of strength was at hand, in which France could only throw in its lot with the West.

Moreover, the adoption of the Marshall Plan by the United States Congress made it profitable for France to accept the Western alliance. On April 3, 1948, President Truman signed the Foreign Assistance Act, which authorized a maximum allotment of $5,300,000,000 to the European Recovery Program for the next twelve months. Of this sum, France was to receive $989 million, and the French zone a further $100 million. The immense sums involved made it clear to all groups in France that by accepting this aid, France was definitely committing itself to alliance with the United States and was weakening its power to take an independent stand against American wishes with respect to Germany. Finally, France completed its alignment with the West European powers by signing, on March 17, 1948, the Treaty of Brussels, by which it agreed to join with Britain, Belgium, Holland, and Luxembourg in the creation of a West European defense system.[26]

Hence, when the deputy foreign ministers reassembled in London, the international situation had greatly changed. Nevertheless, the

French delegation still held firmly to its position on the nature of the future German constitution. It was forced to concede, finally, that the future German government should exercise the power of taxation and that the lower house should be elected by universal suffrage and not by the Land assemblies. By way of recompense, the other powers agreed that an International Authority for the Ruhr would be established and that an Office of Military Security would be set up to supervise disarmament and demilitarization.

The final recommendations of the conference, issued on June 7, were that Germany should be reintegrated into the European economy, should be permitted a democratic, federal government, and should choose a constituent assembly to draw up a constitution. The occupation forces should remain in Germany. An International Authority for the Ruhr should supervise the distribution of coal, coke, and steel, but not their production.

Trizonal fusion was dismissed briefly in a significant paragraph: "Further discussions have taken place between the United States, United Kingdom, and French delegations on measures for coordinating economic policies and practices in the combined zone and the French zone. Agreed recommendations have been reached on the joint control of the external trade of the whole area. It has been recognized that a complete economic merger of the two areas cannot effectively take place until further progress has been made in establishing the necessary German institutions common to the entire area."[27]

The so-called "London documents" prepared by the conference contained directives on the future organization of Germany and were to be handed to the minister-presidents of the western zones by the military governors on July 1, 1948. The documents listed the conditions which the new constitution of Germany must observe, recommended that the minister-presidents examine the question of Land boundaries and report on desirable changes, and noted that an Occupation Statute would be drawn up by the military governors to regulate the relations of the occupation powers with the future German government.[28]

The London agreements, therefore, demolished a large part of the French thesis. No special provisions were to be made for the Rhineland. The Ruhr was not to be separated from Germany, and neither the ownership nor the management of its industry would be internationalized. A central German government was to be set up, with wide powers of legislation and taxation. No mention was made of reparations in the communiqué, as the idea of economic cooperation within the European Recovery Program was predominant. On the other hand, the economic fusion of the Saar with France was tacitly assumed, and France was to maintain control of its zone of occupation until the West German government was legally created. This jettisoning of France's major demands, however, had a profound effect on French opinion.

FRANCE'S ACCEPTANCE OF THE LONDON AGREEMENTS

In making the London agreements, the French government had moved faster in its thinking than most of the politicians in France. A vast tumult of criticism was loosed by publication of the communiqué, and it was in recognition of the vital change of policy involved in the agreements that the French government, alone among the governments which had taken part in the London conference, agreed to submit the decisions for approval to its parliament.[29] There followed one of the longest and most important National Assembly debates of the postwar years.

The most vociferous opposition to the agreements came from the two political extremes—the Communists and the Gaullist RPF. The Communist party was no longer in the embarrassing position of July 1946, when it found itself in opposition to Soviet Foreign Minister Molotov. Having broken with the government of Ramadier on May 4, 1947, it was now able to follow the party line with considerably more fervor than when it was actually a participant in the making of policy. On March 5, 1948, François Billoux, speaking for the party, began the process of rewriting the history of Communist participation in postwar governments. The solution of the problem of Germany was simple, he said. "It is not a question of developing a completely new policy but simply of taking account of the changes in the international situation, of returning to the policy which we defended in 1945-1946, when we were in the Government. . . . That policy can be summarized in this way: security of France, payment of reparations by Germany."[30]

On Sunday, June 29, 1947, Maurice Thorez, speaking at Strasbourg, announced that "the German people must rebuild what it has destroyed"; and two days later *L'Humanité* declared war on the Marshall Plan, on the ground that "Bidault and Bevin are giving up national independence."[31] In this way the Communists laid down the thesis that growing deference to the will of the Americans would lead to the weakening of France's demands on Germany. Pierre Hervé summed up this attitude on July 4, 1947. "It is the massive revival of German might which is planned," he wrote. "Moreover, since the resources of Germany are going to be included in the application of the Bevin-Bidault plan, our demands for reparations are being neatly sponged from the slate. Gone will be the demand for the internationalization of the Ruhr! Quite the contrary, it is the union of the French zone of occupation in Germany with the Bizone which is implied in the new policy."[32] Thus the Communists became, rather ironically, the main opponents of trizonal fusion (in spite of their objections to the military government personnel in the French zone) and the strongest adherents of harsh economic exploitation in Germany.[33]

On June 5, 1948, Georges Cogniot linked the London agreements directly with the need for Marshall aid. Bidault was portrayed in *L'Humanité* as the "American minister for French affairs."[34] In the Assembly debate on the agreements, Billoux summed up the Communist position on June 11. The agreements meant, he said, that France had allied itself with Britain and America against the U.S.S.R. Nothing was said about reparations. The agreements were subject to the demands of the Marshall Plan. The internationalization of the Ruhr was no longer demanded. A Communist fellow-traveler, Pierre Cot, elaborated these views further on June 12, saying that the agreements involved the re-creation of German economic power, and that the sole controls would remain in American hands.[35] The Communist party therefore voted unanimously to reject the agreements; and on Saturday, June 19, the party called for a one-hour general strike. Although the main purpose of the strike was a token of sympathy for strikers in Clermont-Ferrand, the party also gave as one of the reasons that "at the Hôtel Matignon [the premier's mansion] they are more preoccupied with reviving reactionary Germany than the France of the Liberation."[36]

The Communist party also made the curious claim that one of the major agents of this new policy of reviving Germany was General de Gaulle, with the backing of his party, the RPF. Although it was certainly true that de Gaulle had been one of the main formulators of the French thesis in 1944–45, it was far from correct that he had accepted the policy implied in the London agreements. The RPF was as violent in its opposition as were the Communists. In his Strasbourg speech on April 7, 1947, by which he founded the RPF, de Gaulle opposed the division of the world into two power blocs. Germany, he added, must be reorganized so that it could no longer menace world peace, and France must keep the balance between the two great world powers of today.[37]

This did not make de Gaulle the proponent of integrating Germany into a reorganized Europe, as became clear in his important declaration of June 9, 1948. The government, he said, had put France in the position "of agreeing, without preparation, completely, without valid gains, to plans which imply the gravest risks for itself, for Europe, and for peace." By the London agreements, he went on, the division of Europe into two blocs had been made certain. There was a possibility that one day a re-created Prussia, backed by Soviet Russia, would menace the West. There were no guarantees of reparations or of economic fusion with the Saar, no real control of the Ruhr, no guarantees of France's military security. France, he concluded, should reject the agreements, and then concentrate "on reviving the life of the territories in its zone of occupation as it is already doing in the Saar, by orienting them toward France, both politically and economically. That would cost us far less than the irreparable renunciations which have been proposed." In this situation, the present regime could not fulfill its duties, and he therefore offered to take over the government himself. This action of de Gaulle's did not provoke much comment in France, and his offer to take over the government passed virtually unnoticed.[38] In England, de Gaulle's action provoked unfavorable comment. The *Economist* hinted that de Gaulle could not have read the agreements, since "the proposals which he put forward as an alternative are almost precisely those which the agreement in fact secures."[39] De Gaulle's speech, however, had aligned the RPF firmly against the agreements, and his advice that it would be better to preserve independent control of the French zone than to accept fusion on the terms of the London agreements seemed to carry considerable weight with the representatives of the French military government whose task it was to work out the practical application of the London agreements.

In fact, French recalcitrance was to prove a powerful factor in slowing down negotiations and in preserving the separate existence of the French zone for fifteen months longer.

The attitude of the parties in the government coalition was also one of considerable dissatisfaction. Up to this point, the Socialists had been the supporters of a liberal policy toward Germany. They had conceived of the reintegration of Germany into the European community. They had always opposed the dismemberment of Germany, but they had demanded exaction of reparations, the guarantee of supplies of German coal, and the "international nationalization" of the Ruhr mines and industry. On June 9, 1948, Léon Blum wrote in *Le Populaire* that the Marshall Plan involved the resurgence of German industry, and that therefore France should take guarantees for its security. Yet he did not condemn the conference for refusing to expropriate the German proprietors and socialize the industries. There was a good chance, he thought, that a future German government would do both. He was not satisfied with the security system proposed, as he pointed out in his next two articles. He had come to the conclusion that the true guarantee of security was the continuing presence of occupation forces in Germany. "There are military occupation forces in Germany," he added, "the numbers of which are not important from this point of view, their presence alone being significant."[40]

The Socialist point of view was expressed in the National Assembly debate on the London agreements by André Philip. He pointed out the need to think out again, and to redefine, French foreign policy. Two policies coexisted, he said: the older policy of controlling Germany by dismemberment and the like, and the newer policy of creating a plan for Europe as a whole. Europe must be created as an economic unit. However, as to the Ruhr, he still demanded internationalization of all major industries. Finally, in an important aside, he attacked the soldiers of the occupation who, he said, had played too large a part in the formulation of French policy. "In constitutional matters," he declared, "I do not have absolute confidence in military men. . . . In our zone, as in the others, there appears too great a tendency to construct real satrapies, where the commander-in-chief is a master and not the servant of the government." In the London agreements, he concluded, the commanders-in-chief had played too large a part.[41]

Speakers for the Radical-Socialist party pointed out that French security was not safeguarded, since the British and Americans intended to rebuild German power. Paul Bastid, on June 15, noted that the Anglo-Saxons had spared German heavy industry and kept many Nazis in power. He felt that Europe had to be united before the situation would be ripe for an agreement of this sort.[42] Roger Gaborit added that Germany was not yet ready for centralization, since the local work of democratization had not yet been done. In the French zone in particular, he said, the role of the occupation was not only to guarantee France's physical security but also to prepare the Germans for democracy. "Before envisaging German unity," he continued, "it was necessary to lay the basis for democracy, not only by 'denazification' but by 'degermanization.' For doing this, you had two instruments: control of the government and of education. You have not utilized them thoroughly."[43] Here was yet another demand for keeping the French zone of occupation in French hands.

The government's view was set forth by Georges Bidault, the Minister of Foreign Affairs, who spoke at the same time for his own party, the MRP. Bidault had recognized that the moment had come when France should abandon its uncompromising adherence to the French thesis, of which he had been hitherto the most prominent defender. At the same time, he must have been aware of the danger to his own political career in taking this stand before so hostile an Assembly. In fact, Bidault remained in office for only one month after the debate.[44]

Since France had received no support, even from the Benelux countries, for the detachment or the internationalization of the Ruhr, Bidault showed that he had had to give up this demand. The French government, he said, saw that it must come to some agreement, partly to safeguard its position in the Saar and partly to solve the economic problems facing it in its own zone of occupation. He had therefore made three agreements concerning, respectively, the Ruhr, the constitutional organization of Germany, and French security. As for the constitutional question, France had demanded the creation of a federation by the action of the Länder themselves. France would not, in any circumstances, permit its zone to join any form of organization like that created at Frankfurt. This rendered the project of a constitutional assembly much more to French taste. In regard to security, Bidault pointed out that the present military occupation ensured that the

Rhineland would remain demilitarized, that the Truman speech of March 17 (which promised aid to countries threatened by military aggression) prepared the way for a military pact with the United States, and that a Military Security Office in Germany would be created.[45]

Bidault had not given a full-blooded defense of a new policy, but rather a series of explanations of why the government had felt it necessary to give up so many of its aims. It was particularly significant that the most effective support for these agreements came from the former premier, Paul Reynaud, who asked the Assembly to realize that the new situation in Europe required a new approach from France. The United States, he pointed out, was now deeply involved in European defense. France had already cut itself off from the Slav group by refusing to allow the creation of central German institutions in 1945. The wisest course now, he felt, was for France to cooperate wholeheatedly with its allies in restoring the European economy.[46]

The final vote was taken, on an extremely cautious and limited motion, in the early hours of June 17. The motion stated that although the agreements marked a certain progress in the positions of the English and the Americans, they still took only partial account of the French requests. Still, it went on, since a rejection of the London agreements would bring a regrettable loosening of the ties with friendly powers whose cooperation was necessary for peace, the Assembly recommended acceptance of the agreements. It also recommended that the government demand international control of the Ruhr mines and industry, continued reparations, and prolonged occupation of Germany, and that it prevent the reconstitution of a centralized German Reich.[47] Even with these extremely important reservations, the motion was passed by only eight votes (297–289).

Thus, even following the vote, the position of France remained equivocal. A few factors, however, were clear. First, there was inside France almost unanimous support for the maintenance of the French zone of occupation as a separate unit for as long as possible and at least until other guarantees of France's security had been given. Second, great efforts would still be made to convert the agreement over the Ruhr into a system of control of Germany's economic and military potential. Third, unwilling acquiescence would be given to the re-creation of a German government, but considerable attention would be paid to the definition, in the Occupation Statute, of the powers to be granted to it. France had suffered a change of policy, but not a change of heart.[48]

THE CREATION OF THE FEDERAL GERMAN REPUBLIC

The London agreements provided a mere sketch of the proposed West German state. The next eleven months were spent in the arduous work of preparing a detailed plan. The creation of the new state involved the concurrent preparation of several major constitutional and economic measures. These were: (1) harmonization of the economic and administrative structures of the French zone and the Bizone, so that trizonal fusion could take place with a minimum of dislocation; (2) preparation of an Occupation Statute, which would lay down the relations of the occupying powers with the future German government after trizonal fusion had taken place; (3) establishment of security controls, through an International Authority for the Ruhr and a Military Security Board; and (4) preparation of a constitution for West Germany which would be satisfactory to both the Germans and the occupying powers. Only when all four of these steps had been taken could the creation of the West German state come about.

The French government was much better prepared for trizonal fusion in 1948 than it had been previously, in spite of the strong opposition to such a move in the National Assembly. After the winter of 1947 the French zone was no longer a paying proposition; and one of France's main aims, economic fusion of the Saar with France, had already been carried out. In the debate on the London agreements Bidault took occasion to point out that if the agreements were rejected, "Parliament will have to take the responsibility of making available the necessary credits, at the expense of the national budget, to meet the unfavorable trade balance of a zone which has not been economically viable since we obtained the Saar."[49] Moreover, in the London conference, it had been decided that there should be closer economic coordination between the French zone and the Bizone and, to General Clay's annoyance, provision had been made for consultation of the bizonal commanders with the French military governor before the introduction of important measures in the Bizone which might affect future trizonal fusion.[50] The urgent need for currency reform was felt as strongly in the French zone as in the Bizone. And, finally, the continuing Berlin crisis demanded the closest Western cooperation in meeting Soviet tactics.

Certain measures of economic fusion were taken early in 1948. On April 18 it was announced in Frankfurt that the three Land banks of the French zone had, with the permission of the French military governor, decided to join the bizonal Bank of the German States, thus creating the first trizonal institution. Talks on currency reform had been going on in the Control Council since the beginning of February, but without result. On June 19, after considerable discussion between the commanders of the western zones, a currency reform was proclaimed in the Bizone and in the French zone. The issue, however, had almost been a bizonal measure, as a result of the divergence of opinion between the French and the bizonal authorities and owing to the uncertainty about the outcome of the French Assembly debate on the London agreements.[51] A final compromise made the trizonal issue of the new currency possible, and from June 20, 1948, the three zones enjoyed a common currency and a central bank, the Bank of the German States. On August 24 free passage for persons and goods between the French zone and the Bizone was permitted, and preparation of joint food distribution between the French zone and the Bizone had begun. In October the much discussed merger of the foreign trade of the three zones took place, thereby creating the Trizone as an economic unit although not yet as a political one. The French zone's Office of External Commerce (Oficomex) was joined to the bizonal Joint Export-Import Agency (JEIA). The economic unity of the three was recognized by France on November 18, when a commercial treaty was drawn up between France and the three western zones.

While economic fusion was proceeding in this piecemeal fashion, negotiations for the final administrative fusion proceeded more slowly. They involved settlement of the boundaries of the Länder—especially of Baden and Württemberg, which were split between the French and American zones—agreement on the Occupation Statute regarding the powers to be reserved to the occupation powers, acting jointly, after the establishment of the West German government, and settlement of the details of common administration and harmonization of past legislation.

The American authorities had begun to plan the details of fusion early in 1948. On July 3 an agreement for establishing a Tripartite

Occupation Authority was drafted; but the rest of the summer was spent on preparing the Occupation Statute, and on September 9 the three zonal governments set up a tripartite committee to work on the statute. For three months, drafts of a statute were passed between the military governors and the committee. Further disagreement developed between the French and the bizonal authorities when the French demanded a detailed statute and the others a short, general statement. At the same time, the French expressed fears about the course being taken by the Parliamentary Council, which was then drawing up a German constitution, and were even less willing to hand over to such an assembly a set of wide, ill-defined powers.[52]

The situation had become grave by November 1948, with negotiations almost deadlocked, not only between the military governors themselves, but between them and the Bonn Assembly. At this point General Clay sent a telegram to Washington in which he made very serious accusations against the French authorities in Germany. He had come to the conclusion that the French administration in Germany did not share the views of the Foreign Minister, Robert Schuman, and that it intended to delay the establishment of the West German government and German economic recovery. He therefore appealed for decisions to be made at governmental level, where he believed agreement could be more readily reached.[53]

An intergovernmental committee did meet in London on January 17, 1949, to draft the Occupation Statute. Although it continued its meetings through February 25, no final agreement was reached, for the French still insisted upon a detailed statute. On March 20 Clay paid an informal visit to Schuman in Paris and found the French minister amenable to the idea of a shorter statute, and, apparently, to most of Clay's other proposals.[54] The matter was finally decided in the Washington agreements of April 1949.

The implementation of the London decision on the Ruhr was undertaken at a conference in London which began on November 11, 1948. However, on the eve of the conference, the bizonal commanders took the undiplomatic step of publishing bizonal Law No. 75, by which they reorganized the management of the mines and metalworks of the Bizone. Its preamble announced that "Military Government has decided that the question of the eventual ownership of the Coal and Iron and Steel Industries should be left to the determination of a representative, freely elected German government." The Law handed over administration of the mines and metalworks to the Germans.[55] In this way, the bizonal military government, within the text of the London agreements, forestalled in advance any attempt of the French delegation to demand international control of the production and administration of the Ruhr industries, as apart from controlling the distribution of their products.

The effect of this action was very great. The French foreign minister and the French delegate to the London conference protested immediately. On November 18 the Foreign Affairs Committee of the National Assembly voted a motion of protest against the British and American action.[56] On November 20 the French government, in an official communiqué, pointed to the need for international control of the Ruhr mines and industry. Every section of French opinion was outraged. In his Armistice Day speech at Compiègne, President Auriol himself protested, and the British and American press echoed his annoyance. Finally, as a sop to France, a share in the Anglo-American control groups, known as the Essen groups, was offered to France on November 25. On the other hand, the London conference did little to lessen French objections to Law No. 75. An International Authority for the Ruhr (IAR) was created to control only the distribution of coal, iron, and steel and to safeguard foreign interests in the Ruhr.[57]

The final step toward trizonal fusion and the creation of the West German government was taken in Washington in April 1949, concurrently with the most significant security agreement of the postwar years, the signing of the North Atlantic Pact. With its security assured by direct promise of American involvement in European defense, the French concurred in the signing of eight agreements on Germany, which completed the sketch made in London the previous year. First, an Occupation Statute listed the reserved fields which would remain outside the power of the federal German government. These reservations included disarmament and demilitarization, foreign affairs and foreign commerce, displaced persons, security of the occupation forces, and matters concerning the Ruhr, restitution, and reparations. Second, the governments of Britain, France, and the United States agreed "to enter into a trizonal fusion agreement prior to the entry into effect of the Occupation Statute. The representatives of the three occupying Powers will make the necessary arrangements to establish tripartite control machinery for the western zones of Germany, which will become effective at the time of the establishment of a provisional German government."[58] At that time, the occupation powers were to be represented by three high commissioners, and not by military governors. With these agreements, the end of military government was in sight.

Meanwhile, the long process establishing a West German state had been going on. After considerable disagreement with the military governors, the Parliamentary Council produced a draft for a constitution, which was approved by the military governors on May 8, 1949, and ratified by all the Länder except Bavaria on May 23, 1949. Elections throughout West Germany were held on August 14; and in September Theodor Heuss was chosen President and Konrad Adenauer Chancellor of the new state. The West German government was then ready to begin its duties.

By September 1949 the high commissioners had taken over the exercise of the supreme Allied authority in Germany from the military governors. The Charter of the High Commission of June 20, 1949, had laid down the duties and powers of the high commissioners in the new West German republic.[59] The form of the zones of occupation was to be retained, and the occupying forces of each power were to remain in their respective zones. Each high commissioner was to be responsible, in his own zone, for coordination of policy with other zones, for the implementation of High Commission decisions and for the annual formulation of a budget of occupation costs for incorporation in the total budget of the occupation authorities submitted to the German government. General Koenig handed over his powers to the French high commissioner, André François-Poncet, on August 10, bringing to an end the era which had begun on July 31, 1945, when he had assumed power in Baden-Baden.

On September 21, 1949, the three high commissioners received Chancellor Adenauer and members of his government, and, in a short ceremony, declared that the Occupation Statute was legally in force and that trizonal fusion had taken place. Thus the same ceremony by which the West German government came into power also put an end to the military government of the French zone of occupation in Germany.

The German zones of occupation had been of great importance in the international politics of the four years following the end of the war. The changing status of the French zone was dependent upon the international developments of this period, and most particularly upon the growing rivalry of the Cold War. In this conflict, France's attempt to enforce its own solution to the German problem had failed. Yet, the development of the Cold War had brought about a change of opinion in France itself, as a result of which France accepted American economic aid and alignment with the Western powers. When once this decision had been made, France resigned itself to the necessity of participating in a tripartite solution to the German problem.

CHAPTER IV

The Instruments of Occupation:
Army and Military Government

IN the Second World War, the occupation of a conquered country
was not a simple matter of invading soldiers taking over the administration of civilians; behind the fighting man came the trained
administrator. The first stage of the French occupation of Germany
began with the arrival of the invading troops of the French First Army,
the Army of the Rhine and Danube.[1] The second stage began with
the establishment of the military government, staffed by civilians-in-
uniform.

THE FRENCH FIRST ARMY: ARMY OF RHINE AND DANUBE

The French army that invaded Germany was a motley group.
Even before the liberation of France, it had been a mixture of races
created by the chance byplay of events in the early war years. There
were, first, the veterans of the Free French Forces who had responded
to de Gaulle's appeal of June 18, 1940. In November 1942, the "Darlan deal" had brought over the whole of the French North African
army which, in June 1943, had been fused with contingents from the
colonies in central Africa and Oceania that had early rallied to de
Gaulle. To these were added the native troops who had been con-
scripted in the colonies and some 20,000 Frenchmen who had fled
from France, usually through Spain, to join the forces in Africa.[2]
From December 1943 this army was commanded by General Jean
de Lattre de Tassigny.

The liberation of France made available for the army large numbers of Resistance fighters and thus brought about a great problem of amalgamation. As de Lattre pointed out, the nature of the regular French army made the fusing of the Resistance forces with the First Army extremely difficult. "The 'regular' army was justifiably proud of its uniform, its discipline, and its strength. . . . To the regiments we had landed, the extreme variety of the F.F.I. organizations, their at least peculiar discipline, the differing quality of their groups, the poverty of their equipment, the crying inadequacy of their armament and supplies, the heterogeneity of their officering, the facility with which superior ranks had often been assigned, and in certain cases the ostensibly political nature of their aims, ran counter to the classical military outlook of many officers."[3] In particular, many of the Resistance officers were active members of the Communist party, notable among them being General Joinville, head of the COMAC organization in the Resistance and later a Communist deputy.

From the time of the Liberation onward, all groups within the Resistance demanded the creation of a truly national army. In the fall of 1944, *L'Humanité* called repeatedly for the adoption of a *levée en masse* similar to the great movement of 1792, or, better, to the Red Guards of 1917. The amalgamation of the Resistance forces with the regular army must take place, the Communist party urged, by merging into the French Forces of the Interior (FFI) formations from the African army.[4] The Socialist party was deeply concerned with the need for a thorough purge to remove from the army all those suspected of collaboration with the Vichy regime. From the end of 1945 onward, it was the Socialist party rather than the Communist party that led the attack on the military policy of the various governments, this dissatisfaction of the Socialists being due to what they considered the insufficient scope of the army reforms undertaken at this time.[5] The MRP was also concerned with the need for a popular army, in order to remove, as it stated in its manifesto of November 8, 1945, "that spirit of caste which was as harmful to discipline as to morale in the army."[6] In short, among the groups of the Left and Center there was a demand for a new type of army which would be founded by embracing the popular elements of the Resistance movement.

This desire was recognized by de Lattre, and in 1944 some 137,000 members of the FFI joined the 250,000 soldiers of the French First Army. Although various methods were tried to fuse the two groups, as in the replacing of colored regiments by FFI troops in the winter fighting of 1944, or in the grafting of FFI infantry onto regular artillery regiments, still there remained a wide schism between the two types of troops. This deep division within the army that invaded Germany was to cause serious problems in the occupation. The army became a source of dissension among the political groups in Paris. Their criticism, combined with the army's own internal division, undermined the morale of the army during the first year of the occupation; and, according to a Socialist observer, the attitude of the German population quickly changed, as a result, from subservience to amusement and finally to contempt.[7]

Nazi propaganda in the last months of the war had portrayed the French soldier, according to the war correspondent James de Coquet, "as a hideous African molesting blond Aryan women."[8] The first troops to enter Germany were rather frightening in appearance to a population impressed with this propaganda picture. They were a task force made up of Algerian infantry and Moroccan Tabors who, crossing the Lauter River on March 17, 1945, captured the village of Scheibenhardt. These Tabors were Berbers from the Atlas Mountains. They were a fearsome group, according to the troop review, "with black turbans, white gloves, white gaiters . . . in massed battalions, warlike, with brown cloaks flying."[9] De Coquet described these colonial troops in his diary on April 20. "When the inhabitants of a conquered village see the 'goumiers' arriving," he wrote, "they are terrified. The truth is that with their loose cloaks, their bronze features lit up by the excitement of the battle and their guttural cries, they are impressive. . . . But these Tabors behave in a becoming manner. For if the Moroccans are terrible in battle, they let themselves be tamed quickly."[10]

The 2nd Division of Moroccan Infantry crossed into Germany at the same time, and moved south through the central Black Forest to Austria. This division was a mixed group of FFI troops, Algerians, and Moroccans. It was supported by the 9th Division of Colonial Infantry, composed largely of Resistance troops, which captured the southern Black Forest region and closed the Swiss border between Basel and Konstanz. Two tank divisions, also largely mixed in composition, provided the striking power for the army, one taking part in the dash on Ulm and the other in the capture of Stuttgart.[11]

The region of north Baden and north Württemberg was captured by divisions which were largely Tunisian and Moroccan in makeup. Central and south Baden was captured by divisions which were mainly Resistance troops but which also had large numbers of Moroccan soldiers. It is not true that one-third of the French army was composed of Senegalese Negroes, as one critic suggested. During the invasion, the colonial troops were largely Arabs and Berbers from Morocco and Tunisia. Yet these North Africans formed a sufficiently large proportion of the invading force for the German population to have believed that the propaganda threats of a wild African invasion had been realized.

Immediately after the capitulation, divisions of the FFI were sent to Germany to replace some of the colonial divisions which had taken part in the invasion. Among these were the 14th Infantry Division, a completely FFI division created in February 1945 under General Raoul Salan, which included among its officers such eminent figures as Denoyer de Segonzac and André Malraux; the 10th Infantry Division, formed from the Resistance groups in Paris; and the 1st Motorized Infantry Division. The army was redeployed between July 4 and July 10, to take over the northern triangle of the French zone from the American troops then occupying it. Three more divisions from France were brought into Germany at this time, with the result that only one wholly colonial division remained in Germany after October 1945.[12]

There can be no doubt that the invading army committed extensive depredations in Germany during the period of hostilities. French sources later referred to this behavior somewhat obliquely as consisting of "errors" and "indiscretions." In reporting for the committee of inquiry sent by the Constituent Assembly to the zone in December 1945, Max Juvenal noted, "It is incontestable that the first occupying troops in Germany committed regrettable errors. They can be explained by the composition of our troops and also by the feeling of vengeance which could affect men who had suffered."[13]

These abuses took many forms. Those committed by the ordinary soldiers were of the kind that accompany most invasions, ranging from excessive requisitioning of foodstuffs and clothing to black market activities and to more violent actions. De Coquet, the correspondent, commented on the attitude of the invading soldiers. "For many Frenchmen," he wrote, "it is a pleasure to see the panic that seizes the civilians who are being suddenly turned out of their houses. While the occupier is unloading his equipment and preparing his means of transport and communication, the Germans are hurriedly piling up everything they need for day-to-day existence: a little bedding and crockery, a few clothes."[14] In day-to-day relations with the German population, the French began by being much more harsh than the British or American forces. General de Lattre's discipline was firm and immediate. After a wave of sabotage in Konstanz in May 1945, twenty Germans were seized as hostages. When a fourteen-year-old "werewolf" shot a French lieutenant in Lindau on May 25, the slayer was at once executed, the major part of the town evacuated within twenty-four hours, and refugees from Alsace moved in. Drew Middleton, the American war correspondent, became convinced that the series of murders of French military personnel in Baden in May was due to the harshness of French occupation. In June the *New York Times* said that the French occupation was typified by the situation in Stuttgart, where German civilians had to raise their hats to French soldiers and move off the sidewalks for them.[15] But that was not the full story. As one French observer remarked, "The French back there acted just as at any other time—generous and blundering, humanitarian and conceited, chivalrous and meddlesome"; the day after the capture of Bruchsal, Moslem troops were seen walking through the park hand in hand with German children.[16]

MILITARY GOVERNMENT FOLLOWS THE INVADING ARMY

Behind the invading army came the military government teams. Organized in Paris in the winter of 1944–45 under the command of General Louis-Marie Koeltz, these groups of the French Military Administration in Germany (known as AMFA) had been trained to take over the administration of conquered territory from the army itself.[17]

The recruitment of these teams had presented considerable difficulty. The army in the field needed the most active soldiers and, in particular, the battle-trained officers of the Resistance and the First Army. Hence, the early recruits to AMFA were over-age officers or, worse, officers who had been relegated to the rear through suspicion of their past connections with the Vichy regime, and civilian administrators from industry and civil service. Each ministry was ordered to provide a contingent. It was not to be expected that the ministries or private industry would send their best men at a time when France's own reconstruction needs were so great, unless they stood to gain by the dispatch of their experts to Germany. This was, of course, the case where firms or ministries hoped to profit from the vast restitution of goods removed from France—as did the French railways, which hoped to retrieve much of their stolen rolling stock, and the Peugeot firm, which hoped to regain its machine tools. Moreover, large private industries undoubtedly permitted some of their experts to join the military government in the hope of profiting from the influence they would exercise over the industries of the zone. However, while the fighting continued, little attention was paid to the nature of this recruitment.[18]

As the First Army advanced into Germany, it administered conquered territory through its own Fifth Bureau. When the army moved on, the administration was then turned over to AMFA groups sent from Paris.[19] The area thus administered was redefined several times between March 19, 1945, when the army entered Germany, and the capitulation on May 8, 1945. At first, the French army held only the sector between the river Lauter and Speyer, a forty-kilometer bridgehead. During the first three weeks of April they established themselves through almost the whole of Baden. Between April 18 and May 7, they extended their control over south Württemberg.

A period of confusion followed the capitulation. Officially, all the armies were still under the command of Supreme Headquarters (SHAEF), but the main object of the supreme commander, General Eisenhower, was to dissolve the central organization as rapidly as possible. Eisenhower had noted that the end of the fighting meant that the Western allies would be faced with the great task of breaking up into its separate national components the highly integrated combat force that had invaded Germany. He himself had recommended that the western section of Germany be occupied "on a unified basis"; but his government had rejected this recommendation.[20] SHAEF was finally dissolved on July 13, 1945, and the dissolution of the French First Army followed two days later.

Command in the French sector of operations during the fighting and in the French zone of occupation immediately following the capitulation was exercised by the commander-in-chief of the French First

Army, General Jean de Lattre de Tassigny. It fell to de Lattre to bridge the gap between the wartime and peacetime administration of the French sector of Germany. This interim period lasted from the capitulation on May 8, 1945, until General Pierre Koenig took over command from de Lattre on July 31. During this interval the French government in Paris set up the legal framework of the organization of the occupation. On July 7 control of German affairs was taken over by an Interministerial Committee for German and Austrian Affairs, which was to supervise the occupation from Paris. On June 15 the French government announced that the occupation in Germany would be headed by a commander-in-chief who would have under him three deputy or associate generals (*général adjoint*), one to serve in Berlin on the Coordinating Committee, one to command the army, and one to run the administration of the zone. On July 23 General Koenig was named commander-in-chief, and the following day Émile Laffon, director general of the central administration of the Ministry of the Interior, was named administrator general. Meanwhile, General Koeltz had installed the AMFA groups in the Hotel Stephanie and other luxury hotels of the undamaged spa-town of Baden-Baden, and the military government groups were preparing to take over full control of the zone from the army. General Koeltz told an interviewer in June that there were between 1,200 and 1,500 people already trained, each of them going through a four-week course in which he received lectures on Germany from professors of the Sorbonne and the School of Political Sciences.[21]

The boundaries of the zone were not officially announced until June 23. Since the major part of the northern triangle of the French zone was then in American hands, an agreement was made on June 25 on the manner in which the French should take over from the American armies. The redeployment was carried through in the first two weeks in July. On July 31 Koenig arrived in Baden-Baden, followed the next day by Laffon. From that date, the permanent military government began to function.

The interlude between May 8 and July 31 was, however, of considerable significance. During these eleven weeks, General de Lattre and the First Army enjoyed a free hand in the running of the zone. The result was a period of occupation based on entirely different principles from those that were to be applied later, for de Lattre had a policy of his own derived from his personal attitude toward the German people. The execution of this policy resulted in his recall to Paris after eleven weeks.

DE LATTRE AT LINDAU

With the end of hostilities, the attention of France focused on the exceptional man who was commander-in-chief of the French zone of Germany. For eleven weeks, General de Lattre de Tassigny was in supreme control of policy in his part of Germany. He received few important policy directives from Paris, and so was able to give full play to his own ideas about the fate that should be imposed on Germany.[22] So grandiose were his schemes that a storm of criticism broke in Paris, and he was recalled to Paris to become inspector-general of the army.[23] The eleven weeks during which de Lattre ruled from Lindau form a curious episode in miniature, a sudden focusing of attention on the characteristics of occupation rule; and de Lattre's removal had the effect of worsening the abuses suspected by critics at home.

De Lattre's first concern was to restore the discipline of his troops. The moment the fighting ended, he demanded the firmest discipline and order in his army. The divisions were at once set to work on reconstruction in their zone, especially upon rebuilding the bridges and roads. The bearing of this battle-worn army was remarkable. De Lattre himself later praised these qualities, noting that "this essential discipline, at once external and mental, is accompanied with a kind of coquetterie of which the most notable sign is the refusal to accept the not quite perfect or the almost right."[24] Others commented favorably on the behavior of the troops. De Coquet remarked that "this victorious army, which has not had time to stretch, is working all out. Something is worth noting: it is working with good order and discipline. What strikes the visitor to the First Army is the perfect bearing of the troops."[25] Paul Garcin, another correspondent, described later how the army deteriorated in the months following de Lattre's dismissal, but in July he found everything in excellent order. "Nothing reminds one of a barracks," he wrote. "Everything is clean, tidy, and pleasant to look at. Strict discipline is kept, but it is a contented discipline without the slightest harshness."[26]

De Lattre, moreover, had a plan for the re-education of the Germans, and it was the execution of this policy that brought upon him the wrath of the Parisian political circles. De Lattre acted in the grand manner. He believed that the Germans had been educated to be impressed only by magnificent displays that acted upon their emotions rather than on their intellects. He therefore organized the French occupation to rival and surpass the displays of military grandeur to which the Germans had become accustomed. As General du Souzy remarked later, "Our ceremonies and military displays ought also . . . to have as their aim to show the Germans that we too knew how to conceive big ideas, to carry out huge schemes, to achieve the beautiful, but by means where man, the individual, was not crushed by the mass but raised up."[27] De Lattre's plan was not only for the re-education of the Germans. He also had the idea of bringing about, in the French zones of Germany and Austria, a French renaissance. The young men of the First Army would be removed from France and would forget its defeat, and the faults which had increased the misery of the last four years.[28] Carl Burckhardt witnessed a typical de Lattre fury when the general turned on the mayor of his home town for reviving old political divisions and snapped at him that he, de Lattre, "had created in the First Army the spirit of unity. . . . I had, Mister Mayor, once and for all cleared away, in the First Army, all those political prejudices which have poisoned our national life."[29] De Lattre took continual care to ensure that the officers around him understood the philosophy behind his policy, and many testified later of the hours of discussion in his headquarters, either at Karlsruhe or at Lindau, during which he explained his conception of the duties of the occupying forces.[30]

He went to extraordinary lengths to carry out this policy. He ordered his villa at Lindau specially landscaped. The National Opera Company was brought from Paris to play for him there. Regal receptions were given to the Sultan of Morocco and the Bey of Tunis. And when General Devers, who had been his immediate superior in the invasion, came to pay a farewell visit, "the torchlight parade which was held in his honor, was talked about in Paris and even in America, because two thousand Algerian cavalrymen carrying torches lined the route of the American general."[31] De Lattre's lavish use of German resources was extended even to the artists of the Villa Médicis, the French art school in Rome. Robert Rey, director general of fine arts, in describing his reception at Lindau, said that de Lattre had offered

to set the architects of the Villa Médicis to building barracks, the paint-
ers to decorating them, and the musicians to composing military music,
while all were to receive lodging, access to an army mess, and military
uniforms. His care extended, however, to all French people who had
suffered at German hands. He made great attempts to bring the
French deportees and concentration camp inmates to the French zone
as rapidly as possible, and there he set up rest camps and sanatoriums
for those who were too sick to be immediately transported back to
France. The relatives of those in the sanatoriums were brought from
France to see them. Moreover, camps for children were set up in the
Black Forest and along the Bodensee, and thousands of French children were brought there to enjoy their first summer holiday, at German expense.[32]

However, de Lattre's policy had certain grave failings. He encouraged the army in habits of extravagance and wastefulness, especially,
for example, in the use of gasoline, which contrasted harshly with the
conditions of life in France itself. He permitted the army to develop
a contempt for the civilian administrators of the military government,
and thus prepared the way for the internal division in the administration at Baden-Baden, when duplicate administrative bodies were maintained by the civilian and military authorities.[33] He roused in the
German population very strong antipathies, both by his extravagance
with German resources in labor and materials and by his arbitrary
decisions. Finally, no clear policy was observable to critics in Paris;
they saw only a willingness to turn over the major part of policy-
making to the military governors of the different regions of the zone.
As Garcin pointed out in July, "The capital error which is being made
at the moment and which leaps to the attention of all observers: no
occupation policy has yet been laid down; no precise directive has yet
been given. Too large a personal initiative is left to each of the military governors. Each one follows his own policy, and applies his own
methods."[34]

Parisian political groups, especially those of the Right, refused to
believe that this extravagance was part of a policy designed to win the
Germans over to a new way of thinking. De Lattre was likened to
Wallenstein, settled in Germany in the midst of his victorious army.
Some went so far as to believe that he was "already fancying himself
as the head of a French People's Army," or that he would return to

Paris to another "18 Brumaire." Perhaps the Gaullist movement did not have enough room for two de Gaulles. Whatever the cause, de Lattre was removed from his command on July 24, and on July 27 he handed over his post to the reliably Gaullist General Koenig.[35]

BADEN-BADEN: MILITARY GOVERNMENT TAKES OVER

The choice of Baden-Baden as the seat of the French military government was not an altogether happy one. The delightful spa, nestling in a sheltered valley in the central Black Forest, was an anachronism in the war-torn Europe of 1945. Its luxury hotels were virtually undamaged, its orchestra continued to play Waldteufel waltzes in the polished ballroom of the Casino, and its whole atmosphere of luxuriant repose was quite alien to the misery of bombed-out Ludwigshafen or Mainz, or, perhaps more pertinently, to the hardships remaining in Brest, Caen, or Rouen. Since the military government and regular army were already suspect to the Left Wing groups in France as being more than tinged with Vichyite sympathies, the choice of a spa as the center of administration stimulated unpleasant parallels. Many thought that they could see the creation of a "Little Vichy," and the Communist papers spoke of the curious "nostalgia for watering places" which the Vichyites seemed to have. The French press quoted frequent descriptions of the teeming horde of officers and their families who had moved into Baden-Baden to enjoy the amenities of luxury living.[36]

At the head of this administration was General Pierre Koenig. A career officer from Normandy, Koenig had served in World War I in the occupation of the Rhineland and in Morocco. In June 1940 he was one of the first to join de Gaulle in London. In 1943, as head of the general staff, he had been closely concerned with the fusion of the Free French and the North African armies. In March 1944 he became de Gaulle's representative at SHAEF and at the same time head of the French Forces of the Interior. From 1944 to 1945 he was the military governor of Paris, a position whose purpose, according to Left Wing sources, was to hold down the FFI and in particular to prevent the Communist party from taking over power.[37]

At the head of the occupation, General de Gaulle had placed one of those closest to him, a career officer who also had a record of devotion to the Free French cause. Moreover, on the German question

Koenig was, and probably remained, a firm upholder of the French thesis. Speaking to the American Legion Honor Committee in Chicago on November 18, 1945, he said that the occupation must be lasting, since Germany was like a firm which had gone bankrupt several times and could not be put back in the hands of its owners. In a press conference in Berlin on February 21, 1946, he strongly supported the position of Foreign Minister Bidault on the Ruhr, Rhineland, and Saar, and at the same time opposed the creation of any central institutions in Germany until the question of the German boundaries was settled.[38]

Koenig later stated that the first aim of the occupation was to seek France's "traditional guarantees" and to punish the guilty. But the military government had further aims. "To free the German population, and above all its young people, from its illusions; to give to a Germany plunged into chaos a suitable organization for this order-loving country; to be inspired in setting up this organization by the principles of the democratic countries in the West and America; to attempt to orient toward our ideas the teeming youth which tomorrow will take charge of the revival of this country; to lay down with an indestructible firmness the bases of a Franco-German *rapprochement*, which is indispensable for the reconstruction of Europe—these were the main aims . . . of the heads of the French military government," he concluded.[39] In attempting to carry out these aims, Koenig was to become the center of many controversies. He objected to Berlin as the seat of the Control Council, believing it was "mistakenly chosen as the seat of the inter-allied government of Germany."[40] His vetoes in the Control Council roused considerable animosity against him on the part of the American representatives, General Clay becoming more and more convinced that Koenig was one of the major stumbling blocks in the way of German recovery.[41] At the same time, Koenig became increasingly unpopular with the Left Wing groups in Paris. In December 1946 the Socialist paper, *Le Populaire*, accused him of permitting the formation of a Vichy underground in the French zone, and as late as June 1948 a leading Socialist, André Philip, saw the tendency to create veritable "satrapies where the commander-in-chief would be a master and not the servant of the government." The Communists came to regard him as a thinly disguised Fascist, who was using the zonal forces to prepare a *coup d'état* in Paris, and who, in any case, took his orders from General de Gaulle rather than from the French government.[42]

The three associate generals under Koenig were Louis-Marie Koeltz in Berlin, Goislard de Monsabert, who commanded the troops of occupation, and Émile Laffon, the administrator general. Koeltz was an old-time soldier, who had remained with the Vichy army until the Allied invasion of North Africa. Probably on account of his age, he had been put in command of the AMFA groups in Paris in the winter of 1944. As an old-line officer and a former Vichy soldier, he was suspected by the Left of being opposed to the FFI forces and of sympathizing with Vichy.[43] De Monsabert was also a career soldier, a product of the Saint-Cyr military academy. He had served in World War I, and later in Morocco and Tunisia. He had remained with the Vichy army until the landings in North Africa in November 1942, after which he had played a distinguished part in the French First Army as head of the 3rd Algerian Infantry Division and as commander of the 2nd Army Corps. De Monsabert, as commander of the occupation troops, was to feel most strongly the great struggle over the reorganization of the army which took place during the first years of the occupation.[44]

Émile Laffon was an entirely different person, in background and opinions, from these three career officers. Younger than his military colleagues, he was only thirty-eight upon taking over his duties. The son of a Paris lawyer, he had combined the careers of mining engineer and lawyer and had practiced in the Paris courts. He had been a member of the French Committee of National Liberation in Algiers in 1943–44, and after the Liberation he had joined the civil service, becoming director general of the Ministry of the Interior. As a member of the Resistance, he was concerned with the need to crush the spirit of militarism in Germany. From his work in the Ministry of the Interior, he knew that the French zone could help in the reconstruction of the shattered French economy. But, at the same time, he believed that "it was necessary to ask the French in Germany and the French in France to make an effort to control themselves, so that they could adopt an attitude of cool-headed firmness and objective severity toward the Germans."[45] From the start, there was to be animosity between the military and the civilians in the occupation, and this was reflected in the animosity between Koenig and Laffon.

Among the other administrators, there was considerable difference of background. On one side were the highly skilled representatives of French commerce, industry, and banking. This group included such men as the commissioner general himself, René Mayer, René Sergent, head of the Economics Directorate in Berlin, and Georges Glasser, head of the Reparations-Restitution Directorate. Such men were criticized by the parties of the Left, not for their relations with the Vichy government, but because of their positions in the capitalist economy of France.[46] In particular, it was suggested that they would use their influence in the zone for the benefit of individual companies rather than for the benefit of the French economy as a whole.

Others in important office in the zone found themselves attacked for their relations to the Vichy regime. Maurice Sabatier, head of the General Directorate of Administrative Affairs, had been prefect at Bordeaux from 1942 to 1944. Jean Filippi, head of the General Directorate of Economy and Finance, had been an official in the Ministry of Production during the Vichy period. Jean Cabouat, head of the Directorate of Security, had been a prefect under Vichy, as had the director of personnel, Jean Lacombe. The Left Wing attack was concentrated especially on these people, and the parliamentary committee of inquiry in 1946 went so far as to recommend the dismissal of thirteen of the top officials of the zone on the ground that their connections with the Vichy regime seriously impaired their efficiency as administrators of French policy.[47] This problem of the significance of a man's relationship to the Vichy regime was to be one of the most troubled questions in the history of the zone of occupation, as well as of postwar France itself. In the period of social and economic dislocation that followed the Liberation, France was torn by social recriminations of the harshest kind, and the effects were felt just as strongly in the zone.

The first problem facing the administration in Baden-Baden was to define more clearly the relations between the military under de Monsabert and the civilian administrators under Laffon. This was done in part by the decree (*arrêté*) No. 2 of August 22, 1945, which stated that the representatives of the military government alone were responsible for the administration of the zone, under the orders of the administrator general. The troops could be called upon for help and might intervene where their own security was threatened. Further clarification followed, as in the decree of September 4, 1945, which

TABLE I

ORGANIZATION OF THE MILITARY GOVERNMENT OF THE FRENCH
ZONE OF OCCUPATION

(January 1946)

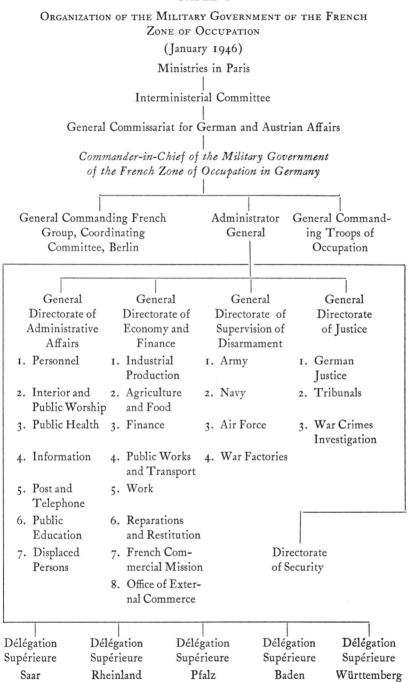

Ministries in Paris

Interministerial Committee

General Commissariat for German and Austrian Affairs

*Commander-in-Chief of the Military Government
of the French Zone of Occupation in Germany*

General Commanding French   Administrator   General Command-
Group, Coordinating   General   ing Troops of
Committee, Berlin   Occupation

General Directorate of Administrative Affairs	General Directorate of Economy and Finance	General Directorate of Supervision of Disarmament	General Directorate of Justice
1. Personnel	1. Industrial Production	1. Army	1. German Justice
2. Interior and Public Worship	2. Agriculture and Food	2. Navy	2. Tribunals
3. Public Health	3. Finance	3. Air Force	3. War Crimes Investigation
4. Information	4. Public Works and Transport	4. War Factories	
5. Post and Telephone	5. Work		
6. Public Education	6. Reparations and Restitution		
7. Displaced Persons	7. French Commercial Mission	Directorate of Security	
	8. Office of External Commerce		

Délégation Supérieure Saar   Délégation Supérieure Rheinland   Délégation Supérieure Pfalz   Délégation Supérieure Baden   Délégation Supérieure Württemberg removed all control of the economic life of the zone from the army.[48]

Second, an administrative machine had to be created. As shown in Table 1, the zone was divided into five areas corresponding to the German administrative divisions within the zone. Each Land or section of a Land within the zone was named a *délégation supérieure*, and was placed under a military governor or *délégué supérieur*. These five areas were subdivided into Regierungsbezirke, Landkreise, Stadtkreise, and Gemeinden; and at each level, representatives of the military government were appointed.*

Third, a central government was created. In place of ministries, four General Directorates were set up to supervise, respectively, administrative affairs, economy and finance, justice, and disarmament. A Directorate of Security was attached directly to the office of the administrator general.

Thus, the outstanding features of this newly created military government organization were: (*a*) that the French used, as far as possible, the former administrative divisions of their zone as the basis of their organization, with the intention of creating a new German democracy on a federal basis from the local areas up; (*b*) that many of the officials brought from France were among the most efficient and sincere of the French civil service, as the London *Times* testified;[49] (*c*) that, from the very beginning, rivalry existed between the military and civilian groups of the occupation, which resulted in duplication of functions, uncertainty of purpose, and inefficiency in executing the duties of occupation; (*d*) that large numbers of military officers and civilians who were compromised by their previous connections with

* Hereafter, the German administrative terms will be used rather than English or French translations of them, since an attempt to find equivalents to the German units of local administration in the administrative organization of another country is misleading. Weimar Germany had been divided into sixteen *Länder*, or states, deriving from the historic states of pre-Bismarckian Germany. The Nazi regime had attempted some simplification by creating thirteen administrative districts, called *Gaue*, but within this new structure the identity of the majority of the states was preserved. The organization of the state of Prussia was slightly unusual, in that the many scattered territories of Prussia were divided into ten *Provinze*, or provinces. These *Provinze*, as well as the Land of Baden, were divided into *Regierungsbezirke*, or administrative areas. All the German *Länder* were divided into smaller units called *Kreise* or circles, the large cities being called *Stadtkreise* or city circles, and the rural districts *Landkreise* or rural circles. The smallest division of all was the *Gemeinde*, or municipality. These divisions are very significant for the occupation period, since self-government was instituted from the smallest units up. See James Kerr Pollock, *The Government of Greater Germany* (New York, 1938), pp. 128–38, and United States Department of War, *Civil Affairs Guide: German-English Dictionary of German Administrative Terms* (War Department Pamphlet No. 31–169, Washington, D.C., 1944).

the Vichy regime found employment in positions of trust in the zone, with the result that all occupation personnel were suspect in the eyes of at least moderate and Left Wing Frenchmen; (*e*) that many of the administrators were high officials of the great banks, trusts, and business companies of France, with the beneficial result that the zone enjoyed the services of some of the most efficient administrators from France but with the undesirable result that the military government was vulnerable to attack from the Left Wing parties in France on the ground that the interests of France in Germany were being subordinated to those of the companies whom the administrators had previously served.

These weaknesses became obvious during the first six months of the occupation. Hence, in the winter of 1945 a major attack was launched in France against the occupation personnel of both the army and the military government.

"EXTRAVAGANCE IN LITTLE VICHY"

The invasion of Germany had been welcomed throughout France as a major epic of French arms, yet by December 1945 both the occupying army and the military government of the zone were the subject of almost universal criticism from French circles. Why had this change come about?

The five major criticisms made against the army and the military government were summarized in the Constituent Assembly on December 21, 1945, by Pierre Bourdan, the reporter for the subcommittee of the Foreign Affairs Committee appointed to study the situation of the French zones in Germany and Austria. The subcommittee, Bourdan said, felt it necessary that a committee of inquiry be sent at once to the zones of occupation in Germany and Austria. The reasons for sending a committee were the lack of unity of action at the summit regarding the occupation, the undemocratic attitudes of the French personnel employed in Germany and Austria, the nature of the German personnel in contact with the French authorities, the unnecessary numbers of French personnel employed, and the insufficient exploitation of the occupied zones in Germany and Austria "at a moment when they might reduce greatly the burden which weighs on the shoulders of all Frenchmen."[50] The motion was supported by all parties of the Assembly.

These criticisms fell into three categories: belief that a refuge for purged Vichyite elements had been created in the zone, annoyance at the extravagant way of life of the army and the military government, and feeling that the government of the zone was inefficient in achieving the aims of the occupation.

The vexed problem of "collaboration" had caused much trouble in France since the Liberation.[51] For many of the Resistance groups, only active participation in the Resistance could be called patriotic. Active and even passive support of the Vichy government was accounted treasonable. However, during 1944–45, the French government had attempted to bring some order into the situation by creating purge committees (*comités d'épuration*) which reviewed the cases of all accused of collaboration with the Germans, whether directly or through the Vichy regime. The parties of the Left were convinced by the summer of 1945 that this process had been far from effective.

The army was especially susceptible to these charges. The spirit of loyalty to established authority which had been an ingrained feature of the French military spirit had led the majority of the French army to accept the orders of Pétain until these were countermanded by Darlan after the North African invasion. The patriotism of these men was acknowledged by General de Gaulle, but not by the majority of the political groups, as was seen in the parliamentary opposition to the confirmation, in December 1945, of the grant of the Legion of Honor to men who had resisted the American invasion of North Africa in 1942.[52] Critics pointed out that others, more gravely compromised, had later fought with the Resistance or with the First Army, and in this way had made less evident their first acceptance of the Vichy regime, while still others had been able to resume their positions in the army through the complicity of friends.[53] Finally, the work of the purge committees had been slow and ineffective. The blame for this was laid to the Minister of War, André Diethelm, who had become so unpopular by the end of 1945 that he was dropped from the cabinet in the ministerial reshuffle of November 21, 1945. In April of the following year, Diethelm was still the Communists' whipping-boy. On April 3, 1946, Paul Tubert declared that there was still need for changing "all the arbitrary decisions taken by former minister [Diethelm], who was held back by no control, bound by no rulings, and not even stopped by the voice of conscience, either in matters concerning collaboration, promotion, or decorations, or in judicial proceedings and disciplinary action."[54] And in its final report the committee of inquiry noted that there was a tendency to use the need to reduce numbers to get rid of the FFI officers in the army, while leaving in place many of the former servants of the Vichy government.[55]

Even after the army reforms of early 1946, carried out by the Minister of Armies, Édouard Michelet, the critics were not satisfied. In November 1946 the Socialist paper *Le Populaire* attacked the minister for allowing a "white army" to be constituted, and published a long series of articles to show that a Vichy army was being created in the zone.[56] In 1947 the discovery of the so-called *complot bleu* gave the Communists a chance to revive the attack. The plot itself was organized by Comte de Vulpian in France and General Guillaudot, inspector-general of the gendarmerie, and was supported by various soldiers and civil officials, though none of very high rank. The aim of the plotters was to create the impression of a Communist coup, which they themselves would destroy by bringing in tanks and troops from western France and from the French zone in Germany. Several arrests put a very quick end to the plot, and the majority of French newspapers treated the incident as of minor importance.

For the Communist and Socialist groups, however, the plot seemed proof that their criticisms of the army had been justified. *Le Populaire* announced that it had been the first to announce the discovery of the plot, but put its trust in Édouard Depreux, the Minister of the Interior, for dealing with it. The Communist party, which had been forced out of Ramadier's government only a few weeks before, seized upon the incident as the occasion for waging a major campaign. The plot, it claimed, was the result of the nature of the organization of the occupation, where the power was shared between the representatives of the great French trusts and ex-Vichyites. And *L'Humanité* suggested that Koenig himself should be questioned in this connection. *France d'abord*, which had been banned in the zone by Koenig after it had opened a strong attack on the zonal administration in its issue of May 29, 1947, went further and announced that 500,000 Wehrmacht soldiers were ready to join in the march on Paris, a claim which was based on the fact that there were 500,000 ex-soldiers in the zone.[57] This crisis proved to be a storm in a teacup, however, and was soon forgotten by the Communists themselves. After mid-1947, the army of occupation was no longer in the limelight, the focus of interest moving from that point to events in Indochina rather than in Germany.

The same charge of "Vichyism" was also leveled at the military government. The method of recruitment in 1944–45 had made it possible for many who were compromised by their past associations with the Vichy government to find employment in the zone. As the storm over the insufficient purge in the army grew, repercussions were also felt in the military government. In January 1946 Pierre Cot complained that denazification could hardly be successful in the French zone. "Among those who represent us," he claimed, "there are men in whom we cannot have confidence for accomplishing this denazification, because we are not sure that in their very hearts they have not been, and have not remained, fascists."[58] In March 1946, Alfred Biscarlet, a Communist member of the committee of inquiry, testified that "the zone of occupation has been, and is still, the refuge for thousands of Vichyites who went there either to be forgotten or to carry on with their work of treason."[59] Salomon Grumbach, reporting for the committee of inquiry in April 1946, recommended the discontinuance in their posts of all who had served the Vichy government for any continuous period. Thirteen in particular were named, including some of the highest officials in the zone.[60] However, by the end of 1946, with the reduction in numbers of personnel and the waning of French interest in the problem of collaboration, the criticism was largely silenced.

The second major source of criticism was the extravagant way of life being pursued by the army and the military government. During the first six months following de Lattre's departure, the morality of the army had collapsed. A vast black market had already developed by June 1945, with German goods being traded across the Rhine. The occupying forces had descended upon the pleasant, undamaged towns of the zone in hordes. Garcin noted that in Offenburg, 800 officers and 2,000 men were living in a town which had only 18,000 population in normal times. This period saw the worst excesses of the occupying troops, especially by the men of the FFI who had strong personal grievances against the Germans. The upper ranks settled down to enjoy the economic privileges of occupation. Baden-

Baden became the mecca of the officer class and a byword in Paris for military extravagance. Biscarlet reported to the Chamber that in Baden-Baden alone there were 1,284 officers, of whom 800 were colonels. At this time, in the whole of the occupying force there were only 6,911 officers, so that just under one-fifth of the total number of officers was stationed in Baden-Baden itself.[61]

Jean Planchais, war correspondent for *Le Monde*, remarked in 1958, "How beautiful Germany was in the years that followed 1945, if not for the Germans, at least for the army of occupation. . . . Thanks to Germany paying occupation costs, it was able to keep up its units, to train them and to mold recruits, free of the supposedly debilitating influence of the French climate. But the occupation also accentuated the split between public opinion and the officer corps. They got into the habit of enjoying a high standard of living, and, on returning to the restricted conditions of life in France itself, they felt the change more painfully and deeply, since they felt they were the victims of ingratitude."[62] The high living expressed itself in many ways. A cartoon in *Le Populaire* on January 5, 1946, showing two officers drinking, bore the caption: "Don't worry! We'll always have wine in the mess." Officers brought their families over from France. Trucks and gasoline were available for the numerous military parades, and, it was suggested, for less justifiable uses. It was pointed out in the parliamentary debate of December 12, 1945, that one-third of France's entire gasoline supply was being used by the military.[63]

The scandals of the army were recognized to exist by the Ministry of Armies itself, in the General Directive No. 1 of December 4, 1945, which announced: "The Army is passing through an unprecedented crisis which is sapping its material strength, affecting the morale of its best elements and alienating public opinion. . . . A plan of basic reform is herewith laid down. . . . Too much time has already been lost. We must *act quickly and everywhere at once*. The main reason for the ankylosis of our military machine lies essentially in the excessive centralization of command. . . . *To restore discipline* means first to command and also to obey. It is to *demand* the immediate carrying out of orders, to *demand* cleanliness and absolute neatness in appearance, to *demand* that the external marks of respect be shown."[64] A wholesale program of reform was put into effect, which involved first the restoration of discipline, then demobilization accompanied by cutbacks in expenditures of all kinds, and finally a new attempt to bring about a full purge of the officer corps.

These reforms took effect rapidly. The numbers in the occupation army fell from over a million at the capitulation to 200,000 on January 5, 1946; to 75,000 on May 13, 1947; and finally to 53,000 on May 31, 1948.[65] A new organization was introduced, based on a fusion of the principal of conscription and of maintenance of a permanent career army, with the aim of ending the quarrel between the FFI and the regular army. After 1947 the quarrel over the army was transferred to other areas, especially to the armies in Indochina and Algeria. The declining number of troops in Germany made the problem of their makeup insignificant.

The same criticisms of extravagance and waste in the army were applied with equal force to the military government. As the committee of inquiry noted, the personnel was far too numerous for the task it had to perform. The administration, the committee said, was "drowned in an ocean of paper."[66] In December 1946 the London *Times* reported that there were 11,000 men in the military government of the French zone, giving a density of 18 French administrators for every 10,000 Germans, compared with 10 for every 10,000 in the British zone and 3 for every 10,000 in the American zone. The *Times* added that 40,000 wives and relatives had been brought to the French zone compared with 10,000 in the British zone.[67] André Philip, the Socialist Minister of Finance, gave notice on March 26, 1946, that he intended to put an end to the situation in which the French personnel in Germany were better off than those in France, as had been the general rule. This was to be achieved by cutting down the budget of the General Commissariat for German and Austrian Affairs, and by severely supervising the expenditures of the military government.[68]

The third criticism was that the zonal government was inefficient because of its incoherent organization and the failure of the government in Paris or in Baden-Baden to formulate a policy for the zone. The structure of the occupation was indeed weak at several points. In Paris, control lay with the General Commissariat for German and Austrian Affairs, an interministerial body created by René Mayer during his brief period as commissioner general; the commissariat's duty was to coordinate the relations of the different ministries in Paris with the zone. However, this body lacked sufficient control in Germany itself, since it could only work through the omnipotent commander-in-chief, and even in Paris its functions were so ill-defined that it was unable to create a coherent policy out of the demands of the different ministries.

In Germany itself, there was considerable duplication of work. The office staff of the commander-in-chief, consisting of three hundred officers, paralleled that of the administrator general, while the decisions of the latter were again reviewed by the director general in charge of each department of government.[69] The maintenance of the offices of the commander-in-chief in Baden-Baden made Allied cooperation difficult, as Clay complained and Laffon corroborated.[70] Finally, the conflict between the civilian administrators and the military was visible throughout the zone. The committee of inquiry gave as an example of this the arrests by the military authorities of security officers of the military government. In a revealing lecture given at Freiburg in 1945 to the principal officers of the 36th Infantry Division, Colonel de Tarragon, aide to the military governor of Baden, pointed out that the troops had to work with the military government. Requisitioning by the troops without military government authorization had to cease, he said. The soldiers had to stop killing off the cattle, or there would be less milk and butter. And the troops were not to impose fines themselves, either on a town or on an individual.[71] It was clear from this talk that the military government was having difficulty making the army keep to its own sphere. The army even forced the military government officers to wear special badges indicating that they were merely civilians-in-uniform, which did away with any prestige value the military government officials may have gained by wearing the army uniform.[72]

Most serious of all was the continual conflict between General Koenig and the administrator general, Émile Laffon, who was reputed to be attempting to carry out in Germany some of the ideals that had come to the fore in the Resistance movement, particularly the view that a new approach must be found to the German question by reconciling the opposing interests of the two countries.[73] The final crisis between the two groups followed months of growing opposition. Early in November 1947, Laffon had offered his resignation to Bidault but had been persuaded to remain until the end of the London conference.

However, on November 15, General Koenig informed him of the abolition of his post. *Le Monde* took an extremely serious view of this action:

> It has been known for a long time that General Koenig and Administrator General Laffon had different ideas on the French policy for Germany. . . .
>
> Well, it would seem that M. Laffon was directly informed the day before yesterday by General Koenig that his position had been abolished. Such a decision appears at first sight only to be within the power of the government. If this decision were not reversed, it would bring about a far-reaching reform in the structure of the organization of the French zone of occupation: in fact, it would leave the French commander-in-chief entirely free to act as he saw fit.
>
> It is not impossible that the divergence of opinions between M. Laffon and the general has an importance beyond its local application to the French administration in Germany and that the Baden-Baden incident has come along to add a further detail on the plane of general policy to other signs of disagreement between the government and certain high officials.[74]

Le Figaro noted that General Koenig "chafed at the presence beside him of a civilian administrator general" and tried to prevent the appointment of a successor. Three days later, *Le Populaire* added the information that Koenig's note to Laffon had ordered him to transmit his powers to Maurice Sabatier, the director general of administrative affairs. *Le Populaire* was outraged at this action by the "very Gaullist General Koenig, who would like to play at being a proconsul."[75]

The resignation of Laffon was followed by those of Jean Arnaud, the director of information, and of C. Bourthoumieux, the supervisor of German justice. Koenig himself took over the duties of Laffon on December 12, 1947. On April 12, 1948, the office of administrator general was abolished and the directorates placed directly under the authority of the commander-in-chief, working through a secretary general and four counselors.[76] From this point on the military were predominant in the zone, and even though the government in Paris moved toward an increasingly flexible point of view on the German problem, the zonal authorities maintained a much less pliant attitude. General Clay was even convinced that the French administration in Germany "was determined to delay if not to thwart the establishment of [a] West German Government."[77] The predominance of the military in the zone came to an end in August 1949, with the appointment of André François-Poncet as high commissioner.

To French observers in the early months of the occupation, it seemed that the incoherence of governmental structure and the lack of harmony among the administrators had the effect of preventing the establishment of any policy for the zone. In particular, it was felt that economic exploitation must be made more effective, an attitude expressed concisely by the MRP deputy, Philippe Livry-Level, on March 29, 1946: "Germany is still rich, and we can exploit it."[78] This criticism was probably the least just of all. The occupation authorities, although undoubtedly overstaffed and hindered by their internal conflicts, did produce a practical policy for the economic regulation of their zone, for its re-education, and for its political revival. What is clear, however, is that this policy was two-sided. On the one hand was the policy of the French thesis, which involved the dismemberment and the exploitation of Germany. On the other hand was the highly developed program of re-education, both cultural and political, intended to fit Germany again to take its place in the political life of Europe. The sources of these contradictions may be found in the internal divisions existing among the authorities in the French zone.

CHAPTER V

The Zone in 1945: Formulation of Aims and Stocktaking

IN 1945 the major question of international affairs, the one which concerned the French people most, was how to find a solution to the "German problem." At the international level, France was taking a share in making the settlement to be imposed on Germany; and in its own zone of occupation, France had to formulate a policy to be applied by its military government. The French view on the settlement at the international level was expressed first in the French thesis, and later in the compromise of the London agreements. What policy did the French attempt to apply in their own zone of occupation?

French thinking about Germany was in several ways contradictory, and the effect was, as many military government officers admitted, to make policy in the zone also appear contradictory. Here, more than ever, the appearance of France was Janus-faced. Perhaps the most immediate reaction of the French was one of bitter hatred springing from their sufferings under the German occupation of France. As Hermann Karl Weinert points out in his study of "the picture of the Germans in postwar French literature," the early French attitude of tolerant compassion for the ordinary German soldier at the front, who presumably wanted the war no more than any Frenchman, slowly gave way to implacable hatred of the savage opponents of the Maquis, who used women and children as hostages and burning and torture as weapons of war.[1] From the Liberation onward, this attitude was expressed, and magnified, by many books and newspaper articles on

German atrocities. Survivors described the crimes of Buchenwald and Ravensbrück, and illustrated descriptions appeared of such atrocities as the burning of Oradour and Mouleydier villages in France itself. This literature of horrors, made more eloquent by the photographs which were printed daily by all types of newspapers, made the French people strongly determined to punish the perpetrators of such crimes.[2]

Faced with this catalogue of human cruelty, Frenchmen attempted to find an explanation by re-analyzing the German character. This analysis was of importance for the occupation. The French conception of the German character, especially in terms of its historical development, would determine where they would place the guilt for the crimes committed and in what manner they would find it necessary to re-educate the German people. Certain general, widely held ideas emerged from this analysis; and public opinion polls showed that the French people as a whole were in fairly close agreement with the ideas being expressed by writers on the German problem.

Most French writers seemed agreed that the German people were basically militaristic. Some, like Georges Rul in his book *The Fourth Reich or the Coming War*, believed that this character was derived from the Teutonic knights and impressed on the rest of Germany by Prussia.[3] These views were expressed with great virulence in a book by Léon Daudet entitled *Acquaintance with Germany*, which was re-published in 1947.[4] For Daudet, German aggression was rooted in Germany's philosophers, especially in the "philosophy of the unconscious" of Kant and Fichte. This conception was developed with greater finesse by Edmond Vermeil, who, through his work in the Center of Studies in Foreign Policy and the National Foundation of Political Sciences, was able to influence directly many of the administrators of the zone.[5]

Many writers were convinced that the German spirit was so imbued with Prussianism that there was no hope of ever changing the German character. The information bulletin for military government officers pointed out, in March 1945, that "one must not forget that the German is, in his inner nature, sensitive only to force. Every manifestation of force is deeply pleasing to him."[6] Pierre Benaerts, in his book *Division of Germany*, claimed that there were two dangerous myths about Germany: "that of democratic Germany and that of Prussianized Germany. . . . The interpenetration of Germany by the Prussian spirit is so advanced that it would be vain to sort out the good and the bad provinces."[7] Many French people must have shared this feeling as late as 1947; when asked in a public opinion poll whether they thought that Germany would become a warlike or a peaceful nation, 63 per cent replied warlike and only 10 per cent thought peaceful.[8]

However, the majority of writers believed that the division between Prussia and the rest of Germany should be revived. This theory, expressed in such works as Robert Minder's *Germanies and Germans*, suggested that each of the provinces of Germany had its own ethnic and historic character, which had been submerged by the dominance of Prussia.[9] In particular, many felt that the least Prussianized of all Germans were those of the Rhineland, Baden, and Württemberg, where French influence had been strongest and which in fact formed the area of the French zone of occupation. Benaerts saw the solution in dividing Germany into three "great hydrographic networks: that of the Rhine, that of the Elbe, that of the Danube."[10] Paul Olagnier, in his book *The Three Germanies*, thought that Germany should be divided, for "racial, mental and cultural reasons," into the Roman, the Germanic, and the Slav Germanies.[11] Wladimir d'Ormesson, the journalist and ambassador, wanted to shift the center of gravity of the Germanic world away from Berlin and to create a federal system around Vienna.[12] Again, the French people echoed these views. Asked in a poll in August 1945 whether they thought Germany should be divided or maintain its unity, 78 per cent wanted it divided. (In the same poll, 71 per cent of those questioned wanted to make Germany into an agricultural state.)[13]

On the other hand, as Weinert points out, the German occupation of France and the French occupation in Germany had brought French and Germans face to face as human beings and the result had been, in some cases at least, to enable them to discover their common humanity. "Where the Frenchman in Germany (as a deported worker) during the war meets a member of the German opposition or even a passive opponent of the party, the tendency to push away the Germans seems to be broken, and a first bridge to understanding to be built."[14] Even in the concentration camps, some Germans were willing to risk their own lives to help the prisoners. And the experiences of young French soldiers of the occupation forces in their relations with the German population varied from the kind of serious attempt to understand the turbulent and inchoate thoughts of a German youth described in Jean-

Louis Curtis's novel *Siegfried* to the sort of love affair described in Georges Auclair's *A German Love*. From these innumerable personal contacts the French were able to decide for themselves whether the theorizings had any basis in fact. The result was to humanize the French approach to the occupation and to encourage Frenchmen in their natural inclination to treat all human beings as individuals with the right to their own idiosyncrasies.

When these views came to be translated into action at the international level, they produced the French thesis so untiringly put forward by Georges Bidault. In the zone itself, several main lines of reasoning may be discerned, closely related to the attitudes described above. This reasoning may be summarized as follows:

Since militarism is a basic German characteristic, Germany must be demilitarized, by destroying its war factories, by lowering its industrial potential, and by maintaining permanent security guarantees.

Since all Germans must be held at least partly responsible for the Nazi era, all must help pay for the damage done. The zone must restore whatever has been taken from France. The French economy must be aided by reparations payments and by the orientation of the German economy toward the service of France. Above all, France must pay nothing to aid the recovery of Germany.

Since most Germans are tainted by Prussianism, and many by Nazism, a long process of re-education must follow denazification.

Since the provinces along the Rhine and in the southwest of Germany are the least imbued with the Prussian spirit and possess individual historical and ethnic character, a new Germany must be created with these provinces as the basis of federalism.

Since the Saar has close economic and historical ties with France and since its economy, and especially its coal, would be of the greatest value to France, every effort must be made to detach the Saar permanently from Germany and to attach it, economically at least, to France.

An attempt must be made to treat the Germans as individuals in such judicial matters as denazification but more especially in cultural and educational matters. They must be exposed to the best of European and particularly of French culture. Young people must be taught the values of democratic society.

With these firm and often contradictory aims, the French proceeded to take stock of their zone.

STOCKTAKING: THE NATURE OF THE FRENCH ZONE

The French were disappointed with their zone as it was finally delineated on June 22, 1945. Although Stalin may have felt that it was greater than the French deserved, since they had "opened the gates to the enemy," it was far less than the French had demanded.[15] In particular, the French had not received Cologne, which they often thought of as the "keystone of French security," and which General de Gaulle considered the northern limit of the "march" of France.[16] Neither had France been given the whole of Hessen-Kassel and Hessen-Nassau, as it had demanded in the European Advisory Commission. Furthermore, on the insistence of the United States War Department, north Baden had been detached from south Baden, and north Württemberg from south Württemberg.[17]

The territory that France did receive was a source of complications. As a result of long haggling in the European Advisory Commission, France received a territory "shaped like an enormous hourglass," which had been cut from eight different German provinces.[18] Its two tapering sections met only at one point, the juncture of the Lauter and Rhine rivers. Yet this zone, if disappointing to the more demanding of French politicians, offered certain solid advantages to France; and the stocktaking which the French military government undertook in the fall of 1945 was not altogether disheartening.

The northern section of the zone

In spite of de Gaulle's assertion that the natural division of the territories on the left bank of the Rhine occurs at Cologne, there was considerable geographical unity in the great triangle of the northern section of the French Zone. The main unifying features of this territory were the mountains and the rivers. The Rhenish Uplands dominated the area. These uplands, 150 kilometers long and 250 kilometers wide, were divided by the rivers into the Eifel, Hunsrück, and Pfälzer Bergland mountains on the left bank of the Rhine and the Westerwald and Taunus ranges on the right bank. The Mosel, Rhine, and Lahn valleys were of great importance, since they provided not only transport but also the major agricultural areas of the territory. There were few mountains of any great height in the area, the highest point of the Hunsrück being only 755 meters. This geographical configuration dominated the economic and social nature of the area. These mountains were rocky, often covered with rough heathland, broken occasionally with forests or meadows, and the majority of the population lived in the fertile river valleys or on the Rhenish plain. There were two major groupings of population, around the mines and factories of the Saar and along the Rhine at Mainz and Ludwigshafen. The northern section of the zone was made up of parts of five separate administrative divisions: Rheinprovinz, Hessen-Nassau, Hessen, Saar, and Pfalz (or Palatinate).

The Rheinprovinz was acquired by Prussia in 1815 and received only slight alterations of boundary before 1945. In 1945, however, the Provinz was divided between the British and French occupation zones, with the British retaining the great industrial areas of the Ruhr and Aachen. The French section consisted of two Regierungsbezirke only, Trier and Koblenz. The French themselves admitted that this area was not linked organically to the rest of the Rheinprovinz and that this division was justifiable.[19] There was a clear demarcation between the Eifel Mountains in the French zone and the beginning of the North German Plain in the British zone. The northern section, in the British zone, contained the greatest industrial concentration in Germany, with a population density of over 400 per square kilometer, while the southern section, in the French zone, was largely agricultural, with a population density of between 25 and 75 per square kilometer. The types of farming differed, and even the dialect varied, the British zone speaking a Low Franconian and the French zone a Middle Franconian dialect.

Although the British took the rich industrial area of the north, the French section was not lacking in value. Regierungsbezirk Trier, with an area of 5,322 square kilometers and a population in 1939 of 495,730, included the fertile upper valley of the Mosel. Regierungsbezirk Koblenz included the lower stretches of the Mosel and part of the middle Rhine from Bingen almost to Bonn. Neither Regierungsbezirk had any important industry or, over the major part of the mountains, anything beyond subsistence agriculture and forestry. In the valleys, agriculture flourished. Considerable amounts of cereal and potatoes were grown, and cattle, sheep, and pigs were raised. The names of the towns—Bernkastel, Trarbach, Bacharach, Boppard—were a wine-lover's dream.[20]

Closely linked with the Rheinprovinz were the four Landkreise of the Prussian province of Hessen-Nassau, which were added to the French zone to provide it with a bridgehead on the right bank of the Rhine. These four Landkreise, with a population in 1939 of only 217,243, were 10 per cent of the area of Provinz Nassau, created by Prussia in 1866. They spread across the slopes of the Westerwald, with only three towns of any size (Montabaur, Westerburg, and Bad Ems). Agriculture here also was predominant, with viticulture in the Rhine valley and considerable cultivation of potatoes and beets.[21]

Once again, the section of the Provinz given to France was the more sparsely populated. The great urban centers of Wiesbaden, Frankfurt, Fulda, and Kassel were all kept within the American zone. The French were considerably annoyed by the American desire for Wiesbaden, since the French thought that they should be given that section of the Provinz to complete their hold on both banks of the Rhine as far as Mainz.[22] On the other hand, the four Landkreise the French received were easily assimilable to the Rheinprovinz, while possession of the more eastern areas of Hessen-Nassau would have brought them a population whose ties were with north and east Germany along the valleys of the Weser and the Main. This area, moreover, had a slight Catholic majority (53 per cent), as opposed to the Protestant majority (60.6 per cent) in the Provinz as a whole. Thus, there was little problem in linking this area with the predominantly Catholic rural area across the Rhine.

From Land Hessen, the French were given all territory lying south of the Rhine, comprising the right-angle bend at Mainz. This area of four Landkreise and one Stadtkreis was the famous district of Rhein-hessen, known throughout Germany for its historical heritage and throughout the world for its Liebfraumilch, the most famous of German wines. Rheinhessen occupied 20 per cent of Hessen, with a population in 1939 of 439,431. The slightly rolling plain, with its clearly defined northern boundary on the Rhine, had a rich soil, mild winters, and warm summers, and hence rich agricultural produce in wheat, barley, and grapes. The rural population was very dense, with over 200 inhabitants to the square kilometer. Industry was found in the city of Mainz, an ancient episcopal city with a population of 158,306, which, with its outlying towns, produced metal goods, machinery, and railroad rolling stock. The only other towns of any size were Worms (population 50,628), a lovely cathedral city where the

Imperial Diets had met, and Bingen (population 59,539), one of the centers of the wine trade.[23]

The Pfalz, or Palatinate, was one of the richest areas of the French zone. When the former state of the Electors Palatine was divided in 1815, the section on the left bank was taken by Bavaria, and this section, called the Pfalz, remained a Regierungsbezirk of Bavaria until 1945, although widely separated from the rest of Bavaria. The area consisted of thirteen Landkreise and seven Stadtkreise, with a population of 1,050,120 in 1939. Although the area was typically Rhenish, with wide mountain plateaus and fertile valleys, it was considerably richer than that to the north. The mountains were heavily forested, and the woodland industries of paper-making, furniture-making, and wood sculpture flourished. Elsewhere in the mountains, good pasturage encouraged the raising of animals. In the Rhine plain, there were not only grapes, but fruit, tobacco, vegetables, and hops.

In spite of the richness of the agriculture, only 25 per cent of the population made its living from farming. The majority (61 per cent) were engaged in industry, trade, and transportation. The main industrial ties of the Pfalz were with the Saar, a fact the Nazis had recognized by placing the two under a single planning association. The major industries lay along the Rhine. Ludwigshafen, with a population of 144,440, was one of the most important cities of the whole zone, since it was a center of the I.G. Farben company which, before 1939, was the largest chemical company in the world. This industrial concentration had been at the basis of many Nazi war industries, especially in production of synthetic rubber. The section of I.G. Farben in Ludwigshafen, founded in 1865, had employed 19,000 workers and 5,900 scientists before the war. In 1939 this one industrial group had produced the equivalent of 80 per cent of the whole of French chemical production for that year. During the war, the personnel had been raised to 37,500. Other industrial centers were Speyer, with textiles, Kaiserslautern, with textile, tobacco, and leather industries, and Pirmasens, a center of the leather industry.

The Pfalz differed from the other parts of the northern section of the zone in its Protestant majority, its industrial importance, and its economic ties with other areas, especially with the Saar and with north Baden. The individuality of the Pfalz was to prove of considerable significance when France decided to unite the whole of this northern triangle, with the exception of the Saar, as one Land. The Pfalz differed from the rest of the Land in its Protestant and Socialist majority, and it felt that it was being condemned to a perpetual minority status. Moreover, the individualism of the Pfalz was so marked that certain elements of the military government attempted to encourage the revival of a separatist movement in the Pfalz, as had been done after the First World War. The separatists received very little support, however, largely owing to strong Socialist opposition to the movement.[24]

The Saar was by far the most important economic asset of the French zone. The changing political and economic status of the Saar is one key to the changes in French policy toward the zone and toward the German problem itself.

The Saar was one of the smallest of the German Länder, with an area of 1,925 square kilometers in 1939. Its population, on the other hand, was 842,420, giving it a density of over 400 inhabitants to the square kilometer. The predominant physical characteristic was the rising level of the mountains from south to north. In the south, on the French border, was a bare plain of poor soil. In the center was an area of low hills (200 to 400 meters high), where mines and forests predominated. In the north were the outcroppings of the Rhenish uplands, reaching 500 meters. The major grouping of population was in a wide belt across the center of the Land, where the major towns, Saarbrücken (population 133,282) and St. Ingbert (population 60,-243), grew up around the mines. An important metallurgical industry, as well as important electrical installations, were located near the mines.[25]

A Department of State economist summed up the significance of the Saar in 1949. "In 1937," he wrote, "the Saar accounted for only 1 per cent of Germany's population, but included one-tenth of Germany's coal deposits, and 12 per cent of its steel production. At the favorable terms of trade for its principal export products (coal, steel, chemicals, glass) currently prevailing in the world markets, the area is capable of producing an annual surplus of about $100,000,000 over its own needs."[26]

For these reasons, French statesmen demanded the economic fusion of the Saar with France. While French aims for the Ruhr and the Rhineland were not acceptable to France's allies, French demands regarding the Saar were more easily granted. France had already been

in possession of the Saar mines from 1919 to 1935. A separatist movement in the Saar had strongly supported French claims on the Saar
after the First World War and might easily do so again after the
second. Many believed that the plebiscite held in 1935 under strong
Nazi influence had been suspect in its results. The burden of the
French occupation was to fall less heavily on the Saar, since it was the
avowed aim of the French to persuade the Saarlanders to request the
economic fusion of the Saar with France.

The situation of the Saar was even more complicated immediately
after the war by the fact that although in the long run the Saar was
by far the most valuable economic asset in the zone, in the short term
it was an economic liability. It had suffered greater destruction than
any other section of the zone. It required large expenditures of capital
to set its industries and mines in action again and large supplies of
foodstuffs to give its miners the nutrition needed in their heavy work.
It was therefore no advantage to the rest of the zone to be attached to
the Saar during the first three years of the occupation, since part of
the surplus of the other sections of the zone was used to cover the
deficit incurred by the Saar. Once the industry of the Saar had regained its productivity, and only then, was it in the French interest
to remove the area from the zone and to bring about its economic fusion
with France.[27]

The southern section of the zone

The southern triangle of the French zone lacked the historical and
economic unity of the northern section. Here, the strategic considerations that had dominated the thinking of the United States War Department, at the expense of historical and economic logic, were only
too evident. The northern boundary of the zone was delineated in
accordance with the War Department's desire to retain in the American
zone the *Autobahn* running from Karlsruhe via Stuttgart, Ulm, and
Augsburg to Munich. As a result, the historical Länder of Baden and
Württemberg were each divided across the center. The French zone
consisted of the southern area of Land Baden, the southern area of
Land Württemberg, the Prussian Regierungsbezirk of Hohenzollern,
and one Bavarian Landkreis, Lindau.

Geography provided a certain unity in the long western boundary
of the Rhine and the southern border on Switzerland. The northern

boundary of the zone, however, was completely arbitrary and remained throughout the occupation an aggravation to the French in
their desire to create a federal system based on the historic Länder.

The French received 66 per cent of the Land of Baden, a territory
of 9,961 square kilometers with a population in 1939 of 1,233,635.[28]
The area comprised two Bezirke (administrative districts of Baden
each comprising about nine Landkreise) in their entirety, those of
Freiburg and Konstanz, and half of the Bezirk of Karlsruhe. The
French did not receive the capital city of Karlsruhe. The long line of
the Rhenish plain, running from the Swiss border to the northern tip
of this southern triangle, and the mountain mass of the Black Forest
gave a certain unity to the eastern section of Baden. The Rhenish plain,
often subject in the past to flooding, had rich pasturage near the river
and exceptionally fertile soil at the base of the hills. Wheat, fruit,
beets, tobacco, and grapes were grown there.

The Black Forest, a granite massif some 200 kilometers in length
running parallel to the Rhine, was an area of deep valleys and heavily
wooded uplands, with some pasturage but few crops. Here lay the
town of Baden-Baden, in a little valley where the hills opened onto
the Rhenish plain. The third section of Baden, the southeastern corner
which formed the Bezirk of Konstanz, was different in character. The
landscape was rough, broken by jagged outcrops of rocky upland, and
the climate unexceptional, except on the temperate shores of the Bodensee and in the Hegau area around Singen.

As in the northern triangle of the French zone, the zonal boundary
cut off the more industrial section of the Land from that given to the
French. In the French area of Baden, 66 per cent of the population
was engaged in agriculture, producing barley and oats and raising large
numbers of cows, pigs, and sheep. Most important of all was the
forestry industry, the Black Forest producing large quantities of valuable fir, spruce, and beech. There was, even in this section of the zone,
some industry, which was dependent largely upon the Rhine traffic
for its supplies of raw materials. There was textile manufacturing in
the towns near Switzerland, metallurgy on the shores of the Bodensee, a highly developed watch industry in the Black Forest, and important chemical installations of such companies as I.G. Farben and
Société Degussa at Rheinfelden and Waldshut.

The unity of Baden lay not in its geographical or economic nature but in its history. The Grand Duchy of Baden, as recognized at the Congress of Vienna, lasted until 1918, although the history of the area as an independent principality dates from 1130 with the appearance of the first margrave. Baden had been a center of German liberalism in the nineteenth and twentieth centuries, and there, too, the influence of France had been strongly felt. This sense of national identity, deriving from the area's liberal past and influenced strongly by pro-French sympathies, was to prove of considerable value to the French in their desire to develop particularist sentiments in their zone.

Württemberg, like Baden, was split along a line running just south of the Karlsruhe-Munich *Autobahn*.[29] To it were added the Prussian Bezirk of Hohenzollern-Sigmaringen, and the Bavarian Landkreis of Lindau. This section of Württemberg consisted of 48 per cent of the total Land, with a population of 1,029,225 in 1939. Once again, there was no natural unity to the area. The north was a section of rough sandstone hills; the center was dominated by the valleys of the Danube and its tributaries; the south was an infertile glacial plain, with the exception of the lakeshore of the Bodensee. The major cities, including the capital, Stuttgart, had been taken for the American zone. The principal towns left to the French zone were Reutlingen (1939 population 33,000), with firms for the manufacture of machinery; Tübingen (23,300 inhabitants in 1939), with one of Germany's best universities and firms for the manufacture of steel and scientific apparatus; and Friedrichshafen (population 13,300 in 1939), with the Dornier airplane factories. Again, as in Baden, history provided the major unifying feature. Württemberg had enjoyed an independent existence as a duchy since the fifteenth century (1495) and constitutional liberties since the sixteenth. Like Baden, Württemberg offered certain advantages to the French. Its particularism was already pronounced, its agriculture was well developed, and its industry could quickly be oriented to French needs.

Comparative population figures for the French zone are shown in Table 2, and the relative economic value of the different sections of the zone can be seen from Table 3, which indicates the value of industrial production in certain selected industries of the different sections of the zone in 1936. It is clear that the principal mining and metallurgy of the zone was in the Saar. On the other hand, the area of the Rheinland-Pfalz, that is, the whole of the northern triangle except the

Saar, was rich in chemicals, leather, and machinery manufacturing. Baden possessed a valuable textile industry and some paper and chemical production. Württemberg produced textiles, steel, and machinery.

Certain important conclusions were drawn by the occupation authorities from a study of the nature of their zone. On the one hand, there were many obvious drawbacks to this particular area: First, the

TABLE 2

POPULATION FIGURES OF THE FRENCH ZONE[30]

	Rheinland-Pfalz	Baden	Württemberg	Saar	Total
Population 1939 ..	2,866,778	1,233,635	1,029,225	842,420	5,972,058
Population 1946 ..	2,748,039	1,174,374	1,114,232	750,436	5,787,081

TABLE 3

NET INDUSTRIAL PRODUCTION OF THE FRENCH ZONE IN 1936[31]
(RM Millions)

Industrial Group	Rheinland-Pfalz	Baden	Württemberg	Saar	Total
Mines	16.1	4.3	0.0	128.8	149.2
Metallurgy ..	41.3	0.8	0.9	132.8	175.8
Foundries ...	21.7	9.2	4.7	20.7	56.3
Steel products.	27.8	11.0	41.8	19.5	100.1
Machinery ..	74.4	22.0	42.5	12.2	151.1
Precision and optical instruments ..	3.0	13.0	44.4	0.2	60.6
Stones and earth	94.1	12.8	5.5	14.4	126.8
Sawmills	10.7	12.5	10.2	1.1	34.5
Wood	22.5	11.8	16.3	0.7	51.3
Chemicals ...	171.6	20.8	4.9	2.5	199.8
Paper	22.9	25.2	6.6	0.2	54.9
Leather	97.8	5.5	23.2	2.0	128.5
Textiles	26.1	106.3	121.1	0.5	254.0
Total production*.	1,042.4	544.5	516.0	454.2	2,577.1

* Including miscellaneous industries not listed above.

zone lacked constitutional, historical, and economic unity. Nine territories, for the most part shorn off from the administrative units to
which they had previously belonged, were linked, for the first time
in their history, as one political unit. Second, the sections of Germany
upon which it would have been possible to build a new federalism, such
as the Länder of Baden and Württemberg, were divided up, and in
every case (except the Saar) the capital cities were not within the
French zone. Third, with the exception of the Saar, the French zone
was left with the predominantly agricultural section of each divided
Land.

On the other hand, certain desirable features were also noted.
First, the northern triangle of the zone formed something of a geo-
graphic and economic unity, which could finally be transformed into
a new Land. Second, the Länder of Baden and Württemberg, even
in their reduced form, retained their sense of national identity and a
desire to return to their own liberal, French-influenced past. Third,
the French zone was able to provide a larger proportion of the foodstuffs needed by its population than were the British and American
zones. In fact, the French occupation force and its dependents could
in large measure live off the land. Finally, the zone possessed industrial resources of considerable value, including 10.5 per cent of Germany's coal, 20 per cent of its chemical industry, 45 per cent of its
leather industry, and 45 per cent of its precision instrument and watch
and clock industry.[32]

Such had been the value of the zone in the German economy of
1936. The next stage of the stocktaking was to estimate the effect of
the war upon the condition of the zone.

THE CONDITION OF THE FRENCH ZONE IN 1945

Owing largely to its agricultural nature, the French zone did not
suffer as heavily as the other zones from the effects of the war. The
air raids had concentrated for the most part on destruction in the me-
dium-sized and large cities, of which there were very few. In the cities
of over 100,000 inhabitants (i.e., Ludwigshafen, Mainz, Saarbrücken),
German sources estimated that 44 per cent of the buildings were totally
destroyed and 45 per cent partially destroyed. In towns of between
10,000 and 100,000 inhabitants, 16 per cent were totally destroyed

and 25 per cent partially destroyed. In towns of less than 10,000 inhabitants, 87 per cent of the buildings were intact. In fact, throughout the French zone, 75 per cent of the buildings remained intact, in comparison with 65 per cent in the American zone and 43 per cent in the British. This destruction of the large cities brought about the sharp contrast between the conditions of life in the cities and in the country, which was one of the main features of life in postwar Germany and caused many former city inhabitants to flee to the country.[33]

The French authorities later estimated that 30 per cent of the industrial installations of the 1943–44 period had been destroyed. Different sources vary greatly in their estimates, but all agree that surprisingly little damage was done. In fact, for the whole of Germany, it has been argued that the total destruction of industrial installations was only 15 to 20 per cent. Various industries, however, had suffered in very different degrees. Mining and metallurgy were estimated to have suffered only 10 per cent destruction, the chemical industry 10 to 15 per cent, the machinery industry 15 to 20 per cent, and the textile industry 20 per cent. In relation to these figures, the French zone was largely spared, since its major industries were mining, metallurgy, and chemical production. On the other hand, these figures did not hold true for the Saar, which had suffered very heavy losses both from the bombing and from the period of invasion. French estimates held that 60 per cent of the medium and heavy industry in the Saar had been put out of action, with the "coefficient of destruction" of industrial plants given at 30 per cent, of textile plants at 32 per cent, of the chemical industry at 44 per cent, and of precision and optical instrument installations at 80 per cent.[34]

Most devastating of all was the complete breakdown of the transportation system. In the French zone, between 60 and 90 per cent of the marshaling yards and 50 per cent of the railroad tracks were destroyed, and only one-third of the prewar rolling stock remained. All the Rhine bridges were lying in the river, blocking navigation. At Roppenheim, for example, the river could be cleared only by removing two piers of the bridge, which weighed, respectively, 250 and 850 tons.[35]

Agriculture, also, had suffered badly. The French zone had not produced enough food to feed itself even in prewar days. Before 1939, with 9.6 per cent of the German population, the zone had produced

4 to 5 per cent of Germany's cereals, 6 per cent of its potatoes, 6 per cent of its sugar beets, and 5 per cent of its dairy products and livestock. The only agricultural goods produced in excess were tobacco (40 per cent of German production) and wine (75 per cent of German production). The situation in 1945 had been aggravated by the destruction of agricultural machinery and transport, by the wearing out of the soil during the war years, by a shortage of seeds, fertilizer, and labor, and by extremely bad weather. As a result, the 1945 harvest produced only 14 per cent of the normal tobacco crop, 50 per cent of the cereal harvest, 30 per cent of the sugar crop, and 50 per cent of the wine harvest.[36]

Population losses were significant, not only for their total but because they fell most heavily on the productive segment of the German people. Unlike the British and American zones, where the population rose heavily because of the influx of refugees and displaced persons, the population of the French zone actually fell. The French government argued that it was not bound to accept the refugees from the German lands incorporated into Poland and Russia, nor those driven out of the Sudetenland by Czechoslovakia, since it had not participated in the Yalta and Potsdam agreements at which these population movements were sanctioned. The French zone received a total of 175,000 displaced persons, of whom 100,000 had been repatriated by November 1945. The French zone, which in 1939 had a total population of 6,319,958, had in January 1946 only 5,787,081.[37]

Most important, however, was the lack of balance in the population. There was a great excess of the very old and the very young, of invalids, and of women in the vital working-age group. Table 4 illustrates the fact that half of the population in January 1946 was

TABLE 4

POPULATION FIGURES OF THE FRENCH ZONE: JANUARY 26, 1946[38]
(Total Population: 5,787,081)

Age Group	Women	Men
Under 18 years	906,309	931,736
18 to 50 years	1,615,900	905,853
Over 50 years	790,070	637,213
Total	3,312,279	2,474,802

below eighteen or over fifty years of age; that the number of women exceeded men by over 800,000; and worse, that the number of women in the age group eighteen to fifty was almost double that of men.

In spite of all these difficulties, the French found the situation in their zone more encouraging, in many ways, than did the British and Americans in theirs. Damage to buildings was less great. The population had fallen in size. Industrial destruction was not as great as had been expected. The economy of the zone could very quickly be turned to the direct benefit of France, by helping feed its army, by restoring the goods taken from France, by paying reparations in kind, and by producing the raw materials and finished products most needed by France.

The French authorities had developed a clear picture of the immediate aims of their occupation and of the situation in which those aims were to be put into practice. It fell to the various directorates in Baden-Baden to apply these aims in their own particular areas of control.

CHAPTER VI

Restitution and Reparations

THE French military government was able to formulate and carry
out economic policy in the French zone without much reference
to quadripartite agreements. The Potsdam Conference had laid down
several economic principles which were to be observed throughout
Germany, including elimination of war potential, deconcentration and
decartelization of industry, and treatment of Germany as a single economic unit. But the French, who had not been represented at the conference, announced that they did not consider themselves bound by
decisions reached there; in particular, they refused to permit the economic unification foreseen by the agreements. As a result Allied controls over French policy proved applicable only when the French
government had specifically agreed to them.[1]

These restrictions were few. Any removal of goods as reparations
had to be justified to an Inter-Allied Reparations Agency set up by
the conference of Paris in November 1945. All foreign trade of the
zone, including trade with France, had to be paid for in dollars, although exports to Allied countries were sold at a 20 per cent discount.[2]
Industrial production had to be held down to the level agreed upon
in the plan of March 1946—that is, to 75 per cent of 1936 production.
Otherwise, the French military government was free to operate as it
wished.

The French pursued two dissimilar aims in their economic policy,
"on the one hand, a policy of confiscation of equipment, on the other
hand, a policy of exploitation of industrial production."[3] In short, the

French removed the industrial potential of the zone as restitution and reparations, and at the same time tried to develop German industry for the benefit of the French economy. This chapter will deal with the policy of confiscation, and Chapter Seven will cover the policy of industrial exploitation.

RESTITUTION

France's wartime losses must be borne in mind in any evaluation of its occupation policy. In 1945 those losses were estimated at a total of 40 billion dollars (1938) or 4,869 billion francs (1945).* This total was made up of two kinds of losses. French goods which had been destroyed were valued at 2,551 billion francs (1945); the remainder of the losses was due to the transfer of French property into Germany as part of Germany's systematic exploitation of the occupied territories of Europe. The former category of goods was to be paid for, in part at least, by Germany in the form of reparations. The latter category, in which the goods were presumed still to exist, was to be sought out in Germany and returned to its owners as restitution.[4] The French military government determined to make the greatest possible use of its authority in the zone to develop the program of reparations and restitution.

A series of official studies carried out in France immediately after the Liberation showed that the spoliation of French goods had taken several forms. They included the seizure of state and private property; the exploitation of the production of Alsace and Lorraine by incorporation of those areas into Germany itself and by transfer of property across the border into the Pfalz and Baden; and the confiscation of goods belonging to Jews and members of the Resistance. Moreover, a false exchange rate and enforced trade agreements raised the total much higher.

The first major effort of the French military government was to restore to Alsace and Lorraine the goods taken from them which could be identified in the French zone.[5] The method employed in the search for despoiled goods was logical: testimony was taken from those who had lost goods and equipment, and a search in the zone was made. Later, additional funds from France were used to finance a systematic

---

* Henceforth, where the monetary unit is not valued at its current rate but at that of a previous year, the year of valuation will be indicated in parentheses.

search throughout the zone, and Germans were forced to declare their knowledge of despoiled goods. The result of this was that with very limited means the French achieved great efficiency in detecting French goods which had been brought into the zone by the Germans. Foreign goods in the French zone, and French goods in the other zones, were not, however, being detected with the same ease.[6]

As a result of these efforts the military government was able to report that by December 31, 1947, goods valued at $18,200,000 (1938) had been restored to France, of which almost three-quarters had been sent to Alsace and Lorraine. In the same period $7,200,000 worth of goods had been restored to other Allied nations. The Alsthom and Peugeot factories in particular, which had been stripped of machine tools in the last months of the war, had been able to recover some 900 tons of equipment by September 1946.[7]

Frenchmen nevertheless contend that the great bulk of spoliations was never returned to France. A study of the Interministerial Economic Committee, published in August 1951, gave the total restitution which France had received from Germany, including the value of gold recuperated, as 134,413,537,483 francs (1950)—only a very small proportion, the French believed, of their total losses from spoliations, which amounted to some 2,345 billion francs (1945).[8] But they could at least console themselves with the consideration that possession of a zone of occupation had enabled them to act for themselves in recovering part of the goods that the Germans had brought from France into the Rhenish provinces and Baden.

APPROPRIATION OF INDUSTRIAL EQUIPMENT AS REPARATION

The exaction of reparations was much slower than the process of restitution. First, it had been held necessary to determine in advance the share of reparations to be taken by each of the Allied countries. At the reparations conference in Paris in November 1945, the proportion of reparations to be received by France was laid down as 22.8 per cent of the industrial equipment removed and as 16 per cent of all other goods. Second, the occupation powers had to determine the level of industrial production to be permitted in Germany. After much argument among the Allied powers in Berlin, the first Level of Industry plan was published in March 1946. By this plan German industry was divided into three groups. The first, which included armaments and industries useful for production of war material, such as synthetic rubber and gasoline, was completely prohibited. The second, including steel, chemicals, vehicles, and precision instruments, was restricted in output. The third, including bicycles and textiles, was unrestricted, because it was of no military value. It was estimated that German exports by 1949 should reach 66 per cent of the 1936 total. All equipment in the prohibited and restricted industries beyond that necessary for the foreseen level of production was to be dismantled and made available for reparations. Finally, an inventory had to be made of the plants and equipment which would be available for dismantling, and the first such list did not appear until June 1946.[9]

The Potsdam agreement, however, stated that "removals of industrial capital equipment shall begin as soon as possible. . . . Prior to the fixing of the total amount of equipment subject to removal, advance deliveries shall be made in respect of such equipment as will be determined to be eligible." This clause was immediately acted upon in the French zone. The first seizures had been of war material, which was taken by the invading army as war booty.[10] After May 1945, machine tools were systematically taken, especially after technical experts were sent from France to carry out a search for them. General Koenig's directive of August 30, 1945, gave legal sanction to these seizures, and the system was elaborated by further instructions from the military government. This phase ended only on June 23, 1946, with the establishment of the first list of factories available as reparations. The commander-in-chief later reported that the French military government had profited from the delay between the Potsdam agreements, which France did not sign, and the Level of Industry Plan of March 1946, which it did sign. According to the military government, "This delay was put to use to secure for France advance deliveries of reparations and to put an end to the economic union existing between Alsace, Moselle, and the German Reich. From this double point of view, the Reparations-Restitution Directorate achieved considerable progress: on the one hand, a program of confiscation of machinery and isolated equipment, on the other hand, the re-equipping of the agricultural economy of Alsace and Moselle by return of the goods removed from those provinces and transferred to Baden and the Pfalz."[11]

The second phase in the reparations program began in June 1946. It had been estimated at the time of the Level of Industry agreement that 1,800 factories would be available from the three western zones, including 164 from the French zone. However, before shipment of these could take place a long preparatory process had to be completed. This involved the cataloguing in each zone of the factories available; the designation by the IARA of the factories to be dismantled, evaluation of these by the zonal authority, and quadripartite verification; the agreement on division of factories between the U.S.S.R. and the West; the expression of interest by potential acquirers, allocation, final dismantling, and shipment. It was estimated by the IARA that for each factory the process took at least sixteen months.[12]

Accordingly, although the French set about the task enthusiastically, little had been achieved by the end of 1946. The Reparations-Restitution Directorate had worked at the designation of factories available, and the French group in the Control Council had informed the IARA that two hundred factories were available from the French zone. Of these, only sixty had been accepted by the Agency. The process of evaluation by ten expert engineers and accountants from the General Commissariat of German and Austrian Affairs in Paris had just begun. The dismantling had been started in only one factory.[13]

In 1947 the process began to move more swiftly. A wide survey of machine tools available for reparations was made, and the total amounted to some 8,000 articles. By the end of December their evaluation had been agreed upon, but no shipment had yet taken place. Of factories evaluated, the total rose from RM 30,000,000 in January to RM 60,000,000 in December. It was reported in October that dismantling was being carried out at the Mauser small arms works in Obernhof in Württemberg, the Zeppelin works at Friedrichshafen, the Balcke machinery works in Frankenthal, the steel-rolling mill at Slegen, and Junghaus and Kienzle watchmaking plants in the Black Forest.[14]

French plans suffered a significant setback in 1947, however, when the bizonal authorities decided to revise the Level of Industry plan for the Bizone. After the conference of August 22–27, 1947, with France, at which the bizonal authorities offered only the sop of increased coal exports to France, a new Level of Industry agreement for the Bizone was issued on August 29. By this plan, the level was to be raised from 70–75 per cent of 1936 production to between 90 and 95 per cent, and steel production was to be raised from 5.8 million ingot tons for all Germany to 10.7 for the Bizone alone. This was followed on October 15, 1947, by the publication of a reduced list of factories available for reparations from the Bizone, the number falling from 1,636 to 681. The French, assuaged by the greater coal assignments, and fearing bizonal industrial competition, also revised their list, reducing the number of factories available from their zone from 200 to 176.[15]

In 1948 the issue of reparations took on a much larger importance. In April 1946 General Clay had already refused to continue sending reparations to Russia, and the United States military government had become increasingly unwilling to continue subsidization of the Bizone while dismantling continued. With the formulation of the Marshall Plan, the problem entered a new phase. The Herter Committee, sent to Europe by the American Congress to report on German conditions, recommended the end of dismantling, and a new bizonal list of factories available for dismantling issued in July 1948 again reduced the number available. The intervention of Paul Hoffman, the administrator of the Marshall Plan funds, caused Britain and France to withdraw their objections to further reductions. The Humphrey Committee, appointed by Hoffman, reported in February 1949, and its findings were taken as a basis for yet another reduced list on April 19, 1949.[16]

The French position on reparations in 1948 was upheld by Jacques Rueff, president of the IARA itself. Rueff had already argued, in 1946, the need for direction by the Allies of the whole German economy, so that reparations in kind could be exacted from Germany with the aim of raising the productive capacity of countries ravaged by Germany. In 1948 Rueff spoke out against the American position, stating that German reparations reinforced the Marshall Plan by strengthening the economies of the weaker countries of Europe. [17]

Meanwhile the IARA continued its work of evaluation and assignment. In October 1947, at the very time when the revised bizonal list was published, the IARA designated thirty-one factories in the French zone for dismantling. The work of dismantling continued throughout 1948, amid a growing chorus of German protests. The German government of Land Württemberg resigned on August 7, 1948, in protest against the decision of the French military government to dismantle thirty-eight factories in Württemberg. On August 9, half a million workers went out on a twenty-four-hour strike, and a resolution of sympathy was passed in Württemberg-Baden, in the American zone, asking for fusion with the French-occupied section of Württemberg. On August 26, State President Wohleb of Land Baden turned in the resignation of his government as a protest against the military government's announcement that ten more engineering factories would be closed on September 10 for dismantling. Nevertheless, on September 22 the IARA issued a further list of fifty-three factories to be dismantled, of which twelve were in the French zone.[18]

The eleven German minister-presidents met at Rüdesheim in October 1948 to make a concerted demand for the end of reparations, and when Robert Schuman, the French Premier, visited Koblenz on October 10–12, he was again pressed on the matter. The French position was reconfirmed in an official communiqué issued by the Ministry of Foreign Affairs on October 13, 1948, which noted that Schuman had made no change of policy. France was in close agreement with Great Britain that dismantling should continue as rapidly as possible and that the factories listed as reparations should be quickly transferred to the countries which had suffered from the war. In certain cases, however, where dismantling would be inconvenient or pointless, the decision to dismantle would be reviewed. Finally, following the Washington agreements of April 9, 1949, the three Western powers announced a new reparations agreement based on the findings of the Humphrey Committee, reducing even further the number of factories available for reparations.[19]

Throughout 1949, as the date for the founding of the West German state approached, the pace of dismantling increased. In 1949 alone, 268 factories were partially or wholly removed from the three western zones, the figures amounting to a total of 42 per cent of the whole value of dismantling since 1945.[20] A final summary of the dismantling carried out appeared in the report of the Assembly of the IARA in June 1951. Table 5 illustrates the situation in the French zone.

France received only a small proportion of the equipment dismantled in its own zone. For example, in 1946, it took only part of two factories from the ten dismantled. In all, France acquired only sixteen complete factories and the major portion of six other factories

TABLE 5

DISMANTLING IN THE FRENCH ZONE, 1945–1949[21]

Year in Which Plants Allocated	Number Dismantled in French Zone	Number Taken, in Whole or in Part, by France
1946	10	2
1947	9	2
1948	40	5
1949	51	13

from its own zone, although one hundred ten factories were shipped from the zone, in whole or in part, to the nations receiving German reparations. However, the French also shipped equipment from the rest of the zone into the Saar, in preparation for its economic fusion with France, in amounts very difficult to ascertain.[22]

The effect of the dismantling on the productive capacity of Germany is hard to estimate. German sources have since claimed that in the three western zones dismantling reduced productive capacity by 8 per cent, with higher losses in certain industries, including a 20 per cent loss in gasoline production, a 25 per cent loss in metallurgy, a 15 per cent loss in cast iron, and a 20 per cent loss in precision and optical instruments. A United Nations agency, on the other hand, stated that the highest estimate of loss of capacity from dismantling in the western zones was 5 per cent, and that little serious harm had been done. In fact, one major effect had been to remove worn-out equipment, which was replaced shortly afterwards by new machinery paid for by Marshall aid.[23]

The French zone, however, did suffer heavily from the dismantling, not so much from its effect on the total economy of the zone as from its local effects. The French zone lacked the large concentrations of industry found, for example, in the British zone, and the dismantling of many of the factories in the French zone had the effect of throwing the skilled working population of many small towns out of work and leaving them with no hope of finding other employment in their own locality. When the watch factories of the Black Forest and of the Swabian Alps in Württemberg were dismantled, it caused great and localized hardship for the population of those areas. The

French military government officers at times joined in the complaints of the Germans against the Reparations Agency, which, they said, failed to take local conditions into account in determining which factories should be dismantled. Relations between the French and the Germans were much embittered by this conflict, and the development of German self-government was hindered.

Yet, on the whole, it can be said that dismantling did not greatly weaken the industrial capacity of the French zone. It was a constant irritant rather than a major amputation.

ECONOMIC FUSION WITH THE SAAR AS REPARATION

The British and American governments had agreed in April 1947 that the Saar should be linked in economic union with France. The opposition of Soviet Russia prevented the fusion from taking place at that time, and it was only in February 1948 that the Western powers decided to permit the fusion without further haggling with the U.S.S.R. On April 1, 1948, the Saar was joined in an economic union with France.[24] Since this fusion had the effect of reducing the number of German factories available for dismantling as reparations, as none could now be taken from the Saar, the Inter-Allied Reparations Agency decided in January 1949 that the fusion should be regarded as part of France's share of reparations. France was considered to have received $17,500,000 (1938) as reparations by its fusion with the Saar.

When the Inter-Allied Reparations Agency estimated that fusion with the Saar was the equivalent of a credit to France of $17,500,000 in reparations payments, it was making a completely unrealistic judgment. The true value of the Saar to France lay not in the equipment which might be dismantled but in the immense surplus of exports of the Saar's economy and in the Saar's production of those industrial goods that France needed most.

PAYMENT OF FRENCH OCCUPATION COSTS

The Control Council had decided in September 1945 that the costs of the occupation forces in Germany should be borne by the Germans. The Germans could not but recognize that the occupying powers, since they exercised supreme control in Germany, could use German possessions as they wished.[25] Allied as well as German circles were perturbed over the legal justification for such actions, and much

was written for the purpose of clarifying the legal basis of the power
exercised by the occupation regime, but the fact remained that the
occupying forces were able to enforce their will in these matters; and
it is necessary to ask how great was the burden which the French laid
upon their zone in forcing the Germans to pay the direct costs of the
occupation.

TABLE 6

FRENCH ZONE OCCUPATION COSTS[26]

(RM/DM Millions)*

Year	Cost
1945	117
1946	1,007
1947	773
1948	544
1949	551
	2,991

* Rounded figures.

Table 6, compiled by the Institute for Occupation Questions in
Tübingen, gives occupation costs in the French zone during the first
four and a half years of the occupation. These payments were of two
kinds—those known simply as "occupation costs," which were the payments necessary for the direct needs of the occupation army, military
government, and dependents, and further payments, known as "mandatory expenditures," which were to further the aims of the occupation
by covering the cost of such things as disarmament or aid to displaced
persons. Table 7 gives a detailed analysis of occupation costs in the
French zone. This itemization raises several important questions, the
most important of which is the significance of the so-called "cash payments" (*Pauschzahlungen*). It can be seen from Table 7 that direct
cash payments constituted the major part of the occupation costs in
the French zone. These cash payments were unknown in the American zone and were only introduced in the British zone in 1950, even
then consisting of a very small sum in proportion to the total occupation costs of the British zone. In the French zone cash payments composed 63 per cent of the total occupation costs in 1946, 49 per cent in
1947, 41 per cent in 1948, and 52 per cent in 1949.[27]

This large sum had to be provided from the budget of each Land
in the French zone, and the Land governments had great difficulties

TABLE 7

USE OF OCCUPATION COSTS IN FRENCH ZONE OF OCCUPATION[28]
1945–1949

(RM/DM Thousands)

I. *"Occupation Costs"*

1. Labor service	370	
2. Provision and maintenance of property	404	
3. Stores, supplies, and services	310	
4. Transportation		
5. Communications	2	
6. Occupation damages (claims)	3	
7. Cash payments to occupying power	1,521	
Total	2,610	
Of which the French did not recognize		104

II. *"Mandatory Expenditures"*

1. Displaced persons	165	
2. German prisoners of war	36	
3. Civilian internees	18	
4. Subsidiary costs in connection with		
a) Reparations and restitution	34	
b) Demilitarization	60	
5. Other mandatory expenditures	67	
Total (rounded)	381	
Of which the French did not recognize		3
Total occupation costs	2,991	
Of which the French did not recognize		107

producing it. Before the currency reform of August 1948, the Land governments were forced to take up loans in order to find the money. After the currency reform, when cash was even more scarce, every source of credit had to be exhausted to make the payments; and, as a result, the Land governments pressed ever more insistently for reduction of the occupation payments. The Germans felt additionally aggrieved by these cash payments, in that they had no means of accounting for the use that was made of the money.

The French, again unlike the British and the Americans, paid for very large amounts of their purchases directly in German money. For example, German foodstuffs delivered for use of the troops and the military government were paid for in Reichsmarks, as were the services of the railroads and the post. More important still, direct compulsory deliveries of goods produced in German factories, which often amounted to 30 per cent or more of total production, were paid for in German money at fixed prices. German sources calculated that the payments for German goods bought from agricultural and industrial production far exceeded the amount available to the military government in the "cash payments" and in the payments for acquisition of German property. They therefore assumed that the additional currency was found in occupation marks—that is, in the currency printed for use of the occupying troops—or in Reichsmarks taken as booty or seized later. In the period before the currency reform, it was calculated that 750 million Reichsmarks were spent which were not covered by occupation costs. After currency reform, the Germans assumed that the additional currency was found in the military government's holdings of Deutschmarks from the first printing. In short, German sources maintain that not only were the occupation payments, especially the cash payments, burdensome on the French zone, but that the French military government made large expenditures on German goods with other revenue which also was taken from German sources. The extent of this additional expenditure is impossible to calculate.

Second, there is no doubt that the burden of the occupation was felt very heavily as a result of the requisitioning of property and the use of agricultural production. Not only did the Germans have to pay French expenses; they also lost the use of their own property and the consumption of their agricultural produce. It was calculated by the Land governments that in September 1948 the French were in possession of 1,228 hotels, inns, and sanatoriums in the zone, 2,788 garages, 3,862 villas and houses, 19,082 single houses, and 31,216 single rooms. But despite some complaints in the French zone that the property was not always fully used, the Germans did at least appreciate the fact that the French were willing to share their houses with them rather than put them out on the street, as did the Americans and the British.[29] The Germans felt, however, that they were starving while the French army and its dependents lived off the fat of the land. There is no doubt that certain classes of agricultural produce were reserved almost exclusively for occupation personnel, or for export. For example, in Württemberg-Hohenzollern, the occupation forces took 74.6 per cent of the meat supply in 1945, 57.5 per cent in 1946, 36 per cent in 1947, and 27 per cent in the first quarter of 1948. Germans complained that whereas they had a meat ration of 200 grams per month in 1948, the French army and dependents had a daily ration of 225 grams. There were other causes of the shortage of food in the French zone, as will be seen in the following chapter; but the high standard of living of the French occupation personnel was a cause of bitter conflict between the German governments and the French military government.

The occupation costs paid by the Germans had a double value for the French. In the first place, the burden of maintaining an occupation force in Germany was much lighter for France than it was for Great Britain or for the United States. In 1946 the occupation of Germany was costing France nine billion francs a year in direct payments for

TABLE 8

OCCUPATION COSTS IN THE BRITISH, AMERICAN, AND FRENCH ZONES,
IN COMPARISON WITH LAND INCOME FROM TAXATION[30]
1945–1949

Year	Land Income from Taxation (RM/DM Thousands)	Occupation Costs (RM/DM Thousands)	Occupation Costs as Percentage of Land Income from Taxation	Cost per Inhabitant (RM/DM)
	BRITISH ZONE			
1946	6,146	2,462	40	112
1947	7,269	2,785	38	123
1948	7,394	2,055	28	86
1949	8,251	1,855	22	77
	AMERICAN ZONE			
1946	4,689	1,604	34	95
1947	5,591	1,968	35	112
1948	5,194	1,995	39	112
1949	5,643	1,661	32	92
	FRENCH ZONE			
1946	1,163	1,007	86	200
1947	1,591	773	49	149
1948	1,324	544	41	103
1949	1,467	551	38	104

the maintenance of its army and military government, a fact which caused considerable dissatisfaction in the National Assembly, where many deputies felt that the zone should cost France nothing at all.[31] Yet this payment was directly in support of the French army, in contrast to the payments which Britain and the United States were forced to make in order to keep the German population of their zones alive. Second, the occupation payments were used to procure for the French occupation forces a standard of living which would have been unobtainable if the purchases had not been at the command of the occupation regime.

Carlo Schmid, former president of the State Secretariat of Württemberg-Hohenzollern, speaking in the Bonn parliament on January 18, 1951, on the question of occupation costs, looked back bitterly on the burden of the French occupation. He said that the occupation costs, although necessary at first, had rapidly become too burdensome; in Württemberg-Hohenzollern, he noted, they were the equivalent of half of the Land budget.[32] Table 8 illustrates how much more heavily the burden of occupation costs fell upon the French zone than upon the British or American zones.

OTHER ECONOMIC BENEFITS OF OCCUPATION

The French found many sources of income in the zone besides restitution, reparations, and occupation costs. There was undoubtedly some looting in the French zone, as in all three other zones. This pillaging had been at its worst during the invasion months, although here and there an exceptional local commander showed foresight and responsibility in protecting the property in his area. For example, the French commander in Tübingen posted guards on the research laboratories in Tübingen and Hechingen. The looting was followed by what came to be known as "individual recuperation." Georges Auclair remarks in his novel, *A German Love*, that there was a group of *débrouillards* for whom "the army and the military administration were never anything other than admirable organizations for tourism or commerce on a large or small scale."[33] A vast black market existed between France and Germany, in which many of the German people's private possessions, like typewriters and cameras, passed into France in exchange for the necessities of life. The liveliest place of exchange was Kehl, the German bridge-town across the Rhine from Strasbourg, which became the center of this black market. Finally, there was irregular requisitioning, carried out by unauthorized personnel, which was not recognized as part of the occupation costs by the military government. This took the form of forcing Germans to work and of requisitioning personal property and houses. The government of Württemberg estimated in 1948 that such requisitions amounted to a value of over 125 million marks, of which the French military government had recognized only 4 per cent.

But these irregular and wholly illegal actions were far from being the policy of the French military government; where the individual perpetrators were discovered they were punished. Such individual plundering seems to be the undesirable but inevitable accompaniment of any military invasion, and neither the Germans nor the Allies could claim to be free of it. On the other hand, the French military government was able, as a matter of policy, to gain many advantages from its control of the economy of the zone.

Control of the zone's commerce, through the Office of External Commerce (Oficomex), was used to benefit France in many ways. All goods sold to France were reduced in price 20 per cent, and France thus enjoyed a very large advantage in buying goods from the zone instead of on the world market. Oficomex bought German goods with German money at the prices prevailing inside Germany, and sold them to French companies at prices so advantageous that these companies occasionally resold them on the world market at considerable profit. In certain cases, monopolies were granted to French companies for the purchase of German goods.

These actions of the French military government were later debated in the parliament of the West German Republic in several bitterly heated sessions. On April 26, 1951, in the debate on the raising of occupation costs, Carlo Schmid made a harsh attack on the policies of the French in the early years of the occupation. Quoting extensively from a report of the director general of economy and finance of March 8, 1948, he pointed out that the French themselves had listed the advantages they had enjoyed. The 20 per cent reduction on goods sold to France had been worth 10 million dollars to them, he said. Combined with profits to France from other actions of Oficomex, this amounted in benefits to a grand total of $336,715,304.[34]

In 1953 the debate became even more impassioned when the Bonn parliament was asked to ratify an agreement signed between the French and German governments to clear up Germany's debt. Since the zone had been run at a deficit during the last few months, France had been forced to pay $15,789,936 to help cover that deficit. The two governments had agreed that Germany should pay back to France $11,-840,000 (in francs) to cover the total debt. Many members were outraged. Dr. Gülich (SPD) spoke passionately against the methods of Oficomex and ridiculed the idea that Germany should owe France money for the occupation period. "It is generally known," he said, "that the Oficomex bought German goods of all kinds at blocked prices . . . and sold them on the world market for dollars." No German accounting of the export trade of the zone was permitted, he continued; and after an examination of the books of the Oficomex, the American firm of Price, Waterhouse, and Company had declared that the defective nature of the accounts kept by Oficomex made it impossible to produce an accountant's report on the foreign trade of the zone. Therefore, Dr. Gülich concluded, it was impossible to say that Germany owed France money for economic help. The Bundestag temporarily rejected the payment by a vote of 148 to 135, with 18 abstentions.[35]

Finally, the French enjoyed the great advantage of being able to buy German goods directly from current production with payments in German marks. In 1947 the government of Württemberg estimated that the French took 25 per cent of total production. By 1948 the three Länder estimated that total purchases by the French amounted to 1,619 million marks. These purchases were not reparations taken from current production, although such a manner of taking reparations had been foreseen at the Yalta Conference; and no mention of reparations from current production was made in the official study of German reparations payments published in 1951 by the French Interministerial Economics committee.[36] Nevertheless, this method was a means of exacting indirect reparation. Goods which the Germans wanted for themselves were compulsorily delivered to the French. At least part of the cost of these purchases was paid for in occupation costs, and an unascertainable amount was bought with German currency seized or printed by France at no cost to itself. The bitterness with which the Germans regarded these transactions is a sign of their importance, although an accurate estimate of their value to the French cannot be reached.

To sum up, France received direct economic benefits from its zone in several ways: First, large quantities of goods, including vehicles, machine tools, farm machinery, livestock, personal belongings, and art treasures, were recovered as restitution. The amount that France recovered from Germany (i.e., from all four zones), has been valued at $257,500,000 (1938).

Second, the French wholly or partly removed one hundred six factories from the zone as reparation, and from these France itself received twenty-two.

Third, the economic fusion of the Saar with France on April 1, 1948, gave France a territory of vast productive capacity, particularly valuable for the production of those goods most needed by the French economy. The fusion with the Saar was valued by the IARA as the equivalent in reparations payments of $17,500,000 (1938). The value of the Saar to France was immeasurably greater than this figure, however, especially since the cost of reviving the industries of the Saar after their wartime destruction had been largely covered by the other Länder of the French zone, and since valuable factories had been transferred from the rest of the zone into the Saar before the fusion.

Fourth, the costs of the occupation forces and military government in Germany were paid for by the Germans. This payment was estimated, for the period 1945–49, at 2,950 million Reichsmarks/Deutschmarks, or approximately $737,500,000 (1938).

Fifth, the French gained economic benefits from their control of German external commerce through the Oficomex and by their ability to purchase directly from current production in German currency. These benefits were estimated by German sources at $336,715,304.

It is therefore clear that France gained direct economic benefits of considerable magnitude from its zone of occupation. Far more significant, however, was the French attempt to turn the economy of its zone to the aid of the French economy, since this policy was not only more far-reaching in its scope but more successful in its effect.

CHAPTER VII

The Economic Policy of the Zone
and the Interests of France

IN formulating an economic policy for the zone, the French authorities had two main aims: first, to balance the export-import budget of the zone so that no charge would fall to the French treasury; and second, to revive those industries whose production would be most useful to the French economy.[1]

THE ECONOMIC NEEDS OF FRANCE

The economic situation of France in 1945 was disastrous. The country had suffered enormously during the war. In a report presented to the reparations conference in November 1945, the French delegation noted that France's material losses from physical destruction and spoliation were 4,895 billion francs (1945). Of the total lives lost from the eighteen countries represented at the conference, France had lost 40 per cent.[2]

This blow to France's productive capacity followed thirty years of growing stagnation in its economic life. Many factors had been responsible—the losses of the First World War, the high military expenses between the wars, insufficient technical development, lack of population growth, rise in the average age of the population, growing obsolescence of the methods of production in industry and agriculture. As a result, in 1938 France possessed only 600,000 machine tools, against 2 million in England. Its resources were insufficiently exploited, and it had a large deficit in foreign trade.[3]

The zone was able to help the development of the French economy in two ways. In 1945 and 1946, the zone helped France overcome the immediate problems of reviving its production. After 1947 the zone supplemented the long-term modernization of the French economy, called for by the Monnet plan, by supplying France's needs in certain basic industrial goods during the interim period when France was developing its own means of production. Immediately after the war, France's major needs were for sources of power, especially coal and electricity, and for the basic means of production, such as steel, machinery, and machine tools. France also needed products which were difficult or expensive to obtain in France or on the world market, such as wood and chemicals. Finally, it needed some consumer goods to fill the gap left by the years of occupation. Among these the most necessary were textiles and leather goods.[4]

France's long-term needs were laid down in the Monnet plan, drawn up in 1946 and adopted in 1947. The plan was based on the principle that the French economy as a whole could develop only with the growth of six key industries—coal, metal, electricity, cement, agricultural machinery, and interior transport. In these industries alone were targets laid down. The economy of the French zone was able to aid that of France by supplying as reparation machinery for immediate productive needs; by providing power, through coal and electricity, to maintain French industry while France was developing its own sources; and by providing essential materials, like wood and cement, for reconstruction in France. The aims of the Monnet plan thus help to explain France's choice of factories as reparations, and the extent and nature of the exports from the zone.

In 1945 all groups in France were convinced that a major reason for possession of a zone of occupation was the opportunity it gave to exploit Germany. For example, public opinion polls conducted in France in November 1944 showed that 75 per cent of those questioned favored annexation of the Saar and its mines. The Communists were especially vehement in their determination to make Germany pay with "the coal of the Saar, the wood of the Black Forest, the agricultural products of Württemberg and the Pfalz." The Socialist party, while opposing any dismemberment of Germany, apart from the Saar, demanded reparation by exploitation of the zone, as Félix Gouin declared in a widely published speech at Strasbourg in March 1946.

The MRP pressed the same claims through the agency of Foreign Minister Georges Bidault. De Gaulle spoke for the parties of the Right, if not for all Frenchmen, when he told the Germans at Baden-Baden in October 1945 that the French occupation would be a "moral and economic union" of France with those territories of the zone which formed a geographical unity with it.[5]

It fell to the General Directorate of Economy and Finance, installed under the direction of Jean Filippi in the Hotel Europa in Baden-Baden, to satisfy these demands. Nor was the Directorate left uncertain about what was expected of it: the Constituent Assembly, in sending its committee of inquiry into the French zone in December 1945, noted that one of its main reasons for doing so was to investigate "the insufficiency of our economic exploitation of those territories, at a time when they could quite appreciably lighten the burden which weighs on the shoulders of every Frenchman."[6] The Directorate proved far from lax in carrying out its instructions.

RESTORATION OF THE ECONOMIC SYSTEM

Transportation system

The Allied bombing and the invasion fighting had inflicted great damage on the German transportation system. The complete breakdown of transportation in 1945 brought about chaos in economic life. Hence, the first efforts of the French military government were directed toward bringing the transportation system back into use. This task fell largely to the Directorate of Public Works and Transport.

The first objective was to revive river transport, especially on the Rhine, which was the one link between the two sections of the zone. Fifty broken bridges and many sunken ships blocked the Rhine along its whole length, and along the Mosel and the Lahn, bridges and locks were destroyed and the banks were partly mined. Largely through the efforts of the army engineers, the work of clearing the rivers was carried through. By October 1945, the Rhine was open as far as Ludwigshafen, and by November as far as the Bodensee. In 1946 the river fleet began to function again, and by 1947 the traffic was carrying over 2 million tons a year.[7]

In 1945 the railway network was in even worse condition. Bridges were down; all marshaling yards were destroyed; only 500 of the 5,667 kilometers of track were functioning.[8] By December 1945, however, the military government had been able to restore 2,700 kilometers to use. By January 1947, some 5,246 had been restored, and the roadbed was therefore almost back to its prewar state. Repairs to rolling stock were also undertaken at once, with the result that by October 1946 almost two-thirds of the equipment was back in use. The French achievement in bridge building was magnificent and included such large-scale constructions as the Maxau bridge, built across the Rhine to link the two triangles of the French zone.[9]

The major object of this reconstruction was to serve French interests. As the military government pointed out in summarizing its first eighteen months of achievement, "This work—and this is the essential point which must be emphasized—has always been directed toward the maximum development of the products which are intended for the French economy. This is the very special function of the railroad network adjacent to France which has led us to push ahead with the reconstruction of certain bridges, to develop the traffic on particular lines, and to put back into working order that incomparable economic tool constituted by the railroad network of the zone."[10]

Financial controls in the French zone

The French applied in their zone a financial policy very similar to that followed in the British and American zones. Very strict measures were enacted from the start to prevent an inflation similar to the one that followed 1918. Prices and salaries were frozen. Heavy taxes were levied, not only on salaries but on items like alcohol and tobacco. Strict rationing was applied to prevent a rise in prices. Moreover, by Law No. 52 of the Supreme Allied Commander, all possessions of the German state, of the National Socialist party, and of other organizations and persons named by the military government had been frozen—that is, they could not be used by their owners in economic transactions. In this way the military government controlled some of the largest capital accumulations in the zone.

The banking system was reorganized. The German banking system before 1945 had been controlled by the Reichsbank, although a highly flexible system of private banks also existed. The Reichsbank, which had been created in 1864, was regarded by the occupying powers as one of the great financial and industrial agglomerations that seemed to symbolize the Hitlerian system of state hegemony in the financial sphere. The Russians had liquidated the bank in their zone in 1945, and the Western powers followed suit in 1947 in the French and American zones and in 1948 in the British. In its place, four Land banks were created in the French zone, and central bank needs were met by the foundation of a bank in Kaiserslautern for the whole northern triangle, of one in Freiburg for the southern triangle, and of a central administrative bank in Speyer.[11]

The injection into the currency of Germany of 5 billion occupation marks in the three western zones and of over 6 billion in the Soviet zone had an amazingly small effect on prices. Strict controls over prices and wages, as well as the general shortage of goods for sale, ensured there would not be a great immediate inflation, in spite of the fact that in the French zone the occupation marks composed 21 per cent of the currency. The deeper effect of this increased amount of money in circulation, combined with the great inflation that had taken place during the war, was of course to make money lose its value as a means of exchange. It encouraged the black market, including such things as the use of cigarettes as currency, and ensured that a large share of production, estimated as high as 30 per cent, would be used as barter instead of being sold at the fixed prices. The result was to make vitally necessary the adoption of a harsh currency reform. The Americans and the Russians had both demanded an immediate reform in late 1946, but they had been dissuaded by the British and the French, who wished to allow a little time for German production to revive before carrying out so vital a change. In particular, the British and the French argued that there must be some balance between goods for sale and currency issued, and that that situation would only exist when German factories were producing some goods for the home market and when American credit had made possible the purchase of raw materials and food supplies.[12]

Thus, for the first three years of the occupation the financial system of the zone was maintained on a conservative decentralized basis, under strict control of the occupation authorities. But the situation merely disguised an inflation of the currency which could not be permanently accepted if Germany was to revive economically. Currency reform was bound to come.

Revival of agriculture

The agricultural produce of the French zone had not been sufficient to feed the area's inhabitants, even in prewar days. Hence, with wartime destruction of agricultural machinery, seed, and the means of transport, with the great reduction in manpower, and with the harsh winter of 1945–46, a difficult food situation faced the zonal authorities. Agricultural experts in the military government at once proceeded to carry out a survey of the resources of the zone, and to put into action a plan for the development of the available resources.[13]

The aim of the plan for the year 1945–46 was to develop the cultivation of those foodstuffs giving the greatest yield in calories, namely, sugar beets, potatoes, and market-garden produce; to permit a moderate expansion of cereals; to ensure a minimum of necessary foods, especially of fats; and to develop to the greatest degree possible the products suitable for export, such as tobacco, wine, fruit, and hops. The military government intended to make even agriculture bring in foreign currency. The plan for 1946–47 was similar, but it made more allowance for regional variation. The plan for 1947–48 aimed at arriving at the level of production of 1938.[14]

This program could not produce the food necessary even to give the German inhabitants the 1,500 calories a day aimed at by the Allies. The 1945 harvest of cereals gave only 50.8 per cent of the 1939 harvest and the grape crop only 57.7 per cent. For this reason the French authorities contracted with the United States government for the delivery of 550,000 tons of American wheat in the year beginning September 1, 1945. Of this amount, only 220,000 tons was actually received, because of the transportation difficulties. Of 20,000 tons of sugar contracted for at the same time, an even smaller proportion was received. Hence, as the London *Times* pointed out, it was not entirely fair to blame the French alone for the lack of foodstuffs in the first year of the occupation.[15]

The calorie allowance actually received in 1945–46 ranged between 1,000 and 1,300 daily. Exceptions were made for miners, heavy workers, and nursing mothers, and in the Saar a higher ration allowance was given to everyone, the allowance ranging from 1,300 to 1,500 calories a day. The situation was slightly alleviated by the fact that the agricultural population was easily able to feed itself and to barter some produce with foragers from the cities. Besides, most Germans grew something in their own gardens to supplement the ration. Nevertheless, there can be no doubt that the food supply was extremely poor. In November 1946 the bread ration was cut to seven ounces a day, and

TABLE 9

AGRICULTURAL PRODUCTION IN THE FRENCH ZONE[16]

Type of Foodstuffs	Production in Thousands of Tons		
	1938	1947	1948
Potatoes	3,792.7	1,599.9	2,099.3
Bread cereals	801.1	368.4	536.3
Oleaginous products	9.1	5.1	7.8
Sugar beets	460.5	142.8	382.3

the butter ration was two and a half ounces a week, of which only half was actually obtainable. There was no ersatz coffee, no jam, and no fish. The basic food was potatoes. The situation did not greatly improve during 1947, the calorie allowance remaining at around 1,400 per day.[17] By the end of 1948 the ration had climbed to only 1,869. In spite of continually increasing yields each year, agricultural production remained insufficient to meet the needs of the population and the occupation forces. Table 9 gives an impression of the wide gap still to be made up even in 1948 before the production figures of 1938 could be reached, and it illustrates why the major part of the imports into the French zone was foodstuffs. Between August 1945 and December 1947 imports of foodstuffs accounted for $124,722,000 out of total imports of $182,343,000. In 1948 the proportion of foodstuffs dropped to about 50 per cent of total imports, but this merely reflected the growing rate of other forms of importation made possible by Marshall aid.[18]

The reason for the low food supply of the French zone was the low productivity of the land, which was in turn the result of poor seed supply and the lack of fertilizer, machinery, and manpower. It has often been suggested that this low food supply was really the product of French exactions. It was alleged that the French army, the military government, and their innumerable relatives lived off the zone, thereby reducing German rations. This remained one of the most vexed questions of the whole occupation, and the constant publicity given to it both in France and elsewhere did much to create a highly unfavorable picture of the zone, which survives to this day.

French political parties were unanimous in 1945–46 that the French occupation forces lived too well in Germany.[19] Journalists wrote satirically of the standard of living of the military government personnel in Baden-Baden. Germans saw this army as a swarm of locusts and poured stories of its extravagance into willing ears. Experts on Germany added their support to these charges. Gustav Stolper, the economist, claimed that the French in their zone "exploit even its poverty," while Karl Brandt, an expert on food supply, noted that "the food shortage in 1947 was worst in the French zone, where a large occupation force lived off the land."[20]

Several points must be made in reply to these criticisms. First, it was by decision of the Control Council, as well as by normal occupation practices sanctioned in the Hague Convention, that the occupation forces supplied themselves from the zone.[21] Second, the requisitioning of food did not include wheat, sugar, and coffee. In fact, on one occasion barges carrying sugar from France to Germany were blockaded on the canals near Nancy by mobs of working men, who refused to allow sugar to be sent to the zone when France itself was in such urgent need of it.[22] The requisitioning did, however, include almost all the wine and tobacco of the zone, as well as large quantities of meat, butter, and eggs. Third, large quantities of foodstuffs were sent out of the zone as exports to help pay for the zone's imports of raw materials and other foodstuffs. Fourth, the numbers of the occupying army and military government fell rapidly after the first year of occupation. From forces of over a million in May 1945, the occupation army had been reduced to 351,000 in December 1945. By May 1947 the numbers had fallen to 75,000; and in May 1948 the total in both Germany and Austria was only 60,000. Military government personnel in December 1946 numbered only 11,000. These figures were not high in comparison with a German population of six million. The greatest German criticism was roused by the occupation forces' demands for supplies of meat, and even these demands fell rapidly. For example, the occupation forces took 74.6 per cent of the meat supplies of Württemberg in 1945, 57.5 per cent in 1946, and 36 per cent in 1947. Fifth, the findings of the parliamentary commission of inquiry discounted many of the criticisms. The committee noted, for example, that Germans were eating whiter bread than the troops, and that the Germans, unlike the French, had flour for making cakes.[23]

The requirements of the occupation forces did not reduce the food supply available for the German population as greatly as the more exaggerated rumors claimed. A more judicious point of view was that expressed by a visiting correspondent of the London *Times,* who reported in 1946, "Officially the French in Germany consume only 500 calories a day of German produce, and only meat and fats at that. . . . French units are inclined to help themselves. . . . But even if 200,000 French people in the zone ate 3,000 calories a day of local produce, which they certainly do not, they would deprive the local population only of 100 calories a day."[24]

In short, in the first months of occupation, the French set about raising production levels by restoring the transportation and financial systems of the zone and by providing a minimum of foodstuffs for the population. At the same time, the German population was set to work at those industries which would be useful to the French economy.

PRODUCTION IN THE INTERESTS OF FRANCE

Coal

France needed coal more than any other import. Between 1929 and 1939, it had imported between 30 and 45 per cent of its total requirements. Although the French mines had already exceeded their prewar production by July 1945, France was still heavily dependent upon imports. France's normal supplies had come largely from Germany and Britain, but with the universal need for reconstruction all Europe suffered from an immense shortage of coal, the major source of power. The one method that seemed to offer some relief was to reduce Germany's industrial production while developing her coal exports, since lowering the level of production in Germany would leave a greater proportion of coal free for export.[25]

The coal production of the western zones was under central Allied control. The Economics Directorate in Berlin divided among the zones the coal available for their needs. The remaining coal then was divided by the European Coal Organization (ECO) at London among its member countries. ECO also allocated coal made available to it by the United States and other exporting countries. Payment was made in the currency of the exporting country, except that German coal had to be paid for in dollars at 80 per cent of the current dollar rate.[26]

Two aspects of this arrangement greatly annoyed the French. Any increase in coal production from the French zone would go into the pool and could not be taken directly for France or for the zone itself.

Any German coal taken by France had to be paid for in dollars, even though at a 20 per cent discount. It was especially annoying to the French to be largely dependent upon supplies from the Ruhr, which was in the British zone, and this dependence explained much of the French desire for internationalization of the Ruhr and for the fusion of the Saar with France.[27]

Nevertheless, French authorities continued to give top priority to reconstruction of the Saar's coal industry. The special treatment given to the region included sending home prisoners of war from the Saar, transferring to the mines labor from other industries and from other parts of the zone, giving the whole area a higher ration than the rest of the zone, and providing consumer goods. Miners themselves received up to 3,600 calories a day. Production rose from 80,000 tons a month in June 1945 to 606,000 tons a month in March 1946. By November 1946 the figure had reached 813,000 tons, and by March 1947 it reached 891,000 tons. At that time, the Saar was back to 74.7 per cent of its prewar production, whereas the British zone lagged behind at 53.2 per cent.[28]

The French authorities developed the output of the Saar mines for several reasons. First, there was the obvious need to increase Germany's total coal production, even though France would benefit only to a moderate degree from increase in the Saar alone. Second, coal was a very valuable export of the French zone in the first three years of the occupation. Between May 1945 and September 1946, for example, coal exports accounted for 17.1 per cent of all exports from the zone. In 1947 Saar coal accounted for $18,000,000 value in the exports of the zone.[29]

Thus the economic fusion of the Saar with France, which took place on April 1, 1948, was a blow to the future capacity of the French zone to produce for export, but it did not greatly affect the zone's coal supplies, which continued to be assigned by the Allied Economics Directorate in Berlin. The zone's need for coal was a pressing problem throughout the period of occupation. Since the increase in production in the Saar was not supplied directly to the zone, supplies had to be sought from Berlin. The French zone was given an allowance inferior to its needs and proportionately less than was its right. In 1938 the same area used 1,200,000 tons of coal a month. It was permitted only 291,000 tons in October 1945 and 362,000 tons in November 1945. The railways and occupation forces took 100,000 tons, leaving only 191,000 for private industry. Since only 82,000 tons in fact reached the zone's industries, the productive capacity of the zone was severely reduced during this period.[30] Increasing production in the Saar and Ruhr did, however, remedy the situation somewhat as greater allotments became possible.

Electricity

A great effort was made to develop the electrical production of the zone for the benefit of France. This was one major source of power that was controlled by France alone, and it was exploited to the full. Two principal power lines (Freiburg-Kembs-Schwanstadt and Koblenz-Merzig-Landres) were erected by the military government to carry the zone's electricity to France. By February 1946 the zone was already exporting 100,000,000 kilowatt hours a month to France, the equivalent of 100,000 tons of coal.[31] The zone continued to export 175,000,000 kilowatt hours a month during the first half year of 1947, although its total production was only 170,500,000 kilowatt hours. Since the zone itself had an average consumption of 188,000,000 kilowatt hours a month, it was forced to import large quantities of electricity to cover its own needs.[32]

Chemicals

In 1936 the production of chemicals in the area of the French zone accounted for almost 10 per cent of the zone's exports. Chemicals were second only to textiles in value of industrial production in the zone. The chemical industry was centered in the great factories of I.G. Farben at Ludwigshafen and Rheinfelden, in the Chemische Fabrik at Kreuznach, and in the Degussa works at Rheinfelden. Well before the formulation of the first Level of Industry plan, the French had set these factories to work again, even though these great industrial combines were part of the assets frozen under Law No. 52, previously described. At Ludwigshafen, the factory was set to turning out buna (synthetic rubber), fertilizers, and plastics. By July 1946 the I.G. Farben factories were producing 43 per cent of their output in 1938.[33]

Chemicals rapidly became one of the principal exports of the zone. Between May 1945 and December 1946 they accounted for 13.9 per cent of total value of exports. In 1947 and 1948 they accounted for approximately 10 per cent of exports. The extent to which production of chemicals had been favored can be seen in the report of the Marshall Plan administrator in 1948. In June 1948 chemical production in the French zone had reached 91 per cent of its prewar total, but steel production was only at 65 per cent and mining at 48 per cent (excluding the Saar).[34]

Metallurgy

Metallurgy, iron foundries, and steel production in 1936 had accounted for RM331,000,000 and machinery production for RM210,000,000 out of a total value of production of RM2,557,000,000. The iron and steel industry, and the machinery industries dependent upon them, were a very important part of the zone's total production. Most important, the Saar alone accounted for over half of the zone's production of iron and steel, and the loss of the Saar meant not only an almost total loss of coal production but a large reduction in iron and steel production in the zone.[35]

Again, considerable effort was applied to revive the metallurgy of the zone, although this was greatly hampered by the small allotment of coal. Between May 1945 and December 1946 production of metal goods and machinery accounted for 12.9 per cent of the zone's exports. After the fusion of the Saar with France an attempt was made to boost the production of metal goods in the Rheinland, and, as a result, production of iron and steel there almost doubled. Even with this spur, however, metal goods fell in importance as exports, accounting for only 10 per cent of exports in the first three quarters of 1948. In June 1948 foundries were running at 32 per cent of 1936 output, and iron and steel production was only 21 per cent. Nor did the precision instrument industries fare any better; they suffered heavily from dismantling, with the result that by June 1948 they were producing at only 30 per cent of their 1936 output.[36]

The metal industry of the zone lagged behind other branches of enterprise during the occupation. The shortage of coal combined with fear of the metal industry's contribution to Germany's war potential prevented the French from developing an industry which well might have proved a danger to French security.

Leather

The leather industry was of great importance in the French zone. In 1936 it had accounted for 5 per cent of the area's total production, and for 45 per cent of Germany's production of leather goods and shoes. The shoe centers of Pirmasens and Tuttlingen and the leather industry of Worms and Reutlingen were known all over Europe. The French at home, lacking consumer goods since the German occupation, felt especially determined to profit from this industry, and complaints were frequent that not enough shoes were being sent back to France.[37]

Large quantities of shoes were thus dispatched to France: 260,000 pairs by December 1945 and another 300,000 by April 1946, with over a million to follow that year. Leather goods accounted for 4.8 per cent of exports in 1945–46. After this point, production did not increase greatly, and in June 1948 the leather industry was back to only 32 per cent of its 1936 production.[38]

Wood and paper

The wood and paper industries had not played a large part in the economy of the zone in 1936, but after the war, wood was especially scarce on world markets in view of the universal need for it in reconstruction. Hence, the French zone, possessing 12 per cent of Germany's forests and with wood of very high quality, was well situated to profit from this need. In August 1945 the military government established a forestry plan which was at once put into effect.[39]

The program was well under way by 1946. In September it was estimated that wood and paper had so far accounted for 21.3 per cent of the zone's exports, and a year later they accounted for almost 25 per cent of exports. In September 1948, after the loss of the Saar, wood exports rose to 37 per cent of total exports, and paper accounted for another 3 per cent.[40]

The French have been accused of denuding the forests of the zone as a way of rapidly exploiting their area of Germany. Germans in the Black Forest and the Rheinland saw lines of stumps beside the roads, where the wood could most easily be cut, and were convinced that the forests would take generations to recover from this brutal felling. Moreover, the Germans complained, the excessive felling of timber had many other aftereffects. The climate was affected, endangering the agriculture of neighboring areas. The topsoil, no longer held down by the timber, was being eroded, especially as much of the felling consisted in clearing whole areas of woodland instead of selective cutting of individual trees. Since whole stands of timber were being sold to foreign companies, it was alleged that French and Swiss firms often bought the wood and resold it on the world market at a profit. Finally, the crowning blow was that the expenses of the French work-teams cutting the wood were charged to occupation costs.[41]

In return, the French replied that Germany had enjoyed several years during the war when its own timber had been virtually untouched, since the Germans were exploiting the timber stands of the occupied countries, including France. They pointed out that any criticism of this policy had also to face the reality of Europe's need for wood for reconstruction, to repair the damages caused by a war for which Germany was largely responsible, and of the zone's need to use all its resources to find some goods which could be used as exchange for the imports so badly needed. The French zone was not the only section of Europe that was using its capital to pay for the needs of this emergency period. Finally, the military government denied that its cutting was so damaging to the German forests as the Germans alleged. The military government estimated that the annual growth of the zone's forests was 60,000,000 cubic meters, and stated that since the cut for the year between October 1946 and September 1947 was only 10,300,000 cubic meters, it was obvious that the forests were not being permanently harmed. This problem was to be one of the main points of discord between the occupation regime and the elected German authorities, and was again and again to embitter relations in the last two years of occupation.[42]

By June 1948 the French zone had not made a rapid economic recovery. Production had only reached 51 per cent of the 1936 level.[43] However, the restoration of economic life had been made possible, especially through the revival of the transportation system of the zone. Industries whose production was valuable to France had been set to work again, and France had profited especially from receiving coal, electricity, leather goods, chemicals, and wood, all purchased at a 20 per cent discount. But, most remarkable of all, whereas Britain and the United States were pouring increasingly large sums into their zones, the French zone had been run, at least until December 1947, at an over-all profit. The way in which this was achieved becomes clearer from a study of the export and import trade of the zone.

BALANCING THE TRADE BUDGET

The secret of French success in avoiding the heavy charges that fell on both the British and American governments in administering their zones of Germany was summarized very simply by the London *Times*: "Each occupying power in Germany picks from the Potsdam Agreement the phrases that suit it best. The French like best the phrase about the German people 'subsisting without external assistance.' The French make their profit by exporting more than they import."[44]

TABLE 10

TRADE BALANCE OF THE FRENCH ZONE[45]
(Thousands)

Year(s)	Value of Imports	Value of Exports	Over-all Balance
1945–46	69,100	84,353	15,253
1947	113,243	106,077	8,087
1948	181,288	106,912	− 66,289
1949 (January–July only)....	105,570	57,328	−114,531

In 1945 the export industries were encouraged, and imports, especially of food, were kept to a minimum. As a result, the French zone showed a surplus of some $15,000,000 by December 1946 (see Table 10). The situation changed slightly in 1947, when increased imports of foodstuffs gave the zone an adverse balance of $7,000,000 for the year and decreased the surplus for the whole period of the occupation to $8,000,000. In 1948 no effort was made to balance exports and imports, and the zone incurred an adverse trade balance of $75,000,-000, a sum which was almost completely covered by Marshall Plan funds. Thus the zone maintained a favorable balance of trade until it became clear that American rather than French aid would cover any deficit.

France profited greatly from the supplies it received from the zone. In 1945–46, France took 78 per cent of the zone's exports. In the first three quarters of 1947, the proportion had risen to 85 per cent, although in 1948 it fell to 70 per cent as a result of the fusion of the Saar with France.[46]

The French had performed the feat of running the zone at a profit to themselves without appreciably lowering standards of living in the zone below those of the Bizone. After the first eighteen months, however, it became clear that this could only be a temporary state of affairs. If it was true that the French had exploited "even the poverty" of the zone, there was a limit to the extent to which poverty could be exploited. The Germans had lived well until the last months of the war and were able to work well on a low-calorie diet for months before the effect of undernourishment was clear in output per man hour. Stocks of raw materials had been built up in the factories during the war, and the French were able to utilize these during the first months of occupation. Later, however, imports of raw materials had to be arranged to keep the factories working. No capital investment was made in the zone's industry until Marshall Plan funds were made available for this purpose.

It became clear in the first three months of 1947 that the French could no longer count on running the zone at a profit. The successful fusion with the Saar in 1948 made growing losses in the rest of the zone almost certain. In December 1946 the London *Times* could write that the French had no intention of joining a trizonal union, since "to do so would mean merging a profitable concern in a bankrupt one and sharing its heavy deficit." In June 1948 Foreign Minister Bidault warned the National Assembly that if it did not approve trizonal fusion, it would have to find the money to cover the expenses of a zone that was no longer a paying proposition.[47]

A NEW ECONOMIC POLICY, 1948–1949

The year 1948 saw great changes in the French zone. It was marked in the first place by the economic fusion of the Saar with France, which was completed on April 1, 1948. The Saar's population had given an overwhelming majority in the elections of October 5, 1947, to the parties favoring economic fusion with France; and the constitution of December 15, 1947, had proclaimed this economic fusion. The French National Assembly had shown its willingness to accept the fusion by voting the necessary credits for the introduction

TABLE 11

Trade Balance of the Länder of the French Zone[48]
1946
(RM Thousands)

Land	Exports	Imports	Over-all Balance
Saar	27,572	45,945	−18,373
Rheinland	49,951	35,756	14,195
Pfalz	165,028	145,776	19,252
Baden	92,959	89,599	3,360
Württemberg	102,603	84,617	17,986

of the franc into the Saar in November 1947. The surprising fact, which Bidault ignored when he told the National Assembly on June 11, 1948, that the "zone, since we obtained the Saar, has not been economically viable," was that the Saar had been a burden on the rest of the zone up to this point. Of all the Länder of the French zone, the Saar alone had imported more than it had exported; and German officials in the other three Länder, as well as military government officials, were well aware of this fact.[49] Table 11 illustrates the situation in 1946 and shows that the other Länder were covering the deficit incurred by the Saar. The adverse trade balance of the Saar was, of course, partly due to the fact that the French military government deliberately maintained a higher average food supply in the Saar than in the other Länder as well as giving very high ration allowance to the miners, and large imports of foodstuffs were needed to supply the population at this level. The Saar had suffered more heavily than the rest of the zone in destruction of its industrial equipment, and repairing the mines and factories was a very costly operation in the months before the industry of the Saar became fully productive. Finally, the great iron industry of the Saar demanded the import of raw materials before it could be revived. It is therefore not correct to argue that the addition of the Saar to the French zone was of immediate economic value to the zone itself. The Pfalz, with its great complex of chemical factories at Ludwigshafen, was of much greater immediate value. The Saar was nevertheless of great importance to France. Potentially, at least, it represented a source of coal supply which would not be dependent upon the acquiescence of other coal-hungry powers. After the first expensive reconstruction had been carried out, partly at the expense of the other Länder, the productive capacity of the Saar basin could again be used and its vast potential surplus realized.

The economic fusion of the Saar with France thus marks a turning point in the history of the zone, not because the Saar had been the economic power which had turned the zone into a paying proposition, but because actual occcupation of the Saar was the best guarantee of international acquiescence in the future economic fusion with France. Without the Saar, from the sole point of view of the trade balance of the zone, the other Länder were economically healthier.

On the other hand, the policy that had enabled the French zone to run for three years without incurring a deficit was no longer applicable in 1948. Exports from the zone in 1948 barely topped those of 1947, and imports increased enormously. Fortunately for France, however, the economic weakness of the zone was to be the liability of the United States and not of France. The London conference on Germany, in February 1948, had determined that the western zones of Germany should participate in the European Recovery Program; Jean Filippi arrived on March 18 to represent the French zone and in this capacity took part in the creation of the Organization for European Economic Cooperation (OEEC). The French zone authorities thereupon submitted to OEEC a plan for the fiscal year 1948–49, asking for $100,000,000 aid to cover the expected adverse trade balance. Total production in the year 1948–49 was expected to rise 10 per cent above that of the previous year.[50]

Marshall aid came at a most critical time for the zone. By the end of 1947 stocks of raw materials were depleted, equipment was wearing out, and the poor food supply was reducing the working power of the population. In short, the dangers of running a zone on a self-supporting basis were beginning to be seen. Without Marshall aid, the Economic Cooperation Administration noted in 1948, the economy of the French zone "would collapse."[51] Fortunately this aid was forthcoming, and in the first year of the program (July 1, 1948, to June 30, 1949) the French zone received $100,000,000 in aid; the same sum was granted for the following year.

Other factors combined with the aid given by the Marshall Plan to help the economic revival of the zone from 1948 onward. Closer economic ties with the Bizone made possible a more rational economic structure for western Germany. In April 1948 the banks of the Länder were fused. In August free passage of goods and persons between the zones was authorized. In October the external commerce offices of the zones were united. Most important of all, on June 19, 1948, a currency reform was proclaimed in the three western zones. This, according to most observers, was the major event of the whole occupation.

The French had been considerably less enthusiastic than the bizonal authorities in introducing the currency reform. During the months of planning, the French had suggested the so-called Mitzakis plan, named for the French banker who was running the Exchange office in the General Directorate of Economy and Finance. This plan would have introduced a deflation of 75 per cent. The American plan, which was finally adopted, envisaged a deflation of 90 per cent and finally reached 93.6 per cent. The result was a much more stringent reform than the French had wished, with greater immediate economic stimulus but with harsher social consequences.[52]

The reform was vitally necessary. German currency was vastly inflated. It had risen from a total circulation of RM10,400 million in 1938 to RM73,000 million in May 1945. To this had been added the issues of occupation currency, amounting in the west to RM5,000 million and in the east to some RM6,000 million. The Reichsmark had thus lost public confidence, even though the freezing of prices had prevented any great rise in living costs. Nevertheless, the untrustworthy currency had induced people to hoard large stocks of goods. As a result people had no inducement to work harder because the salary increases were of no use either for savings or for purchases.

A necessary preliminary to the currency reform was the creation of a central bank through which the reform could be carried out. The Bizone had created such a bank on March 1, 1948, under the name of the Bank of the German Länder, and the Land banks of the French zone were authorized to join it on March 25, 1948. This central bank took the place of the Reichsbank as an institution for the issue of currency, and through it the currency reform was carried out. The method adopted was the following: Everyone was permitted to change sixty Reichsmarks for sixty of the new Deutschmarks, and to convert the rest of his savings at a rate of ten Reichsmarks for one Deutschmark. However, of this sum, 35 per cent was annulled completely, reducing the level of exchange for holders of bank accounts from 10 per cent to 6.5 per cent. In this way the reform hurt the holders of cash or of bank accounts. It was a great blow to the middle class, and it was struck against the advice of French financial experts. This provision was one of the most criticized by Germans, since it benefited the owners of capital goods or property at the expense of the holders of savings. Salaries and prices were left unchanged, one Reichsmark being converted directly to one Deutschmark.[53]

The result of these measures was astounding. The day following the reform, shops filled with goods which had been hoarded, since the shopkeepers needed more money to pay salaries and to replace stock and since the currency had won confidence by its very scarcity. The black market was wiped out overnight. Production and employment figures rose at once. "From that moment, the decisive revival of the German economy began."[54]

After July 1948, with both the currency reform and Marshall aid helping the economic revival of the zone, the economic situation changed rapidly. In June 1948 production rested at only 51 per cent of the output for 1936. By December it had risen to 66 per cent, and certain individual industries had made even more rapid progress. Mining, iron and steel production, manufacturing of precision instruments, glass, ceramics, rubber and textiles, had all risen 50 per cent or more. The food supply was level with that of the Bizone at 1,900 calories a day. The plan submitted for the year 1949–50 foresaw further rapid improvement. Food supply was to rise to 2,200 calories a day, production was to reach 75 per cent of the 1936 level, with growth particularly in production of iron and steel, leather goods, textiles, and electricity. The zone was able to join in trizonal fusion in September 1949 with an expanding economy, geared to the receipt of Marshall aid, but with excellent prospects of substantial economic progress.[55]

To sum up, the economic policy of the French military government in its zone of occupation fell into two parts, divided quite clearly by the events of April–July, 1948, when the Saar was withdrawn from the zone, currency reform was introduced, and Marshall aid began. From 1945 to mid-1948, the aim of the French authorities was to develop the economic capacity of the zone in the interests of France.

This involved (*a*) the revival of the transportation system, with the especial aim of making possible increased exports to France; (*b*) the maintenance of a conservative financial system; (*c*) the development of a minimum food supply for the German population and of a maximum of agricultural export; (*d*) the expansion of sources of power, especially coal and electricity, which could be exported to France; (*e*) development of industries, such as chemicals, leather, textiles, and forestry, which produce products for export and from which France would profit by purchase at 20 per cent discount; and (*f*) the maintenance of a favorable trade balance for the zone, to prevent any charges falling upon France itself. This system was no longer tenable by 1948.

From 1948 on, the economic policy of the zone was directed toward developing those industries whose rate of recovery had lagged behind the rest of the zone, toward seeking financial aid from the United States for reconstruction in the zone, and toward accepting further cooperation with the other zones, with the eventual aim of ridding France of a zone which might well become an economic burden. Before 1948 the claims of French security and the economic interests of France in possession of a zone were harmonious. After 1948, if France wished to maintain its control of the zone for security reasons, it would have to face growing economic burdens. Here was a major reason why the French government was willing to accept the recommendations of the London conference in June 1948 and to envisage the creation of a self-governing republic of West Germany.

CHAPTER VIII

Denazification and Re-education

THE French occupation was not intended as a short-term venture. The French took seriously their opportunity to remold that section of the German people over which they exercised control. They had three major aims. First, denazification was to weed out the evil influences that might hinder the process of re-education. Second, by remodeling the educational system of the zone and by introducing the Germans to the culture of France and, to a lesser degree, to that of Europe, the outlook of the German people was to be slowly changed. Finally, when the process of re-education had begun to take effect, the German people were to be introduced to the workings of democracy. It was hardly surprising, in view of this ambitious program, that General de Gaulle wanted French troops stationed "permanently" on the Rhine.

DENAZIFICATION

The French did not see eye to eye with their allies on denazification. President Roosevelt had made it clear in 1943 that he did not regard the German people as responsible in the same degree as their "guilty barbaric leaders," although as the war progressed he became increasingly inclined to adopt harsh measures against the whole German people. Even in late 1944, however, he could still make a distinction between the "Nazi conspirators" and the "German race, as such."[1] Roosevelt's acceptance of the contrast between the guilty and the misled prepared the way for Secretary of State Byrnes's Stuttgart speech in 1946, which promised eventual self-government to the German people, since "it was never the intention of the American government to deny to the German people the right to manage their own affairs, as soon as they were able to do so in a democratic way."[2] Denazification, to the Americans, was the necessary preliminary operation required to remove the cancer from German society.

The British government maintained a similar attitude. Although the British people regarded the Germans as militarists, they felt that the major share of the blame for the war should be borne by the Nazi leaders. In 1943 Churchill told the House of Commons that "Nazi tyranny and Prussian militarism are the two main elements in German life which must be absolutely destroyed."[3] After the capitulation, British observers were ready to pity the German people for their sufferings, rather than to asume that German misery was the reward for German misdeeds.[4] The British military government also regarded denazification as the key to restoration of a healthy political life in Germany. Field-Marshal Montgomery, commander-in-chief of the British zone, went so far as to explain to the Germans that "our object is to destroy the evil of the Nazi system; it is too soon to be sure that this has been done."[5]

A large number of Frenchmen were not willing to make this distinction between the Nazi leaders and the people they had misled. Too much bitterness had entered into French thinking as the aftermath of three major wars and a harshly enforced occupation. Many Frenchmen were convinced that all Germans were imbued to a greater or lesser degree with the doctrines and moral characteristics of Nazism. French political theorists delighted in demonstrating the peculiar psychology of the "German race"; and the military government officers were told in their bulletin in March 1945 that "every manifestation of strength is agreeable to him [the German] in his deepest character."[6] César Santelli, an official in the Paris office concerned with educational reform in the French zone, wrote in 1946 that it was impossible to count on the emergence of a democratic Germany. "It betrayed its mission in the past; it will betray it yet again in the future. So, consider that the generation which was intoxicated by Nazism, that is to say, in general, the generation of those aged over twelve, is almost completely lost."[7]

Nor was Santelli alone in this opinion. French observers traveling through Germany found nothing to quarrel with in this diagnosis.

Jean Guignebert felt that the Germans showed no contrition whatever for their crimes and had decided that the atrocities could not have taken place. He concluded that "as long as the Germans do not choose to hate war more than their defeat, to love liberty more than authority, all fears will be justified, all possible vigilance and distrust will remain the permanent duty of the occupying powers."[8] The deputy, Édouard Bonnefous, in a book based on notes taken while he was a member of the parliamentary committee of inquiry in the French zone, was pleased to see that "France fortunately shows more distrust than its allies toward the vanquished, even toward the repentant among them, believing that considerations of prudence should be given more weight than the desire for a democratic re-education of Germany."[9]

The military government as a whole was not clear in its approach to the problem of Nazism. There were present in the zone many who had been sympathetic to the Vichy regime and who had been in agreement with at least some of the aspects of Germany's control of Europe. But in spite of the loud outcry against the presence of these people in the zone, it is doubtful whether they exercised any great influence upon the formulation of policy. There were also present in the zone, however, others who, by background and inclination, found much that was attractive in the aristocratic and industrial elements in German society. Georges Auclair remarks that these officers "talked about genealogical trees, alliances between Baden and France, had themselves received by archduchesses, princes and counts, and considered themselves men of the world. The old German nobility accepted cigarettes and did not think themselves demeaned in spite of the defeat, since one could still see officers' uniforms in their salon and cars with chauffeurs at their door."[10] It was not to be expected that denazification would be pushed so far as to disturb such pleasant relationships. The parliamentary committee of inquiry noted that representatives of private companies in France were using their position in Germany to make advantageous contacts with German business for the sake of their companies at home, and it is possible that this factor slowed down slightly the process of denazification in the economic sector.[11]

A major and rather unexpected factor influenced the French attitude to denazification. The desire for revenge was felt far less strongly among the younger officers of the Resistance than it was among those who were compromised by their relations with the Vichy regime. These younger officers, as many observers have attested, saw that the solution to the problem of Franco-German hostilities was not to embitter relations still further by political persecution, but to seek an understanding between the two peoples which would be a firmer guarantee of peace. As one military governor remarked, these men were able to show this magnanimity of character just because "they were not afraid of the Germans."[12] These men, too, showed to the greatest degree that awareness of the individuality of all men, which is one of the profoundest contributions of the French mind. Pastor Marc Boegner of the Protestant Federation of France noted, after a tour of the zone in 1945, that he was "particularly struck by the great effort of comprehension and humanity which the military government had shown in the difficult area of denazification."[13]

Several important features of the French zone's particular form of denazification emerged under these differing influences. In the first place, denazification was never pushed as far in the French zone as it was in the other zones, since the majority of the French did not believe in the sharp categories of guilt as drawn, for example, in the American zone. Many believed that the way to democracy in Germany was "not only by 'denazification' but by 'degermanisation,'" as the Radical-Socialist Roger Gaborit pointed out in a National Assembly debate in 1948.[14] Denazification would never be carried out in the French zone along the strict lines of classification foreseen in the questionnaire, the famous *Fragebogen*. The French sense of individuality, combined with the greater understanding shown by many of the officials of the military government, ensured that the French would be more willing to treat each case on its individual merits, rather than be bound by the tighter classifications of the American zone. Their apparent laxity in this matter did not, of course, sweeten the relationship between the zones, and it led to the accusation that Nazis were receiving better treatment in the French zone than in the other zones. Carlo Schmid, president of the Württemberg State Secretariat, denied the "legend" that denazification was not as strict in the French zone as in other zones. Speaking in the Consultative Assembly of Württemberg, on November 22, 1946, he ridiculed the idea that a flood of former Nazis had entered the French zone. The system in the French zone, he said, was not as rigid as the American *Spruchkammer* system—and it was faster.[15]

Perhaps most vital of all in determining the relative success of denazification was the attitude of the Germans themselves. Michael Balfour has pointed out that only two groups stood out clearly in Germany. One was the small group of fanatical Nazis, perhaps 10 per cent of the population, and the other was a similar number of active anti-Nazis, again perhaps 10 per cent of the population. There was, as well, a certain number of Nazi party followers who believed the Nazi doctrine with reservations. The remainder of the people, perhaps 50 per cent or more, was largely unpolitical or passively anti-Nazi. The two extreme groups were clearly defined, and as the Allied armies moved into Germany, interrogation of prisoners and of all the German population behind the front line proved that these groups were fairly consistent in size.[16] The great mass of the population was, above all else, stunned by the extent of the defeat. An air of apathy hung over the population, which expressed itself in a distrust of all things political. The slogan, heard repeatedly, was *Man hat uns belogen und betrogen* ("We have been lied to and deceived").[17] Many had seen that the Nazi slogan, "Common good before individual good," had come to mean the individual good of the party before the common good of the people. The Nazi party was not, "as it had promised, a means for serving and helping the German people. It had become, at its highest level, an end in itself."[18] But as the opening of the concentration camps began to prove what many had feared to know, the apathy was increasingly disturbed by self-examination. There were two major questions the Germans found themselves asking, related but far different in their implications. There was first the question of how active a part the individual had played in the work of Nazism. This question was also asked by the military government and by those Germans enlisted in the work of denazification. The second was the deeper one of how much every German, whatever his attitude had been, was responsible for the rise of the Nazi tyranny. The success of denazification, as many realized, was dependent upon the answers being found to both of these questions. But it was only the first question that the military governments found themselves in a position to tackle.

Even before the capitulation, thoughtful Germans had occupied themselves with the question of German guilt. As William Hocking pointed out, "during the early years of the Occupation, the German

mind everywhere, no matter how much or how little it had been involved in the policies of Hitler, was seriously engaged with its own
moral problem and that of the nation"; and the level of this thinking
was high. "Of its own motion—independent of our efforts—it was
recovering its rapport with the spirit of Western life."[19]

Many of the speeches of the early months of the occupation given
by German political leaders read like moral exhortations. Speaking in
Tübingen in January 1946, Carlo Schmid called on the German people
to open their souls to truth. How can we be healthy again, he asked,
if we go on lying to ourselves? He was not going to be afraid of
dirtying the nest, as some people had accused him of doing, since the
nest "is dirty and must be cleaned." The truth was, he continued, that
the Second World War, "from the very beginning, was planned and
desired by Adolf Hitler and his clique, the men to whom the German
people in its confused, indolent blindness gave its trust." Many Germans, he thought, still had the feeling that "Germany has again been
sacrificed by a wicked, jealous and rapacious world—because it is so
pleasant, so wonderfully pleasant, to consider oneself freed from responsibility for one's own wishes and dreams, by believing oneself the
prey of wicked, guilty forces without." Finally, Schmid pointed out,
all the crimes which the German people consider to have been committed against them, such as the "bombing out of millions from their
homes, the displacement of whole populations, the imprisonment of
millions . . . all these crimes were first committed by Germans."[20]
It was notable, too, that at this time the German newspapers gave
great prominence to the Nuremberg trials, and two books published in
the American zone, containing the speeches of the prosecuting attorney
and the court's judgment, sold out at once, although they were published in editions of two hundred thousand each.[21] When Fritz Wan-
del, former Stadtrat of Reutlingen, spoke on his experiences as a pris-
oner in Dachau, a crowded audience questioned him for hours on the
conclusions he drew from this "road of madness" the German people
had followed.[22] Examples of this great national questioning were innumerable all over Germany. Yet against this background of a search
for moral truth came the practical process of denazification; and, in
far too many ways, the two processes were to be contradictory.

Denazification, as laid down in the Potsdam agreement, had four
facets. The National Socialist party and all organizations allied to it

were to be destroyed. All National Socialist laws were to be abrogated. War criminals were to be arrested and punished. And "all members of the Nazi party who have been more than nominal participants in its activities and all other persons hostile to Allied purposes shall be removed from public and semipublic office, and from positions of responsibility in important private undertakings."[23] The French accepted the first three provisions with alacrity; but on the fourth, they had important reservations.

The Nazi party in the French zone was at once dissolved, in accordance with SHAEF Law No. 5 on the dissolution of the National Socialist party, and Control Council Law No. 2 of October 10, 1945, on the dissolution and liquidation of Nazi organizations. Laws of specifically Nazi character were abrogated; and a new judicial system was created to replace the National Socialist legal system.[24]

Responsibility for the creation of this new judicial system in the French zone fell to the General Directorate of Justice under President Charles J. Furby. Furby, with the firm support of General Koenig, set about creating a framework of justice on the French model. He insisted from the first on the separation of powers, especially as far as the executive and judiciary were concerned, a difficult matter to enforce when the military government had been installed by the army. Further difficulties arose from the fact that the justice applied by SHAEF in the early days of the invasion was Anglo-Saxon justice, which differed in certain important respects from French legal procedure. Although they accepted in large part the SHAEF procedure, the French were determined to introduce so far as was possible the juridical influence of France, remembering with a certain pride that the "Napoleonic law codes have gone round the world." For this purpose, it was proposed to influence the legal faculties of the German universities, as well as to change the judicial system itself. Finally, further difficulty arose from the geographical composition of the zone, since all the former appeal courts lay in the British and American zones.[25]

A sound, impartial judicial system was quickly created. Special French tribunals were set up to deal with questions in which both Germans and French were involved, and members of these tribunals were all French lawyers appointed by the administrator general. The courts of pre-Nazi days were revived, for the purpose of dealing with cases in which Germans alone were concerned. To meet the problem of the appeal courts, a separate court was at first created in each Land, at Saarbrücken, Koblenz, Neustadt, Freiburg, and Tübingen, but after April 1946 a high court was set up for the whole zone in Rastatt.

With a working judicial system created, the military government set about the punishment of war criminals with great determination. As early as 1943 the Allies had given notice that at the end of the war all guilty of war crimes would be found and punished. War criminals who had committed crimes in countries outside Germany were to be arrested in the zone and sent back for trial in the country of their crime; and those guilty of crimes committed inside Germany were to be tried in the zone itself. At first, the general tribunals in each Land carried out these trials, but after April 1946 the one general tribunal for the whole zone, in the beautiful old chateau of Rastatt, took over the work. The first case was the trial of thirty-three guards from such concentration camps as Haslach and Gaggenau. By 1949 the French authorities were able to declare that no war criminals were at liberty in the French zone.[26]

Denazification in its strictest sense, however, meant the exclusion of active Nazis and persons similarly hostile to the Allies' purposes from all posts of importance in public or private life; and on this matter the French did not completely agree with the Americans or the British. But since American procedures were "more articulate, verbalized and legalistic than were those of the other three Allies," the American methods of denazification did influence the procedure in the other western zones; and to some extent the French came to model their methods of denazification upon the American.[27] The American attitude was based in the first place upon the secret orders to General Eisenhower, JCS 1067, which laid down very wide categories of employment from which more than nominal participants in Nazi activities were to be excluded.[28] Military Government Law No. 8, published on September 26, 1945, restricted all party members to common labor, a rather too sweeping injunction, as General Clay found, since often the only qualified administrators seemed to be those of more than nominal party allegiance. In March 1946 under the prompting of the military government, the German governments of the three Länder in the American zone passed the Law for Liberation from National Socialism and Militarism. The result was an overwhelming amount of paper work. In the American zone, there were thirteen million questionnaires and three million chargeable cases. The attempt to use Germans in the proceedings finally broke down in 1948, when the Communists, and then the Christian Democrats and Democrats, withdrew from the tribunals. In 1948 Clay was ordered by the American government to reduce the number of cases outstanding on May 1 to 30,000.[29] The questionnaires were a nightmare, not only for the Germans who had to fill them in, but for the Americans and the Germans associated with them who had to deal with them. The immense sales of Ernst von Salomon's novel, *The Questionnaire*, illustrated the widespread disgust with the whole proceeding.[30]

Denazification as practiced in the American zone was treated, to some degree, as a model for the French zone, particularly in the matter of laying down a legal framework for the process. But in practice denazification in the French zone was very different. The effect was to make the process, if not satisfactory, at least more acceptable to both occupier and occupied than was the case in the other zones. Denazification in the French zone went through several clearly marked stages. The first lasted from the entry of French troops in March 1945 until the establishment of German denazification committees in December 1945. During this period, the work was carried out by the French authorities only—in the early months by the First Army, and from August to November by the military government itself. The army had been more concerned with protecting its own security than in safeguarding the rights of the accused; and, at the time of the capitulation, large numbers of Germans were in prison, with very little prospect of an immediate trial. One of the first aims of the General Directorate of Justice was to separate the various kinds of prisoners, dividing war criminals from the rest and bringing as many as possible to a fair trial quickly. Second, a purge of those holding public office, especially of lawyers and teachers, had to be carried out, and this process was well under way by October 1945. At that time the numbers removed from office varied from 30 per cent in the Pfalz to 75 per cent in Württemberg.[31]

It was soon obvious that the most efficient way to carry out denazification was to allow the Germans to do it themselves. With about 10 per cent of the population proven anti-Nazis, it was decided to allow those who had suffered in their person or property, or who were proven opponents of the Nazi system, to be associated in the work. In principle, this stage of the work was to be carried out within the framework of two directives which were issued by the Control Council in 1946 for the purpose of creating uniformity throughout Germany in the denazification procedure. On January 12, 1946, the Control Council, in its directive No. 24, defined more clearly the meaning of the terms "more than nominal participants in Party Activities" and "hostile to allied purposes," as used in the Potsdam agreement. Such persons were to be removed from public, semipublic, and important private offices; but as a loophole, a final clause permitted certain individuals to be temporarily retained "for their specialist knowledge."[32] On October 12, 1946, in directive No. 38, the Control Council classified "war criminals and potentially dangerous persons" in five main categories and established "punishments and sanctions appropriate to each category." The five categories were: major offenders, offenders, lesser offenders, followers, and persons exonerated—the last category consisting of those who could prove that in spite of membership in a condemned organization they had been in active or passive opposition to the Nazi regime.[33] But these directives were not wholeheartedly accepted in the French zone. In the early months of 1946, the Länder of the French zone had worked out systems of denazification which were already in force; and as the military government itself admitted, "Directive No. 38 did not bring about profound changes in our system of denazification."[34]

The determination of the French to allow each Land to develop in its own way, with the least possible enforcement of uniform rules for the whole zone, resulted in each Land producing its own system of denazification. The system adopted in Württemberg was perhaps the most satisfactory to all concerned in the procedure, and it was so admired in the other Länder that the Christian Democratic party of the Pfalz resolved in January 1947 that "the multiplicity of procedures for denazification must be ended, and . . . a procedure similar to that of south Württemberg of June 28, 1946, should be adopted."[35] The method which had been adopted in Württemberg was described in the Consultative Assembly by Otto Künzel, the state commissioner for political cleansing,* the man most responsible for the working of

---

* The German word *Säuberung* is translated as "cleansing" in order to avoid the harsher overtones of the word "purge." All zones had difficulty in finding the *mot juste* to describe this process.

the system.[36] Künzel pointed out that Germans were associated with the process in the winter of 1945–46. The first plan, laid down by the provisional government under the presidency of Carlo Schmid, had led to the creation in each Kreis of an examination committee (*Untersuchungsausschuss*) consisting of five permanent members and three temporary members taken from the professional group whose members were being examined. Above this committee was a cleansing committee (*Säuberungsausschuss*), which made the final decision for each case and passed it on to the military governor of the Land for his approval. The major effort of these committees had been to carry out denazification in the public administration, and less effort had been spent on the sector of private industry. Within a few months, however, it became obvious that there were failings in the system. Most of all, Künzel concluded, it became clear that there was no uniformity of treatment throughout the Land. Each Kreis was adopting its own standards.[37] The result was the Ordonnance for Political Cleansing, passed by the German State Secretariat on May 28, 1946. This extremely important law was the basis for denazification in Württemberg throughout the remainder of the occupation. It differed in several important respects from the American zone's Law for Liberation from National Socialism and Militarism.[38]

The preface to the ordonnance stated that "the cleansing of public, cultural and economic life of persons who, by supporting, furthering or actively participating in National-Socialist and militaristic doctrines, have brought the German people into ruin and distress, is a prerequisite for reconstruction." The first clause laid down the principle which would guide the whole process. "Political cleansing demands energetic action against National Socialism and militarism, but at the same time, thorough and just consideration of every individual case. It must secure the well being of the whole people." The second clause stated that membership in the Nazi party or its subsidiaries would not be *prima facie* evidence of guilt, but nonmembership would not be taken as proof of innocence. The measures to be applied against those found responsible included withdrawal of the right to vote, to present oneself as a candidate for political office, to teach or to publish; dismissal, removal to another office, or compulsory retirement with or without pension; and direct monetary fines.

The organization that was to carry out these provisions was to be headed by a state commissioner for political cleansing, aided by a Land

Political Advisory Council chosen by the Land government on the nomination of the political parties. The major work of hearing cases would be carried out in each Kreis as before by examination committees consisting of five permanent members chosen from members of the political parties and one to three temporary members chosen from the professional groups whose members were being examined. One examination committee would be concerned with the public administration, one with private business. The main work of deciding each case fell on these Kreis committees, since it was believed that they had the close local knowledge needed to decide justly on the individual cases. These committees were more concerned with establishing the facts of an accused's responsibility than with deciding the measures to be applied against him. The decision on sanctions fell largely to the cleansing committees, of which there were three for public administration and three for private business in the whole Land. The final decision as to measures to be taken against each person was reviewed by the Political Advisory Council and by the state commissioner himself.

Although the French military government was not mentioned in the whole ordonnance, the General Directorate of Justice did play its part in the proceedings. As a matter of principle, it kept its share in the process as unobtrusive as possible.[39] Lack of personnel also played its part in producing this welcome reticence on the French side, since the supervision of denazification began with only two officials in the office of the administrator general in Baden-Baden, and even in 1947, the Office of Supervision of German Justice had seventeen officials, of whom only nine spoke German. The major work of the French was to review as many of the decisions taken as possible. The military government would ask the Political Advisory Council to review decisions with which it was not satisfied, especially where French authorities from the other services could throw further light on any individual case.[40]

The Württemberg ordonnance of May 28, 1946, attempted to improve the system of denazification in several ways. It laid down that strict classification by party membership could not be taken as legal proof of an individual's guilt. It attempted to give the accused a fair hearing by holding it in his own locality and by having present in the examination committee members of his own profession—doctors, for example, helping to try doctors. It attempted to speed up the work by increasing the number of committees and to allow the fairest possible review of each case by processing it at four levels. It allowed the accused the right of self-defense and ordered that the case against him be laid down in writing in advance. The system as adopted in Württemberg was fairly typical of the measures applied in Baden and Rheinland-Pfalz. By the end of 1946 denazification of those in public office had advanced rapidly. In all, 248,845 cases had been examined and action taken in 97,517 of these. The greatest stringency had been shown toward teachers, less than 50 per cent of whom had retained their positions.[41]

A further change in the organization of denazification was taken in 1947, after the Control Council had passed its directive No. 38, ordering the adoption throughout Germany of a system of denazification similar to that of the American zone. The major changes implied were the adoption of the American *Spruchkammer* system, and the adoption of the five classifications of degree or guilt. The military government ordered the Land governments to pass laws of denazification in accordance with the Control Council directive, and these new laws were written in April 1947 in Baden and Rheinland-Pfalz, and in May in Württemberg. Yet even at this time neither the Germans nor the military government of the French zone were willing to go along with the full details of the directive. The government of Rheinland-Pfalz increased the flexibility of its law by including seven categories into which the accused were to be divided, and made special note that membership in the party did not automatically classify a person in one of the seven groups.[42] Debating the new law in Württemberg in April 1947, Viktor Renner, minister of the interior, pointed out with pride that the laws for denazification in Württemberg differed considerably from those of the American zone, especially in not containing the five categories into which the population was to be classified. In Württemberg, he claimed, the process was regarded more as a political measure than as a judicial matter, and it was something that had to be done quickly.[43] Nevertheless, the *Spruchkammer*, which differed mainly from the cleansing committees in attempting to introduce trained judicial personnel as judges in the tribunals, were opened with appropriate solemnity. But already the process was beginning to break down.

By 1947 the French military government was prepared to hasten the process as much as possible. In a press conference in April 1947 a representative of the military government admitted that it now seemed "impossible to remove all former members of the Nazi party and its affiliates, without dangerously affecting public life." Yet, he went on, "the administration was cleared at the outset of all former National Socialists in important positions. This action is now over. The purging of business is almost completed."[44] On May 2, 1947, all persons born since January 1, 1919, were amnestied, provided that they had not held the position of "cell leader" or a higher office in the party; and on November 17, 1947, the amnesty was extended to all who had been classified as "followers."[45] At the same time, it was announced that further trials would be restricted to members of organizations declared "criminal" by the Nuremberg tribunal. Trials against others were suspended.[46]

By 1947 the German population of the zone was also becoming increasingly discontented with the slow progress of denazification. In spite of the attempts in the zone to be flexible and speedy, the process had not satisfied anyone. In 1946 Dr. Hermann Geiller had pointed out, in the *Badener Tagblatt*, a commonly held distinction when he reminded those carrying out denazification that there was a basic difference between *Will-* and *Muss-Nazis*, between those who had joined the party because they wanted to do so, and those, like lawyers, academicians, and architects, who joined it because they had to do so. Moreover, he went on, many who became Nazis by choice were quickly disillusioned, but were unable to withdraw. The same theme was echoed by many who could not believe that the Germans were implicated in the crimes of the Nazis.[47] The *Schwäbisches Tagblatt* told how, "in the factories, the German men and women often shared their last bit of bread with the prisoners, and Swabian farmers, who in overwhelming majority asked nothing from Hitler and his accomplices, treated the prisoners who were working for them like members of their own family." Many examples, the paper considered, could be given as "proof of the humane behavior of the German people and of the active opposition of civilians and officials to the brutality and vileness of the Nazis."[48] There was, from the beginning, a feeling that important Nazis should be punished severely, but that the little men should be left undisturbed. A young man came into the office of the *Badener Tagblatt* in Baden-Baden in April 1946 and asked, "How can we believe in democracy and Christianity when . . . millions of innocent people must still suffer for those things which are the responsibility of the men who are facing trial in Nuremberg?"[49] When the verdicts were finally announced at Nuremberg, many felt that they were too lenient, especially in the cases of von Papen, Schacht, and Fritsche. The *Rheinischer Merkur* suggested that, once the main trial was over, a law court of the German Länder should be set up, so that Germans could punish crimes committed against Germans. The little men, the paper added, should be allowed to go free.[50]

The French undoubtedly attempted to follow this policy of punishing major criminals and of treating lightly those who were less implicated. As a result, they came under severe criticism from Allied and even some German circles. From the beginning of the occupation, officials of the other zones believed that the French were allowing Nazis to stay in power in their zone. The *New York Times* reported in October 1945 that at least twenty-seven Germans dismissed from their posts in the American zone had found employment in the French zone, a fact which the French authorities admitted but attributed to error on their part.[51] Some of these complaints lose force in view of the fact that two who found homes in the French zone in 1945 after being refused employment in the British or American zones were Konrad Adenauer and Carlo Schmid. Nevertheless, responsible German groups continued to complain that too many Nazis were being left in office. The Christian Democratic party in the Rheinland, in its manifesto before the Kreis elections of October 1946, noted with pleasure that the Nuremberg judgment seemed to be a "denial of collective guilt," but went on to say that Germans must punish Germans. "One is right when one sees the progress [of denazification] as the touchstone for the future of Germany. . . . It is not valid only for the workers, office staff, and officials. . . . Whoever by way of a well-filled purse, a good-sounding name, or a flourishing factory, and by lucrative payments to the NSDAP, knew how to avoid membership, is no struggler against Nazi tyranny. So denazification in industry is the most immediate concern."[52]

A particularly glaring case occurred in November 1946, when a German criminal court at Freiburg quashed proceedings against Heinrich Tillessen, who twenty-five years before had murdered the cabinet minister, Mathias Erzberger, but had avoided trial under Hitler's amnesty law of March 21, 1933. Tillessen admitted his guilt, and the public prosecutor demanded the death sentence. The court, however, said that the amnesty law was not one of the laws nullified by the Allies, and that Tillessen should therefore be freed.[53] At this point, the French military government stepped in, and with great care not to judge the case itself, created a court with international representation to determine whether the amnesty law had been annulled. The court decided that it was no longer in force, and Tillessen was re-tried and found guilty in another German court in Baden. The incident caused great disgust among many groups throughout the zone. Gunther Markscheffel, speaking at a Socialist party meeting in Baden, pointed out that his party was shocked at the Tillessen affair (but added that they were also shocked at the presence in the CDU of big capitalists who had supported Hitler financially).[54] Ernst Johann, writing in the *Rheinpfalz*, found this just another proof of the failure of the Germans to change. Major Nazis, he said, ever more numerous, are helping each other in the administration, and in industry.[55] And in a recent novel, *The Fear Makers*, Wilfrid Schilling claims that denazification in the French zone was a very temporary and shallow process which has already been reversed.[56]

By 1948 there was an almost universal outcry against denazification, which seemed only to be directed against the little men and to be dragging on interminably. Pastor Niemöller caused a stir with a pastoral letter of February 2, 1948, in which he called on Germans to refuse to cooperate in further denazification. The Communists, too, had come to think that the process was a weapon of the "new reaction." "An end to the Fragebogen war," cried the Communist paper *Neues Leben*. "We have given serious warning to those responsible for denazification: should no change in the methods of denazification used until now be brought about in the near future, and denazification lead further to renazification, then the KPD of Rheinland-Pfalz will be forced to withdraw from its share in the work of the denazification committees." On August 10, 1948, the Communist party did withdraw from the work of denazification in all three western zones.[57]

The French were convinced by 1948 that denazification had been carried out as far as was possible. The method of the French military government had shown certain commendable features. It had been based on the belief that every case must be judged individually. Usually, extremely reliable and fair-minded Germans had been associated in the work and had been trusted with its execution. In the professions by whom the French considered the work of re-education was to be undertaken, especially in the legal and academic professions, the process had been carried out with great thoroughness. Still, there were undeniable weaknesses. The whole system of monetary fines, compulsory retirement, reduction of salary, and similar kinds of punishment tended to give the impression that the payment of a fine wiped away all responsibility for the over-all record of the Nazis. In this way, the process of denazification solved the guilt question in a totally practical way, and tended to nullify the effects of the moral questioning which many had felt the duty to face at the end of the war. *Rheinischer Merkur* summed up the bitterness that many felt toward the process by demanding a political amnesty before the foundation of the West German Republic: "Questionable in its moral foundation, varied between zones and Länder in its legal bases, compromised by false judgments, [denazification] has increased the division in Germany, the uncertainty of the law, and social misery, nourished a costly bureaucracy, widened the division between the parties, weakened still further the sense of justice, and created a new and at the same time illegal category of 'politically persecuted.' "[58]

Professor Edmond Vermeil suggested a different approach, however, when in speaking of Germany in 1946 he asserted that " 'denazification' is a fallacious term. One does not throw off Nazism, like a garment that has gone out of style." What was needed, he felt, was a thorough process of re-education which would destroy "bad Germanism," that character which equated the idea of a national state with territorial expansion.[59] And it was on this program of re-education that the French based their real solution to the German problem. Denazification was an unpleasant necessity. The spread of French ideals and culture was worthy of "that universalism which is the vocation of the French spirit."[60] Denazification was throwing off the past. Re-education would open the way to the future.

RE-EDUCATION

When a United States Educational Mission returned home after spending the summer of 1946 in the American zone, it reported that "the re-education of the German people is an undertaking of the greatest magnitude . . . at once the hardest and most important task facing the Military Government in Germany today."[61] Saul Padover, interrogating many youths as the Allied armies moved into Germany, had already pointed out that "Germans in their late teens and early twenties are the real problem. In this age group there are genuine Nazis. Some of them give the impression of being beyond hope or redemption. They display all the well-known Nazi characteristics— deceit, disloyalty, lying, and cowardice in crisis. . . . Older Germans themselves often suggest that such Nazis, if guilty of crime, should be sent abroad in labor battalions to rebuild countries the Germans destroyed." But he added that a German schoolteacher had once told him that the students in his school were either *verkraenkelte* or *vergiftet*, either sickly with Nazism or hopelessly poisoned—and that most of them were merely sickly and could be cured.[62]

Observers in the French zone came to similar conclusions. Jules-Albert Jaeger, reporting to the Center of Studies in Foreign Policy in Paris on his two years of work with German youth, showed that these young men were still deeply influenced by the ideas that had been drilled into them during the Nazi period, but that they were now waiting in a kind of torpid uncertainty for something to replace the faith that they had been brought up to accept. For Jaeger, the solution was that suggested to him by President Beneš, to create in Germany a diversity of influences, especially regional and social. The spirit of German unity was as dangerous in the mental sphere as in the political.[63] Germans in the French zone were especially worried about the relationship between younger and older people, since the Nazis had deliberately tried to break down family ties and to replace family loyalties with unquestioning loyalty to the party. The *Badener Tagblatt* looked back, in 1946, on the "time of incitement, when young people were flattered with false promises on the future of Germany and driven against their backward parents." Yet now, the paper felt, there was hope again, since "the family is again the healthy germ-cell of our people."[64] The *Rheinischer Merkur* was not quite so satisfied. After it had published a letter asking for help for young people, it had received a large number of letters of despair, all on the theme, it said, that "nobody understands us, and nobody helps us. . . . We have been deceived twice. First, by Hitlerism, which misled our idealism . . . into universal crimes, and the second time by our postwar homeland, which never stretches out the hand of reconciliation to us who are lost and seeking a way." The editor decided that the moment had come for someone to reply to this kind of thinking with a sharp reminder. Youth must remember, he said, that everyone is suffering in some way, that no one who is capable of work and not guilty of crimes is usually refused employment, and that one must expect people to be distrustful for a while in view of the fervor young people showed in swinging to Nazism.[65] A few months later the paper came back to the same theme. Young people, wrote Dr. F. Malburg, are indulging in too many words and not enough deeds. Too many of them are still using the ideas which Hitler gave them, especially of a so-called Heroic Age. They must realize, he wrote, that the true Heroic Age is the one of "consciousness of responsibility." Bravery is the willingness to stand by one's opinions. Above all, he felt, young people must take part in politics instead of complaining about the way others are managing affairs.[66] The *Trierische Volkszeitung* in January 1947 published another typical letter of complaint, from a nephew to his uncle. The young man felt that there was no reason for hope. The world, he said, had collapsed in an unparalleled catastrophe. The conquerors were confused. The conquered, and especially German youth, saw no way out. Destruction, hunger, cold, and moral distress seemed to be impassable obstacles. His uncle replied that the nephew was doing what the Nazis had wanted, with their motto, "After us the flood." He should remember that Germany had always been its own worst enemy, since no other people had had such immense talents that it had not been able to use.[67]

Opinion polls taken in the early years of the occupation were very revealing. The pupils in three secondary schools in Baden-Baden were questioned in October 1945. They displayed curiously little desire to leave Germany, 80 per cent replying that the country they would most like to live in was Germany. When asked whom they considered to be the greatest man in universal history, fifteen replied Frederick the Great, fifteen Bismarck, twelve Goethe, ten Alexander the Great, eight Caesar, three Jesus Christ, and one Hitler.[68] In a wider poll taken in Baden and Württemberg in 1947, 55 per cent of the boys and 69 per cent of the girls questioned still felt they did not want to emigrate, even if they received a good offer of employment.[69]

Polls taken by a German public opinion agency, the *Institut für*

Demoskopie, also illustrated the cleavage between the young and the old, and the uncertain moral values of the young. Asked whether they had a favorable or an unfavorable impression of the young people between the ages of eighteen and twenty-five, 47 per cent of the men and 35 per cent of the women replied that their impression was unfavorable. When 370 young people in Baden and Württemberg were asked in February 1948 whether they thought that older people understood them, 33 per cent replied that they were very seldom understood by older people, and only 14 per cent thought that the older people understood them very well.[70] This break between the generations had the further effect of leaving the youth with a distrust for politics, since the politicians of the older generation seemed to many to have brought on the Nazi regime and all it implied. Asked in a military government poll in December 1947 whether they were interested in the parties then active in Germany, 72 per cent of the young people questioned, excluding university students, said they were not, and 70 per cent had no idea how the programs of the different parties varied. Of the university students, 45 per cent were not interested in German political parties.[71] A similar poll conducted by the German institute revealed comparable results. In February 1948 a group of 370 youths and 100 university students from Freiburg and Tübingen were asked about their interest in politics. Among the youths, 43 per cent had fairly little interest in politics, 23 per cent no interest at all, and 6 per cent thought politics distasteful. Of the university students, however, 61 per cent were interested in politics among other interests, and 6 per cent thought it their main interest.[72]

The problem of German youth thus had several facets. A small proportion of this generation was strongly influenced by Nazism. The majority were bewildered and confused. Their relations with their parents and the older generations were sharply and mutually distrustful. These young people had been brought up to believe in extreme German nationalism, and especially that the great heroes of German history were those who had united the country by force. Their bewilderment and sense of rejection made them distrust all those aspects of German society which could be held in any way responsible for the present intolerable situation, and thus led them to distrust all political power, Allied or German.

The French officials responsible for the educational work of the zone showed great understanding of these problems, and as a result of the work of this body of devoted officials, the educational and cultural achievements of the French zone stand high among the truly positive results of the occupation of Germany.

At the head of the Directorate of Public Education was Raymond Schmittlein, to whom the success of the educational program must be largely attributed. Born in Belfort, close to the German border, and speaking fluent German, Schmittlein was a Germanist of wide experience. He had been a professor in Lithuania between the wars, had commanded disarmament operations in the Levant for the Free French in 1941, and had acted as General de Gaulle's representative in Moscow in 1943. From 1943 to 1944 he had been a member of de Gaulle's cabinet in Algiers, and as a lieutenant-colonel with the 2nd Moroccan Infantry Division, he had taken part in the Italian and French campaigns and in the invasion of Germany. Schmittlein was in close personal contact with de Gaulle and with General Koenig, and he was able to use his personal prestige to ensure the rapid adoption of his educational program for the French zone of Germany.

Schmittlein described the theories upon which the educational program of the French zone was based in an article in *France-Illustration* in 1949. His policy was "to break the chains on German youth." No democrat, and especially no Christian, Schmittlein wrote, can turn the Hitlerian theory to his own profit and seriously think that the Germans are in some sense an inferior race destined to nationalism, militarism, and totalitarianism. "Man is the product of the environment in which he evolves," he continued. German youth had evolved in the intellectual climate of the false nationalism of the nineteenth century, "the nationalism imposed artificially by romantic writers and Prussian soldiers."[73] The environment in which youth was educated had to be changed, since the Nazis had set about creating an educational environment in which youth would be permanently formed in accordance with the Nazi ideology. For example, superbly produced books, with expensive plates, had illustrated their racial theories in the schools, and the teachers had been made to teach whatever the Nazis wished.[74]

Schmittlein was assisted by an able group of young Germanists, many of them from the École Normale or from the School of Political Sciences in Paris. His immediate assistant, Mme Germaine

Giron, had attended the Interpreters' School in Heidelberg; and she, and others like Charles Muller, showed great determination to achieve a mutual understanding with the Germans concerned with educational work. The organization of the educational program was based on the framework adopted in the Ministry of National Education in Paris, yet the work itself was to be something entirely original in the history of the two countries, and the British and Americans were later to admit that in this respect at least the success of the French military government far exceeded their own.

Re-education was planned to affect all age levels. The greatest hope was placed in the education of the children, and the primary school was regarded as the major instrument of re-education. The first problem facing the French was to find adequate buildings and suitable teachers. Of 5,961 schools in the zone, 2,000 had been damaged, and French troops were billeted in many of the others.[75] Worse still was the problem of finding suitable teachers, since 75 per cent of the teaching force had been suspended in the summer of 1945 because of Nazi connections.[76] Nevertheless, Schmittlein demanded that the schools and universities be opened in the autumn of 1945, and, in spite of many protests from the military, General Koenig agreed. The administrator general therefore authorized both primary and secondary schools to reopen on September 17, 1945. In this instance, the French acted more quickly than either the British or the Americans, schools in the other western zones opening on October 1.

The military government took urgent measures to ensure that the opening of the schools would be a success. Appeals were made to retired teachers to return to their profession. Emergency training courses were instituted. Many suspended teachers were restored, without security of tenure, and at the end of the year, while a few were dismissed, the majority were again given tenure. The results of this piecemeal recruiting were, however, plainly unsatisfactory. In December 1945 the average age of teachers in large towns was between fifty-six and sixty, buildings were totally inadequate, and there was still a great shortage of textbooks.[77]

The Directorate of Public Education also began long-term measures to remedy this deficiency. The absolute ban imposed on all school textbooks published since 1933 had caused shortages which temporary expedients, such as the use of Swiss textbooks, had not entirely remedied. The directorate had many textbooks rewritten, introduced others, in French and in translation, that were in use in the French schools, and brought others from Luxembourg and America. The newly written texts set out to emphasize the local characteristics of the zone. The history books, for example, illustrated the quarrels between Baden and Prussia and the ties of France with the Pfalz. The textbook program was of cardinal importance and earned the admiration of the other zones. Robert Havighurst, reporting for the Rockefeller Foundation in 1947 on the conditions in Germany, pointed out that "the Americans have published only 3 million [textbooks] for the 3 million children in their zone. The British have published 12½ million copies for 3½ million children and the French have published 6,300,000 copies for 900,000 children." By 1948 ten million new schoolbooks had been published in the French zone.[78]

The training of new teachers was even more important. The immediate shortage was partially remedied by the establishment of teachers' training colleges on the pattern of the French *écoles normales*. Sixteen of these colleges had been created by December 1946. They offered a two-year course, part of which could be taken by correspondence, and at the beginning they gave short courses, with the aim of training some teachers within six months. About 1,500 new teachers had been trained by 1947, a welcome addition to the 13,000 teaching in all schools in 1946.[79]

The high schools were faced with much the same sort of problems as the primary schools—shortage of buildings and teachers—but again, the establishment of the teachers' training colleges and the revival of university life had begun, in 1947, to supply new teachers. The major changes in the high schools, apart from those in personnel, were in curriculum and examinations. The German school system had previously made a selection at the age of ten between those pupils who would attend the Gymnasium, the secondary school preparing students for college and professional work, and those who would enter the Volksschule, the general school which prepared pupils for more practical work and at which the school-leaving age was fourteen. The military government found this system undemocratic, since there was no possibility of entering the Gymnasium after graduation from Volksschule, no matter how intelligent a pupil had shown himself, because the Gymnasium had begun a full classical course of study which a transferring student could not make up. Moreover, this system favored the children of middle- and upper-class parents, since they alone could support their children during the nine years of nonvocational training offered by the Gymnasium.

In 1946–48 the French suppressed the teaching of Latin in the three lowest grades of the Gymnasium. From the beginning of his fourth year in the Gymnasium, the student was given the choice of three courses of study—a classical curriculum, with study of Latin; a modern curriculum with more science and mathematics; or a mixed curriculum of Latin-mathematics-science. As a result, the better students from the Volksschule could transfer to the Gymnasium without being penalized in way of curriculum. At the beginning of the sixth year in the Gymnasium, the students were given the further choice of one of four specializations: French-Latin-Greek; French-Latin-English; French-Latin-sciences; or French-English-sciences. The students in all four sections had the same courses in French, religion, German, geography, music and gymnastics, drawing, or sewing. The military government set out in this way to lessen the cleavage between the different classes in Germany by breaking down the sharp distinction in German society between those who had been trained in the classical discipline of the Gymnasium and those who had had only a vocational training. Second, they attempted to modernize the curriculum by increasing the emphasis on science and modern languages. And third, they set up French as the one compulsory foreign language, as a necessary prerequisite for better understanding between the two countries.[80]

A further school reform was the stiffening of the *Abitur,* the school-leaving examination which conferred the right to enter a university. The universities in the French zone, and indeed in all of Germany, were quite unable to cope with the flood of applications which poured in on them. The military government was forced to adopt some method of selection which would be more effective than the mere requirement of possession of the *Abitur,* since the *Abitur* was granted by every Gymnasium individually, without reference to any state or national standards. It was not a useful test of a student's capacity for university study, especially in the days immediately after the capitulation when vast numbers of soldiers, many in their late twenties or early thirties, were demanding a graduation certificate from the over-pressed school administrators.

The French attempted to stiffen the requirements for the school-leaving certificate by introducing a system similar to that of the French *baccalauréat*, with common examinations set for each Land and graded by teachers other than those of the school taking the examination. The system of grading was also changed. Candidates were graded on a scale of twenty points. Those with fifteen or more were given entrance to a university. Those with thirteen to fifteen were permitted to spend a year of preparation at a university before beginning their main studies. The others were refused entrance. The results for the Länder in 1947 varied greatly, showing that the grading system was far from uniform in the Länder. In Baden, 15.2 per cent of the candidates were given fifteen or more points, in Württemberg only 1.1 per cent.[81]

These reforms did not pass without a great deal of criticism from German academic and religious circles. Great criticism, especially from the bishops, was leveled at the reduced Latin requirements; and to satisfy them in some degree, the churches were permitted to run their own schools where candidates for the priesthood could be given the linguistic training, in addition to the other instruction that their churches required. The opposition was, however, much more the effect of conservative thinking and derived in many cases from the opposition of established social groups to this democratization which would throw the professions open to all classes. In particular, the stiffening of the *Abitur* raised an amazing storm of protest from German circles of most dissimilar opinions. When the minister of education and public worship in Rheinland-Pfalz issued in July 1947 an ordonnance instituting an examination for entrance to the university, there was an outraged protest from parents, from trade-unions, and from political parties.[82] The Socialist party, for example, objected strongly in the next session of the Landtag, claiming that the schools could not adapt to the choice of subjects by a central committee, that it was unjust to those who had to take an examination shortly after being in captivity, and that there was need to take into account the individuality of the pupil known only to his own teachers.[83]

The conflict with the churches took a much wider form in a debate over the "confessional [denominational] schools," in the discussions during the writing of the Land constitutions in the spring of 1947. The churches, and the Catholic church in particular, were determined to oppose the maintenance of the state schools, which were set up by

Hitler in 1937. The struggle became an all-out conflict between Germans who wished to set up confessional schools and to guarantee the right to do so in the new constitutions and those Germans who wished to keep the schools free of ties to any one confession. The French entered into this conflict, although largely behind the scenes, in favor of the state school system they had known in France since the early 1900's. According to Helen Liddell, secretary of the information service of the Royal Institute for International Affairs, who made a field survey of education in occupied Germany, the churches were "struggling for power against the French over the State school. . . . They use the argument that this bad and unchristian system was part of the Nazism, which the French are setting themselves to eradicate. The French retaliate with the accusation that former Nazis can get posts in confessional schools, provided they declare themselves against compulsory state education. By implication, the Churches cannot be trusted to play their part in the training of youth and in the eradication of militaristic and nationalistic ideas."[84]

The churches set out to apply pressure on the Consultative Assemblies in the different Länder to secure the right to set up confessional schools. Monsignor Groeber, bishop of Freiburg, in the solemn service at the opening of the Consultative Assembly, had announced that the proposed text, which he considered did not guarantee parents' rights in education, could not satisfy Christian consciences. Bishop Wurm, Evangelical bishop of Württemberg, appeared before the constitutional committee in Württemberg to press for the right of parents to confessional schools, and he pointed out that he approved of the constitution of Rheinland-Pfalz. This, he thought, "is the best constitution which has ever come to my sight. In it, as in no other constitution, are assured the natural rights of man, freedom of the church and Christian values."[85]

In Rheinland-Pfalz the issue was finally settled by permitting a separate referendum on the school question to be held at the same time as the referendum on the constitution. The result was unsatisfactory to both sides, since 52 per cent voted for the confessional schools and 48 per cent against. In spite of the narrow margin, the scholastic clauses were adopted in the constitution, with the decision that "the public people's schools are either confessional or Christian 'simultaneous' schools," confessional schools being set up again where they had existed before their abolition by Hitler and new confessional schools being created where requested by a sufficient proportion of the population.[86] In Baden, a compromise was accepted at the time of writing the constitution, but the matter was put to a referendum on December 12, 1948, in which 78 per cent of the population voted for the introduction of confessional schools.[87] In Württemberg, the right to confessional schools was also accepted in the constitution. Thus, by the end of 1948 the school system of the zone was based upon a double system of state interconfessional schools and confessional schools, a complicated system created in accordance with the expressed wishes of the population but against the advice of the French military government.

The stiffening of the *Abitur* examination had been intended to lessen the pressure on the universities, for here the problems already encountered in the lower schools were greatly magnified. There were only two universities in the zone at the time of the capitulation, and both were in the southern triangle. They were the famous old foundations of Freiburg in Baden and Tübingen in Württemberg. Freiburg in particular was heavily damaged, its library decimated by losses through bombing and street fighting and its buildings in ruin. The faculties had been heavily purged by the Nazi government, and few of those professors retaining their positions could be called open friends of the Allied powers.[88]

Nevertheless, the French began at once the revival of university training. In October, Freiburg and Tübingen universities were authorized to reopen. The problem of denazification of the teaching staff presented great difficulties, since the French found it very difficult to replace such skilled personnel. Finally, some 30 per cent of the university professors were dismissed or penalized, a much smaller proportion than in the lower schools, and an attempt was made to supervise the teaching in the universities by the appointment of a French curator who was usually an excellent Germanist well acquainted with the methods of German education. The task of these young men was overwhelming, however, since among their many other tasks they were expected to censor all lectures given in the university. The parliamentary committee of inquiry was shocked to discover that in 1946 only three officers had been appointed to supervise university education in the whole zone.[89]

The first two years were spent in readjustment, with little possibility of beginning full university curriculum. The main problem of
the students remained the difficulty of finding enough food. Every-
body tried to get a little extra, from friends in the country or by
food packages from America and Switzerland. The university *Mensa*
served very cheap and bad meals, which the students used to supplement the meals they bought in restaurants in town. In 1947 the military government decided that the situation was so bad that students
preparing for examinations were to be given extra food cards and that
all university students should be given the rations of heavy laborers.
Finding a room was even more difficult, since the military government
had been forced to adopt Freiburg as the capital of south Baden and
Tübingen as the capital of south Württemberg. Within the universities, a division in the faculty quickly became evident, between the
older members who were still strong in the academic seclusion so
favored in prewar Germany and the younger men, often appointed
under French influence, who maintained much closer and more understanding relationships with their students. At Tübingen, this group
was called the "New University" by the students.[90]

The University and the townspeople of Basel were extremely generous in helping the University of Freiburg. The rector of the University of Basel had taken the lead in 1946 in instituting a scheme
whereby over a hundred students from the University of Freiburg
were invited to attend the University of Basel. These students were
usually between the ages of twenty-four and twenty-eight and in their
second year of university. They were approved by the French military
government and given a clearance. About half of them were lodged
in an old hotel which was about ten minutes away from Basel. Swiss
families in most cases supplied them with their midday meal, usually
without charge. Each student was permitted to spend two semesters
at the University of Basel.[91]

The major effort of the French to meet the problem of university
enrollment was the founding, or rather, as the French preferred to
say, the re-founding of the University of Mainz. In 1946 Tübingen
could take only 3,300 students and Freiburg 2,100; and the universities which students from the northern triangle would normally have
entered—Bonn, Cologne, Heidelberg, Frankfurt, and Marburg—
were equally overwhelmed with the enrollment from the British and

American zones alone. The choice of a site for the new university was made between Speyer, Trier, and Mainz. As well as memories of its former university which had existed between 1477 and 1817, Mainz offered the cardinal advantage of an air force barracks building which could easily be converted into a university. In fact, it was said that, when the barracks was erected in 1938, the Air Ministry had accused the architect of building an academy instead of a barracks. On March 1, 1946, the founding of the university was authorized, and on May 22, 1946, the official inauguration took place.

In founding a new university, the French had the opportunity to mold a new academic life free of the dangerous influences of the recent past. Yet, from the start, the university was to be an autonomous organization. As General Koenig said at the opening ceremonies, in a phrase which is still quoted with admiration by those connected with the university, "I want to tell you openly that here you are *chez vous*." Schmittlein, who had been one of the major moving forces in the creation of the university, pointed out that the university would be based on liberty, "not only the inner liberty which one's conscience alone can give, but also the effective liberty of choosing one's own opinion, and of expressing it, which has as a corollary respect of the opinion of others."[92]

The recruitment of the faculty presented an opportunity for making a new beginning. There was no difficulty in recruitment, largely because of the great number of university professors expelled from the eastern sections of Germany who were seeking employment. And the university also deliberately avoided demanding the full paper qualifications from otherwise qualified persons, attempting in this way to prevent the development of the academic corporatism which had been harmful in other German universities. The result was that the foundation of the university was not received with good will in all German academic circles. Writing in the *Rheinischer Merkur* the day before the opening ceremonies, Oberbürgermeister Kraus of Mainz expressed his gratification at the founding of the university and at the great aid which it had received from the French military government, but he noted that there was opposition from German circles. Some, he said, had challenged the right to, and the need for, a new university. Attempts had been made to keep students and professors away. Suspicions had even been voiced against "their German spirit, their German reliability." These critics, he said, were either open National Socialists or, worse, were "true-blue Great Prussian Conservatives and National Liberals of Bismarckian stamp, who have forgotten nothing and learned nothing. It is these people who identified Germany with Greater Prussia and who now name everyone an enemy of the Reich . . . who will not recognize Berlin as the capital of the Reich." Above all, he concluded, they know nothing of the great value of the Rhineland, "where there has been no Brandenburg and no Hohenzollern, no Prussia and no Bismarck."[93]

The university thrived in spite of all opposition. By November 1946 it had 156 professors and 4,450 students, and it has since developed into one of the major universities in Germany. Two more institutions of higher learning were founded along the Rhine to help produce a new cadre of administrators and professional men. Largely through the work of Mme Giron, a school for interpreters was opened at Germersheim. The curriculum, although built around the modern foreign languages and especially French, English, and Russian, offered a full program of liberal arts and a specialized program of study of the country whose language was being learned. At Speyer, the military government founded a school for administrators, with the aim of filling the gaps left by denazification. The interpreters' school has now become a school of the University of Mainz; and the administrators' school has been recognized by the West German government, and its graduates are sought for positions all over Germany.[94] Several important institutes of scientific research, which had been transferred to the zone by the Nazis as the bombing of Berlin intensified, were reopened under the direction of some of Germany's best scientists; and about eight "popular universities" (*Volksuniversität*), corresponding to night schools granting college degrees, were organized. They were largely attended by people under thirty, and by 1947 they drew about 1,500 students.[95]

The French contribution to university education in the zone was reviewed before the Landtag of Württemberg by the rector of Tübingen University, Dr. Erbe, when General Koenig came to pay a farewell visit in July 1949. The first German reaction to the defeat, he said, was a feeling of overwhelming misfortune, in which they took to the history books to blame their own ancestors. But the occupying powers made things worse by refusing to understand how glad the

Germans were to throw off the ties on intellectual life, "the humiliation of Clio." The first period of the occupation was therefore the time of the "use of mechanical methods" by the occupying power, who attempted to introduce the institutions to which he was accustomed at home. The second phase, however, was that "of the winning back of trust," in which the military government had cooperated fully in the revival of the life of the university.[96]

Other activities for youth were also encouraged. The most important were the church organizations, such as Catholic Youth, with 120,000 members, and Protestant Youth, with 35,000. Political groups also set up young people's organizations, such as Socialist Youth, with 20,000 members, or Trade Union Youth, with 13,000. Finally, great impetus was given to open-air activities, by the Friends of Nature and the Youth Hostels Association. These clubs did much to help the young people of Germany throw off their dependence on the Hitler Youth Movement and to direct their group spirit toward nonmilitaristic pastimes.[97]

Perhaps most effective of all was the organization of contacts with the young people of other nations. Early in the occupation, a few French officers in the military government had the courage to see the need of German youth for contacts outside the zone and the need to bring French and other foreign students into the zone to meet Germans. As early as 1946 the youth service of the military government set about making these contacts possible. In 1946 summer courses were held at the Universities of Freiburg and Tübingen, and approximately 620 French, German, and other foreign students attended. At the same time, contact was made between youth movements in the two countries. An exhibition sent around Germany by French youth groups, entitled "Message from French Youth," was visited by 120,-000 Germans. Summer camps with a program of lectures and discussions were held in the zone for members of French and German organizations, such as church and political groups, in which 1,035 French people took part. In 1947 the program was much accelerated. About 1,500 students attended summer courses at Freiburg, Tübingen, Mainz, and Germersheim, and the livelier students were invited back at Christmas to renew the contacts made during the summer. Further contacts between youth groups were begun, and a particular effort was made to encourage contacts between apprentices in the same type of work, as for example in meetings in Württemberg between textile workers and watchmakers.[98] By 1948, German students were able to take part in some student activities outside Germany. A group of Germans took part in the annual pilgrimage of Paris students to Chartres.[99] French universities were persuaded to accept a few German students, and the success of the experiment encouraged the development of the program.

These activities merged into the program for the re-education of the older age groups. The program attempted to develop in the zone a deep sympathy for, and understanding of, French culture. The French language was taught not only in schools but also in four newly founded French Institutes at Freiburg, Tübingen, Mainz, and Trier. French instructors in large numbers were brought into schools throughout the zone. Visiting Frenchmen, among them such experts on Germany as Edmond Vermeil and Robert d'Harcourt, gave numerous lectures. An important series of cultural events was organized to acquaint the Germans with the achievements of French culture. Eight major exhibitions were organized, including a display of paintings and art objects illustrating the ties of France with Baden. French theatrical companies presented such plays as Anouilh's *Voyageur sans bagages* and Molière's *Le Misanthrope* and *L'Avare*.[100]

The success of the efforts of the French military government to further understanding between the two peoples is illustrated in a remarkable way by a series of developments which followed the foundation of the West German Republic. More than eighty cities and towns in France and Germany have adopted a corresponding town in the other's country; and this program has been carried out through the local initiative of mayors, officials, and townspeople. The origins of this spontaneous movement were in such groups as the Franco-German Union (*Deutsch-französische Vereinigung*) in Ludwigshafen. One of the group's German members ascribed its origin to the fact that "Ludwigshafen on the Rhine had, among the many officers of the occupying power, several persons who recognized, as did a number of Germans in the town, that the peoples of both nations would be best served if the past were surmounted, so that a Franco-German understanding could be created. . . . The result was the founding, in May 1950, of the Franco-German Union of Ludwigshafen on the Rhine."[101]

From such small beginnings, the larger program followed. In 1953 the mayor of Mainz asked the mayor of Dijon if he could bring a group of administrators to study the functioning of city government in Dijon; the visit proved such a success that visits continued to be exchanged, and in June 1958 the official "twinning" of the two cities was announced. A similar series of events—the exchange of visits in 1953 and the official linking in 1956—produced the "twinning" of Mâcon in Burgundy and Neustadt an der Weinstrasse in the Pfalz. A further result of the visits of the officials of Dijon and Mainz was the formation in 1957 of the friendship union between Rheinland-Pfalz and Burgundy. These links have not been for empty show. They have been accompanied by many exchanges of students, administrators, singers, and wine-drinkers between the two countries.

The work of two other organizations should be mentioned. The International Bureau of Liaison and Documentation, set up in 1945 at Offenburg in Baden and staffed by a group of Catholics, Protestants, and laymen, attempted to facilitate understanding between the two countries, especially through its two magazines—*Dokumente,* which sought to spread information of France in Germany, and *Documents,* of Germany in France. Another committee, named the Committee for Exchanges with the New Germany, was founded in France in 1948 under the instigation of Emmanuel Mounier, editor of the review *Esprit.* The committee organized public debates, sent Frenchmen to Germany for conferences, received German groups in France, and published an information newspaper called *Allemagne.*[102]

There can be no doubt of the success of the French educational and cultural program. In spite of occasional opposition from conservative and nationalist groups, from the churches, and even from the universities, and of the complaints that Germans were "stuffed with culture" rather than food, the program succeeded. German youth showed an avid desire for education and took advantage of all openings available in the secondary schools, the teachers' training colleges, the "popular universities," and especially in the universities. International contacts proved invaluable in opening the minds of young people to values other than those inculcated during the Nazi regime. Above all, the German people came to see that the French, or at least some of the French, thought of them as individuals. Day-to-day association with French people and with the cultural achievements of France undoubtedly created a friendliness toward France which was not felt in the other zones toward their occupiers.[103]

CHAPTER IX

The Revival of German Political Life
1945-1947

THE administration of affairs in Germany, according to the Potsdam agreement of July 1945, should be directed "towards the
decentralization of the political structure [of Germany] and the development of local responsibility." Local self-government should be
restored, democratic political parties authorized, and, most important
of all, "representative and elective principles shall be introduced into
regional, provincial and state (Land) administration as rapidly as may
be justified by the successful application of those principles in local
self-government." Enforcement of this policy was left to the commander-in-chief in each zone.[1] With these principles, the French were
in wholehearted agreement.

The French entered Germany with no enthusiasm for handing over
the central government to Germans. Although they were determined
to take sanctions against war criminals and those principally associated
with the Nazi regime, they were not willing to make sharp distinctions
between good and bad Germans, since they felt that all were answer-
able in at least some degree for the Nazi period. Their policy with
regard to German political life was to be, in its own way, as re-educa-
tional as their education policy. Political power, they believed, should
be given to the Germans only in small doses; and the Germans would
have to prove that the last dose had been beneficial before they would
be given a further one. Hence, political life revived only sluggishly

in the French zone and was always several weeks or even several months behind the progress of the American zone.

The revival of German political life in the French zone went through several clearly marked stages, influenced on the one hand by the pressure of international events, and on the other hand by the growing French conviction of the success of their re-education policy.

First, between May 1945 and September 1946, German participation in government was restricted to local administration carried out by nominated officials chosen from the ranks of known opponents of the Nazi regime. Next, in September and October, 1946, elected bodies at the level of the Gemeinde and Kreis were given the administration of these local districts. In November 1946 Consultative Assemblies were chosen and given the dual function of drawing up constitutions for the Länder and of advising the nominated governments in matters of policy. The third stage, extending from May 1947 to September 1949, was marked by popular ratification of the Land constitutions and by the establishment of elected assemblies in each Land. These Land assemblies (Landtage), and the governments chosen by them, remained the highest form of elected government in the French zone until the summer of 1949. At that time, as the fourth stage, the German people were permitted to elect a parliament for the whole of West Germany.

LOCAL GOVERNMENT BY FRENCH NOMINATION

When the Allied armies moved into Germany from the west in 1945, their governments were faced with a vitally important policy decision, which could only be made by taking a position on the extent of German popular responsibility for the Nazi regime. The military government officers had to be told whether, in the opinion of their home governments, there was a group of Germans of such strong anti-Nazi determination that they could be entrusted with the government of Germany.

Several groups claimed to speak for the democratic forces in Germany. The political parties of the Left felt that they were the natural choice for the exercise of political power. The Communists showed themselves ready at once to take part in the herculean labors involved in denazification, and to take a major role in the administration. The Social Democrats, who were especially numerous in the northern triangle of the zone, made a strong claim to represent a "good" Germany. Saul Padover, attached to the propaganda warfare section of the American military government, noted as early as 1944 that the Social Democrats believed that they were the "sound core" in Germany. Georg Thesen, a Social Democrat from Trier who had spent three years in a concentration camp, told him, "The German people themselves . . . must undertake a thorough house-cleaning. . . . There are good people in Germany. Help the good people exterminate the evil." Padover himself gradually came to believe that the Social Democrats had done little that was practical to stop the progress of Hitler and that they were now weak, scattered, and middle-aged. Nevertheless, he felt they were "the best friends the Allies have in Germany, perhaps the only friends."[2] This point was supported by the action of the German Social Democrats who, in exile during the war years, had maintained the view that Germany should be "liberated."[3]

The churches, too, felt that they had a record of opposition which justified their being entrusted with influence in the new Germany. Men like Bishop Wurm and Archbishop Bornewasser had been subjected to strong Nazi pressures. But, as Hans Rothfels has pointed out, the churches were hampered in their opposition to Hitler by the fact that the Lutheran church had a long tradition of close church-state relationships and that the Catholic church had concluded a concordat with the National Socialists.[4] The Allies, although willing to make full use of church recommendations, were far from ready to use the churches in any more extensive way.

Finally, there was the most problematical group of all, the politically disillusioned. Many had come to lose their faith in the regime, either early or late; and the German opposition to Hitler was more widespread than the Allied governments seemed willing to believe. Even the attempt on Hitler's life on July 20, 1944, was played down by the Allies, so that when the military government officials looked around for reliable elements in the German population they sought out individuals rather than large groups.

Yet, in spite of the opposition that undoubtedly existed in Germany, the sanctions exercised by the Nazi regime—especially after the July 20 plot, when some five thousand were killed—reduced immensely the leadership of the opposition.[5] It also increased the average German's overwhelming sense of futility and apathy. The Allied armies found almost no overt opposition from the German population, but also little active support. The people as a whole were stunned. The German's natural discipline, combined with the overwhelming shock of total defeat and ruin, made him a pliant, passive object under the direction of the military government. Only exceptional individuals were found, or sought, to take over the immediate responsibilities of local government. In Stuttgart there was Oberbürgermeister Strölin, who had been entrusted with the task of contacting Rommel in the July 20 conspiracy, and who had dared to countermand Nazi orders for the destruction of the bridges and had made every effort to contact the approaching French in order to surrender the town. In Reutlingen, Oskar Kalbfell had ridden into town on the outside of a French tank as a guarantee that there would be no resistance from the townspeople. But such men were not numerous. The most proven opponents of the Nazi regime were either dead or ruined in health, and it was doubly difficult to find men who were not only long-time opponents of the Nazi regime but capable administrators as well. It was necessary in many cases to regard these men as a caretaker government, chosen to serve during the months while the progress of denazification and re-education sorted out the trustworthy from the politically dangerous among the younger and more active survivors of the war.

Against this background, the French military government began the creation of a functioning government in its zone of Germany. The geographical nature of the zone presented immediate problems of administration, which were complicated even further by the fact that the zone itself was not wholly the conquest of the French army. The northern section of the zone, with the exception of the small French bridgehead between Lauterbourg and Worms, was held by the American forces, and the first administrative machinery was set up there by the American military government. When the northern triangle was handed over to the French on July 9, 1945, certain sections of the zone, such as Trier, had been under American administration for almost six months. The French thus suffered the disadvantage that they seemed to arrive, like Louis XVIII, in the baggage trains of the Allies, or as de Gaulle had feared, "as a so-called conqueror who has not fought."[6]

The first task of the military government in reviving German political life was to create a workable administrative framework for the truncated provinces left to them by the zonal division. At the lowest level of the Gemeinde and Kreis, the administrative boundaries were left untouched. In each area, a nominated Bürgermeister was given the task of relaying to the German population the orders of the military government and of carrying out the various administrative tasks assigned to him. The method of appointment of these men was haphazard. A family doctor in Singen related that a French officer appeared suddenly at his door one evening and said, "You are the Bürgermeister." Strölin arranged with the French for his successor as Oberbürgermeister of Stuttgart. Kalbfell, who had ridden into town with the French tanks, became Oberbürgermeister of Reutlingen.

Above the level of the Landkreis, problems of reorganization were felt immediately. Only the Saar was an administrative unit in its own right. Every other section of the zone was a shorn-off section of a Land whose remaining area lay within the British or the American zones. To remedy this, the southern sections of Baden and of Württemberg were erected into Länder in their own right, the former being called Baden and the latter Württemberg-Hohenzollern, since the Prussian enclave of Hohenzollern was fused with the surrounding region of Württemberg. In the northern triangle, five administrative units were created: the Saar; Pfalz-Rheinhessen; Hessen-Nassau, consisting of the four Landkreise on the right bank of the Rhine which were part of the French zone; and Trier and Koblenz, the two Regierungsbezirke from the Prussian province of Rheinland.

The northern triangle of the zone was more varied than the southern in its economic, religious, and cultural make-up, and for that reason its political life displayed greater variety and conflict than did that of the predominantly conservative, agricultural south. From the earliest moments of the occupation, a sharp division was obvious between the Pfalz, with its strong Protestantism and its large industrial complex of Ludwigshafen, and the predominantly Catholic and agricultural Rheinland.

It was unfeasible, however, for these five units composing the northern triangle to remain separate entities. The economic difficulties of the zone were only compounded by the maintenance of such administrative complexities. The first simplification took place on January 2, 1946, when the two Regierungsbezirke of the Rheinland were united with Hessen-Nassau, to form the Oberregierungspräsidium of Rheinland–Hessen-Nassau, with its administration in Koblenz. This situation lasted only six months. On August 30, 1946, General Koenig announced that the whole of the northern triangle, with the exception of the Saar, would be united to form an entirely new Land, to be called Rheinland-Pfalz. Ordonnance No. 57 of the same day put this decision into force. The seat of the Land was to be moved to Mainz as soon as possible, although temporarily it would be at Koblenz. A Consultative Assembly for the whole Land was to be set up after the elections of September and October 1946, and a mixed committee from the Pfalz and the Rheinland was to prepare a draft constitution for the Land.[7]

The period of caretaker governments in the northern triangle thus falls into three parts: From May 1945 to December 1945, the area was divided into five administrative units (Saar; Pfalz-Rheinhessen; Hessen-Nassau, sometimes called Regierungsbezirk Montabaur; Regierungsbezirk Trier; and Regierungsbezirk Koblenz). From January 1946 to August 1946, the five were consolidated into three administrative units (Saar; Pfalz-Rheinhessen; Rheinland–Hessen-Nassau). Finally, after August 1946 these were made into two units (Saar; Rheinland-Pfalz).

The nature of these caretaker groups can be seen from the composition of the Oberpräsidium of Rheinland–Hessen-Nassau, which was installed in office in Koblenz on January 2, 1946. At its head was Wilhelm Boden, who had studied law and political science at the Universities of Bonn and Berlin and had been a member of the Center party and a local administrator until 1933. During the Nazi regime he had been a counselor to the Archbishop of Cologne and a representative of a Berlin insurance company. His opinions made him a welcome ally of the French military government. A strong Catholic and known anti-Nazi, he believed in the need for federalism in Germany and in the value of cooperation with the French military government. Boden's government consisted of four Christian Democrats, two Socialists, one Communist, and one independent. None had been a member of the Nazi party. Johann Dötsch, director of work and social insurance, had spent six years in a concentration camp and was so weakened that he died in October 1946. Dr. Kurt Haupt, director of justice, aged sixty-four, was one of the older generation who had been politically active before 1933. He had already been a counselor of the Land

court in 1922, and a Center party member, and had only stepped in to
tide the government over the initial period of the occupation. Similarly, Dr. Gerhard Lichter, aged fifty-five, director of food and agriculture, and Heinrich Hupper, director of finances, aged fifty-nine,
were Catholics who had been dismissed from their posts in 1933 and
reinstated by the British and American forces respectively. On the
other hand, Willy Gräfe, the Communist member of the government,
was only forty-five, and a militant member of the party. He had
fought in the Spanish Civil War and had been active in clandestine
activities against the Nazis. Gräfe, the director of public works and
reconstruction, was regarded by the French as a man who would push
denazification rapidly and effectively.[8]

The period of caretaker government ended in August 1946 with
the formation of a cabinet for the whole Land. The officials nominated
by the French for service in this cabinet were career politicians of a
new type, and the majority of them have remained in political life in
the West German Republic. Of the former cabinet of Rheinland–
Hessen-Nassau, only Wilhelm Boden remained. The new cabinet, as
remodeled after the elections of autumn 1946, was as follows:

President: Dr. Wilhelm Boden (CDU, Rheinland)
Justice: Dr. Adolf Süsterhenn (CDU, Rheinland)
Education and Public Worship: Dr. Ernst-Albert Lotz (CDU,
    Rheinhessen)
Food and Agriculture: Oskar Stübinger (CDU, Pfalz)
Social Security: Hans Junglas (CDU, Rheinland)
Economy and Finances: Dr. Hans Haberer (CDU, Pfalz)
Interior: Jakob Steffan (SPD, Hessen)
Work: Paul Rohle (SPD, Rheinland)
Reconstruction and Communications: Willy Feller (KPD, Pfalz)

This cabinet was to carry on the work of government, as a nominated instrument of the French military government, until the adoption of the constitution of the Land and the election of a Landtag in
May 1947. The men coming to the fore in this period of nominated
governments were later to take over political power as elected representatives of the German people; it speaks well for the political wisdom of the military government that such men were entrusted with
power so early.

Many who were to grow in stature gained their experience and reputation during the early days of the occupation. Among the Christian Democrats was Boden himself, who nevertheless failed to gain the support of parties other than the Christian Democrats after the election of May 1947, and who moved into administrative work as head of the Land bank in Mainz. In 1946 the head of the Regierungspräsidium of Montabaur was Peter Altmeier, who replaced Boden as minister-president in July 1947 and has held that position since. Also coming into prominence, especially through his cogent articles in papers of federalist inclinations such as the *Rheinischer Merkur*, was Dr. Adolf Süsterhenn, a lawyer and former Center party member who in 1946 became minister of justice and culture for Rheinland-Pfalz and one of the main drafters of the constitution of Rheinland-Pfalz. Dr. Süsterhenn was to move on later to take a share in the writing of the constitution of the West German Republic; he became a member of the Bundesrat in 1949–51 and later served as president of the constitutional court of Rheinland-Pfalz. The most prominent Socialists were from the Pfalz. Franz Bögler, who had been forced to flee in 1933 at the age of twenty-one as a result of his anti-Nazi activities and had spent the war years in exile or captivity, became Stadtrat of Speyer in 1946. He came into further prominence as first vice-president of the Consultative Assembly of November 1946, head of the Socialist party in the Pfalz from April 1947, and Oberregierungspräsident of the Pfalz in July 1947. Bögler was a man of fiery character and uncompromising honesty who, through occasional goads to the French administration, guaranteed that the German administration would not be regarded as a mouthpiece of the military government. The Democratic party's most prominent member, Fritz Neumayer, after serving as president of the Land court in 1945–46 and as minister of the economy and communications in 1947–48, was to become a member of the first Bundestag and federal minister of housing and justice from 1952 to 1956.

A similar development took place in the southern section of the zone. Here, for various reasons, the task of the military government was easier. The two sections of Baden and Württemberg, although separated from their traditional administrative capitals of Karlsruhe and Stuttgart, still felt a sense of their individual identities. Even with the addition to South Württemberg of the small enclave of Hohenzollern and the Bavarian Landkreis of Lindau, there was little sense of the antagonism that remained between the Pfalz and the Rheinland. Moreover, these areas were traditionally antagonistic toward the influence of Prussia and were still influenced by contacts with the French. Finally, the agricultural, conservative complexion of the region gave it an immediate sympathy for the decentralization the French intended to introduce. On the first anniversary of the French invasion, the *Badener Tagblatt* observed somewhat wryly that although it was disappointing to find that the end of the war did not bring the immediate start of peacetime relations, at least it was a slight consolation to "be occupied by a power which shares our own cultural background."[9]

The predominant figure in Baden was Dr. Leo Wohleb, a Christian Democrat of pronounced federalist leanings. Dr. Wohleb was born in Freiburg and had been a Gymnasium professor of classics between 1920 and 1930. During the Nazi period he had been principal of the Baden-Baden Gymnasium. With the establishment of the French occupation, he became an official of the education ministry and then chairman of the Christian Democratic party. Wohleb was nominated as head of the State Secretariat in Baden in 1946; in 1947 he was elected state president. His passionate insistence that Baden should not be united to Württemberg was later to win him much animosity, but he retained the support of his own party in south Baden and was able to delay the formation of the South-West state (Baden-Württemberg) until 1952. Friedrich Maier, president of the Socialist party in Baden, was a former schoolteacher who re-entered politics as a member of the advisory councils of the Gemeinde of Gengenbach and the Kreis of Offenburg. He took part in all the elected assemblies in Baden, acted as the Baden representative to the Parliamentary Council in Bonn, and became a member of the Bundestag in 1949. Wohleb's coalition government was remodeled in November 1946; the State Secretariat was composed as follows:

President, Education and Public Worship: Dr. Leo Wohleb (CDU)
Justice: (interim) Dr. Leo Wohleb
Interior and Work: Dr. Marcell Nordmann (SPD)
Agriculture: Anton Hilbert (CDU)
Economy: Dr. Friedrich Leibbrandt (SPD)

Finances: Dr. Paul Wäldin (DPD)
State Commissioner for Denazification: Streng (CDU)
State Commissioner for Food: Anton Dichtel (CDU)
State Commissioner for Reconstruction: Erwin Eckert (KPD)

In Württemberg, the natural candidate for political power was Dr. Carlo Schmid. Son of a French mother and German father, himself born in France and speaking French as well as any occupation officer, Dr. Schmid was a translator of Baudelaire and a professor of law. He was at once appointed president of the State Secretariat of Württemberg. Around him he gathered a group of associates of all parties, who took it upon themselves to safeguard the interests of Württemberg, at the same time collaborating as fully as possible with the French. This government demanded that the French lay down from the beginning what its legal status was, and this was done in a provisional constitution granted in the early months of the occupation.[10] Working with Schmid at this time were Dr. Paul Binder, a Christian Democrat who became minister of finances; Dr. Theodor Eschenburg, a world-famous professor of political science and law at the University of Tübingen, who became commissioner for displaced persons; Viktor Renner, a Socialist from Tübingen who became minister of the interior; and Eberhard Wildermuth, a Democrat who took over the ministry of the economy. This group of friends, who were all men of considerable intellectual eminence, was to remain a strong force in German political life. The State Secretariat of Württemberg was composed as follows:

President and Justice: Dr. Carlo Schmid (SPD)
Interior: Viktor Renner (SPD)
Education and Public Worship: Dr. Albert Sauer (CDU)
Finances: Dr. Paul Binder (CDU)
Work: Clemens Moser (CDU)
Economy: Eberhard Wildermuth (DPD)
Agriculture: Dr. Frank Weiss (CDU)
State Commissioner for Political Cleansing: Otto Künzel (SPD)

The problems facing the nominated governments were outlined by Carlo Schmid on November 22, 1946, when he set out to give the newly chosen Consultative Assembly an account of his stewardship. The German government had been constrained to start from nothing, he said. The administrative machinery of Württemberg, and its personnel, had all remained in Stuttgart. Only the Gemeinde and the Kreis still existed as functioning administrative units. It took three months to create the present six divisions of government—justice, interior, culture, finances, economy, and work. Denazification had been carried out and schools opened. Close relations had been maintained with north Württemberg in the American zone. He closed with a very revealing insight into the problems facing a nominated government. "Just as before," he said, "the government remains responsible solely to the military government, and just as before it has to accept its ordonnances and have its own measures approved by the military government. Many of the measures which go out into the Land under our signature are not the fruit of our own decisions; much would have been different if we alone had been responsible. . . . [When our objections were not accepted by the military government,] we have carried out the orders in spite of our misgivings, because we are convinced that in relation to the circumstances in which we live, it must be done in this way for the well-being of the Land."[11]

It can be seen that the period of nominated governments was far from being, as some critics have claimed, a period of puppet governments. The French chose wisely in the majority of their important nominations, balancing the needs of Germany itself against the desire of the military government for cooperative administrators from among the Germans. It is significant for the long-term success of the occupation that the French found it possible from the very beginning to appoint qualified, reliable politicians and administrators who could work with the occupation regime and at the same time win the confidence of their own countrymen.

POLITICAL PARTIES AND LOCAL ELECTIONS

The French believed that German political life must grow naturally from strictly localized organizations. On September 15, 1945, they permitted the nominated Bürgermeister to appoint advisory committees for the Gemeinde and the Kreis, so that he would be aided by groups of supposedly representative background. Two days later, permission was given for trade-unions to be formed. Any group of workers that wished to form a trade-union was to present itself at the local town hall, where preliminary permission was given. The group was then to draw up a list of members and a constitution for further approval. Three months later, similar permission was given for the formation of political parties. In no case, however, was it foreseen that a group could extend its competence beyond its own Land, and the effect was to atomize both the labor and political movements. Although the trade-union movements numbered some 124,000 members by January 1946, they belonged to 163 separate groups. In April 1946, the political parties, in spite of their allegiance to several national organizations, were registered as 1,052 separate groups.[12]

From the start, the French military government acted strongly to prevent the formation of any ties beyond the Land. The ordonnance of December 13, 1945, had stated that permission would be refused for any party to form a unit larger than one Land. When the New Germany party attempted to form a union of all anti-Fascists in the French zone, irrespective of which party they belonged to, the military government refused to license it. There was to be nothing comparable to the central committees in either the British or the Russian zones. Repeatedly, the French intervened to prevent the beginning of interzonal contacts. For example, they refused to allow two members of the Communist-dominated Socialist Unity party to come from Berlin to attend a Communist meeting in Ludwigshafen on March 11–12, 1947; nor would they allow Dr. Schumacher, the head of the Socialist party in the British zone, to address a Socialist meeting in Speyer in April 1947. Moreover, when the minister-presidents from the whole of Germany met in Munich in June 1947, the minister-presidents of the French zone found themselves in the embarrassing position of having to say that they were not permitted to discuss the possible unification of Germany.[13]

The political life of the French zone had to conform very strictly to the plans the French laid down for it. Above all, the French intended to use to the full the federalist, and even the separatist, sentiments which had been stronger in the past in the Rheinland, Baden, and Württemberg than anywhere else in Germany with the exception of Bavaria. The party that seemed in most ways acceptable to the French was the Christian Democratic Union, which, with the Communist and Socialist parties, was authorized in the Rheinland in January 1946, in Baden and the Pfalz in February, and in Württemberg in March.

The Christian Democratic Union, although inheriting much from the old Catholic Center party, was a new political creation, which attempted to unite all Christian parties. It found support from the Catholic clergy throughout the zone, but only in Württemberg was full understanding with the Protestants reached and a compromise program agreed upon. In general, the party aimed at furthering the interests of the Christian churches, especially in the matters of education, social conservatism, and the federalization of Germany.[14] Its religious bias and its emphasis on avoiding excessive centralization made the party seem more trustworthy in the eyes of some military government officers than its major rival, the Socialist party; the French military government was thus often accused of unduly favoring the Christian Democrats. Since, however, the French military government was also accused by some Germans of being radically Socialist at one time and of being separatist at another, one must assume that at the very least no partiality was shown as a matter of policy.* Local partiality was a matter of course throughout Germany.[15]

The Socialists, in spite of French pressure, looked to Hanover for their leadership. The personal dominance of Dr. Schumacher was very strong, and it increased greatly as it became obvious after 1947 that the unification of western Germany was only a matter of time. The Socialists aimed at the union of the working class and middle class in a program of social reform, which would include socialization of the sources of power and of key industries such as metal, chemicals, and transport, land reform, and equalization of the burden of reparations.

---

* The four principal parties in the French zone bore a confusing variety of names during the early years of the occupation. (1) The Christian-Democrat Union was known as the Christian-Democratic Party in Rheinland–Hessen-Nassau, as the Christian Democratic Union in Pfalz-Rheinhessen and in Württemberg, and as the Baden Christian Socialist Popular Party (Badische Christlich-Soziale Volkspartei, or BCSV) in Baden. The BCSV changed its name to Christian Democratic Union Baden on November 25–26, 1947. (2) The Socialist party was known as either the Social Democratic Party (Sozialdemokratische Partei or SP) or as the Social Democratic Party of Germany (Sozialdemokratische Partei Deutschlands or SPD). (3) The Communist party was similarly known as either the Communist Party or the Communist Party of Germany (Kommunistische Partei or KP and Kommunistische Partei Deutschlands or KPD). (4) The Democratic party was known in Rheinland–Hessen-Nassau as the Liberal Democratic Party (Liberal-Demokratische Partei or LDP) and in Pfalz-Rheinhessen as the Popular Social Union of Hessen and Pfalz (Sozialer Volksbund Hessen-Pfalz or SVHP). These two parties united in 1947 to form the Democratic Party of Rheinland-Pfalz. The Democratic party in Württemberg was known as the Democratic Popular Party (Demokratische Volkspartei or DVP), and in Baden as the Democratic Popular Party South and Middle Baden (Demokratische Volkspartei Süd- und Mittelbaden). For convenience, the local names of these parties will be used only when local characteristics of the parties are referred to. Otherwise, the national name of the party will be used, i.e., Christian Democratic Union (CDU), Social Democratic Party of Germany (SPD), Communist Party of Germany (KPD), and Democratic Party of Germany (DPD).

Only in the Pfalz, however, did the Socialist party have a majority, and, as a result, in Rheinland-Pfalz it fought its most bitter battles with the dominant Christian Democratic party. The Socialists found themselves in an ironical position after the formation of Rheinland-Pfalz had swamped the Socialists of the Pfalz with the Christian Democrats of the Rheinland. From that point on, the strongly centralist Socialists were forced to demand local autonomy for the Pfalz in order to preserve their control over the one area where they were in a majority.[16]

There can be no doubt that certain groups within the French military government in the Pfalz hoped to encourage a separatist movement there similar to the one in the Saar. Several of the officers of the French military government had taken part in the occupation of the Pfalz following the First World War and had actively furthered a separatist movement there. In the 1920's this movement had led to considerable bloodshed, culminating in the rioting in Pirmasens in 1933. Moreover, the first nominated officials in the Pfalz were known separatists, who had already worked toward this goal in the 1920's. The Pfalz was therefore in the curious political position of witnessing first a struggle between the Socialists and the separatists, and later between the Socialists and the Christian Democrats.[17]

The Communists were never able to win much support in a zone that was predominantly rural and Catholic. The interests of the population, especially in Baden and Württemberg, were too sharply opposed to the Communist party's aim of national unification, agrarian reform, and separation of church and state. The party was further weakened by the refusal of the Socialist party to join it in a unity party similar to that of the Russian zone and by its ties with the Soviet Union. However, in certain localities like the industrial agglomerations of Ludwigshafen, Reutlingen, Pirmasens, and Friedrichshafen, the Communist party found loyal support.[18]

The Democratic party set as its aim the furthering of the interests of the middle class. Individual liberties were to be guaranteed, church and state were to be separated, and above all, state control of industry was to be avoided. While the party's voting strength was rarely above the Communist party's, it was often able to hold the balance between the Socialists and the Christian Democrats; and in Rheinland-Pfalz and Württemberg, it later joined in the governmental coalitions.[19]

But in 1946 the development of political parties struck several major obstacles. The first and most important fact was that the parties were mere exercises in democracy, since they possessed no power at all. As Carlo Schmid pointed out, they could not even mold public opinion and thereby influence government policy "for the good reason that the occupying powers have a legitimate interest in this matter, in order to preserve their security and to create a more favorable climate of opinion before freeing our press." But Schmid went on to say that no real public opinion existed because the Germans themselves were no longer taking an interest in politics. "The predominant feelings . . . of our people are lethargy, a sense of loss of unbelievable proportions, and corresponding worry for a bit of bread and a bed for the morrow. . . . And so there can be no such thing as public opinion in Germany at this time."[20]

This theme was repeatedly echoed. In Germany in 1945 there could be no facile shift from the shock of Nazi rule and the disillusionment of the total defeat to the lively day-to-day jockeying of a long-established democracy. Ralph Jennet, in a leading article in the *Badener Tagblatt* of March 23, 1946, entitled "Quo vadis, Germania," cited a letter he had received in order to show the political lethargy of the population. "We all have very little hope," the correspondent had written, "that things can get better again. We don't believe in parties who are again promising every possible thing. . . . One can scarcely open a newspaper without reading wearying party talk."[21]

What many Germans were wrestling with, however, was the problem of their own responsibility for the excesses of the Nazi regime. For this reason, many of the political speeches in the zone at this time were concerned with the relationship between freedom and responsibility. Adolf Ludwig, former Bürgermeister of Pirmasens, speaking to a crowded Socialist meeting in Neustadt in the Pfalz, was enthusiastically supported when he stated that Hitler was brought to power by the politically indifferent.[22] In an article in the *Schwäbisches Tagblatt* in December 1945, Dr. Dieter Roser spoke out more harshly: "We Germans showed ourselves unready for freedom because we were not fit for it. Freedom means two things—freedom from external restraints but also freedom of thought within ourselves. This is what we Germans were afraid of."[23]

The French military government decided to permit elections in the localities in the autumn of 1946. By Ordonnances 50–54 of August 5, 1946, elections in the Gemeinden were permitted; by these elections, an assembly would be created in each Gemeinde to replace the consultative committees which had been nominated in January of that year. An important French innovation in this law was the rule that the Bürgermeister and his assistants would be chosen from these assemblies, or would be installed in office by them if, as in the case of Württemberg, they had already been chosen by universal suffrage. During the Nazi period, the Bürgermeister had been a closely supervised agent of the party, though not always a direct nominee, whereas before 1933, the method of choosing a Bürgermeister had varied between direct election by the voters and choice by the council. The adoption by the French of this form of election of the Bürgermeister was not well received by the Germans, for it seemed to attack the principle of a professional executive. The system has been considerably modified since the end of the occupation.[24]

Local elections had already taken place in the American zone on January 20 and 27, 1946, and so the French had a precedent to follow. They made minute preparations for the success of the elections. In May 1946 preliminary electoral lists were drawn up by a committee presided over by the Bürgermeister and including members of the political parties, the consultative committees, and the denazification committees. An appeal committee was to be set up in each Kreis, to deal with appeals from those disqualified from voting because of their past political records.[25] The French noted with some pride that "one should emphasize here the very remarkable nature of our legislation and its superiority to solutions employed elsewhere. . . . In this manner, France showed the respect for the individual case which is the true spirit of justice."[26] In August still more detailed instructions were given on the method of running the elections, specifying even the color of the envelopes to be used.

On September 2, 1946, the military government announced that the Gemeinde elections were to be followed within a month by elections at the next highest administrative level, in the Landkreis and Stadtkreis. The average Kreis had a population of some 80,000 to 100,000. These assemblies were to be given supervision over such matters of local administration as local roads and railways, hospitals, public works, and administration of the Kreis budget.

The two elections were made the occasion for a full-scale political

TABLE 12

Gemeinde and Kreis Elections in the French Zone[27]
(Gemeinde: September 15 and 29, 1946)
(Kreis: October 13, 1946)

	Rheinland–Hessen-Nassau		Pfalz–Rheinhessen		Baden		Württemberg	
	Gemeinde	Kreis	Gemeinde	Kreis	Gemeinde	Kreis	Gemeinde	Kreis
Per cent voting..	86.4	79.5	86.41	79.3	83.7	67.3	86.6	68.6
CDU	49.9	65.6	40.5	42.2	53.5	60.4	39.1	63.3
SPD	17.4	25.9	31.8	35.5	13.9	17.6	13.7	19.9
KPD	3.8	5.2	8.5	1.1	5.9	7.7	4.8	6.5
DPD (or LPD)..		3.3	2.1	1.5	14.8	14.4	5.4	10.3
Independents ...	28.9		15.9		8.3		29.6	

campaign in the zone. The political parties seized upon the opportunity to present their programs, and the interest of the electorate was shown in the large turnout at the polls. The election results (see Table 12) gave a decided majority throughout the zone to the Christian Democratic party, although in the Kreis elections in October the Socialists showed considerable gain in strength.

THE LAND CONSTITUTIONS, NOVEMBER 1946–MAY 1947

Five days before the Kreis elections, the French military government had made it clear that they intended the Gemeinde and Kreis elections to have a wider significance than the mere election of local assemblies of limited powers. Ordonnances Nos. 65–75 of October 8, 1946, ordered the creation of Consultative Assemblies for each of the three Länder. The duties of these assemblies would be to advise the nominated governments until the creation of an elected government in each Land, and to draw up a constitution which would be put before the people of each Land in a popular referendum. The method of choosing these assemblies was by a complicated use of electoral colleges, as Table 13 indicates. The assemblies were to be elected on November 17, 1946, by two electoral colleges, the first containing all members of the Kreis assemblies, the second all members of the Ge-

TABLE 13

METHOD OF ELECTION OF CONSULTATIVE ASSEMBLIES IN THE FRENCH ZONE[28]
(November 1946)

	Baden	Württemberg	Rheinland-Pfalz*
Deputies elected by Kreis assemblies	40	38	88
Deputies elected by assemblies of towns over 7,000 population	21	27	39
Total members	61	65	127

* In Rheinland-Pfalz, the choice was made by four electoral colleges, two each in Rheinland–Hessen-Nassau and Pfalz-Rheinhessen, respectively.

meinde assemblies of towns of more than seven thousand inhabitants. In this way, it was hoped to attain a balance between the rural areas, which were favored in the Kreis assemblies, and the larger towns.

This indirect method of election prevented the choice of the Consultative Assemblies from becoming the source of yet another electoral battle, since the membership of the electoral colleges was laid down by the election results of September and October 1946. As a result of the voting in the electoral colleges on November 17, 1946, the representation shown in Table 14 was gained by the different political parties.

With the choice of these Consultative Assemblies, an entirely new situation came to prevail in German political life. Although the governments of the Länder were still nominated by, and owed responsibility to, the French military government, they were in fact remodeled

TABLE 14

PARTY MEMBERSHIP IN THE CONSULTATIVE ASSEMBLIES OF THE FRENCH ZONE[29]
(November 17, 1946)

	CDU	SPD	KPD	DPD	Soziale Volksbund
Rheinland-Pfalz	70	41	9	2	5
Baden	37	11	44	9	
Württemberg	40	14	4	7	

to harmonize with the political strength of the parties as expressed in the elections. Moreover, it quickly became the custom for the Land governments to inform the assembly of its policy and to invite debate on its actions. One of Carlo Schmid's first actions, for example, was to give the Württemberg assembly a full report of the policy of his government from the end of the war on.[30] On December 4, 1946, General Koenig called the three heads of the Land governments, Drs. Boden, Wohleb, and Schmid, to Baden-Baden and announced that their governments were authorized to make ordonnances which would have the force of law; the only stipulation was that they must respect the decisions of the Control Council and must not take any decision which would be "contrary to the ordonnances and decisions of the French general Commander-in-Chief in Germany or of the Administrator General or in a more general way to the policy of the French government in the occupied zone."[31] However restricted this right may have been, the German governments were nevertheless being given the power of making laws, and this step was a major move toward self-government.

Perhaps most important of all, however, was the task given to the assemblies of writing the constitutions for their own Länder. The assemblies used this opportunity for a far-reaching debate on constitutional principles which foreshadowed in many particulars the debates on the writing of the Basic Law of the West German Republic two years later.[32] The constitutional debate brought political interest in the Länder to a high pitch, and the interest which in more normal times would have been stimulated by debates on foreign policy and the like was transferred to the more esoteric realms of the nature of natural law and the origin of natural rights.

In Rheinland-Pfalz the constitutional battle was already well under way when the Consultative Assembly met in November 1946. The ordonnance of August 30, 1946, creating the Land of Rheinland-Pfalz, had also provided that a committee composed of members of the governments of Rheinland–Hessen-Nassau and Pfalz-Rheinhessen should be given the job of preparing a constitutional draft, to expedite the work of the assembly that would meet in November. A constitutional committee was set up in September under the direction of Dr. Adolf Süsterhenn, a qualified jurist and convinced federalist.

Dr. Süsterhenn made no bones about presenting his opinions with the greatest possible force. In a series of articles in the *Rheinischer Merkur* in the autumn of 1946, he gave a very persuasive statement of his views. His opening article, "The First and Highest Task," provided an eloquent description of the significance of a constitution to a country. The writing of a constitution was not going to be treated as a task ordered by the occupying powers which must be done as quickly and as sullenly as possible, he wrote. Germany must realize that writing a Land constitution was the means of founding a new society. This society, he continued in his next article on "The Basic Rights," has certain natural rights which must be at the basis of any constitution. Tracing the history of the conception of natural rights from early Christianity, the English Independents, the American and French revolutions, and the Frankfurt parliament, he noted that these rights exist independent of, and not because of, the state. At this point, Süsterhenn struck a basic point of disagreement which was to be aired at greater length in the discussions over the Basic Law of the West German Republic. The theorists of the Christian Democratic party tended to base their thinking on the Catholic idea of natural law, whereas the Socialists, although not opposed to the idea of basic rights, preferred the view that the state was the guarantor of rights.

The constitution, as Dr. Süsterhenn envisaged it, would be based upon the separation of powers into a two-chamber system, with the second chamber representing the natural units of society, such as the family, the municipality, and the workers. There would be not only a minister-president at the head of the cabinet but also a state president. The right of parents to choose the schooling for their children would be protected by the provision of confessional schools run by the churches, as well as the "simultaneous schools" or interdenominational schools desired by the Socialists.[33]

These views were embodied in the constitutional draft drawn up by Süsterhenn's committee. There was to be a head of state separate from the president of the cabinet; two chambers, one of which would represent local collectivities and religious and cultural organizations; a supreme court; a financial council and an economic council; and provision for popular initiative. But perhaps most irritating of all to German national feeling, the strong federalism of Dr. Süsterhenn and his associates in the Christian Democratic party was seen in the fact that nowhere was there any mention of a German republic.[34]

There was an immediate wave of annoyance when these views were made known, not only in Rheinland-Pfalz but even in the British and Russian zones as well. Nationalists felt wounded at the disparagement of Germany. Critics said that the draft had ten articles more than the "celebrated constitution of Weimar." When the Consultative Assembly met in November, it decided to set up a constitutional committee to consider the draft and named fifteen members (eight Christian Democrats, five Socialists, one Communist, and one Democrat) to produce a draft constitution.

In January 1947 the committee announced that the draft had gone too far in leaving out all mention of a German republic; and the members agreed that the preamble must point out the affinity of all the Länder of Germany and that the Land of Rheinland-Pfalz was at least a "member" of Germany. When the preamble was finally written, it contained only the mildest reference to the idea of Germany, stating that the aim was to "form a new democratic Germany as a full member of the community of peoples."[35] Among other ideas discarded were the state presidency, the second chamber, and the supreme court, which was replaced by a constitutional court. The greatest arguments, however, came over the school question. The Socialists demanded categorically that they be interdenominational, simultaneous schools, but the Christian Democrats remained adamant on the need for separate confessional schools for each religion.

The debate was finally carried to the Consultative Assembly itself on April 15, 1947. The Christian Democrats, who had for the most part been able to impose their views, approved the draft but suggested that the question of confessional or simultaneous schools should be submitted in a separate referendum. The Socialists rejected the constitution completely. They objected to the very creation of Rheinland-Pfalz, claiming that as a unit it was too small for reconstruction needs. They demanded simultaneous schools and immediate nationalization of certain basic industries. Finally, on a clear party vote, the Christian Democrats voted through the adoption of a special referendum on the school question. The third reading on April 25 was followed by the adoption of the constitution by the assembly by the disquieting vote of 70-31 with 26 abstentions, the Socialists and Communists voting against the draft and the Democrats and Christian Democrats voting for it.

The result of this vote was an election campaign of great virulence, since the Socialists now found themselves opposed not only to the major party in the Land but also to the very form of government which that party wished to adopt. It augured badly for the democratic future of the new state that the two parties of the Left felt themselves aggrieved by the constitution within which they would be expected to work. The Christian Democrats and many moderates at once reproached the Socialists for their obstructionist attitude and set out to argue their way to success.[36] Dr. Süsterhenn approached the school question in a leading article in the *Neuer Mainzer Anzeiger,* in which he once more stated that natural rights exist prior to the state, that one natural right is the right to avoid violation of conscience, and that therefore parents must have the right to send their children to the school of their choice.[37] Replying to him on April 25, Rector J. Rudolf hinted that Süsterhenn was behind the times, that, at the present time, the confessional school was not the best form of education. In any case, he added, somewhat wryly, education is passing out of the hands of the parents.[38] On the day before the election, Dr. Boden, the minister-president, made a last attempt at persuasion. The interest in the election was obviously and encouragingly very great, he said, especially since the political parties in the last meeting of the Consultative Assembly placed the issues at stake "on the last, most basic questions of principles and aims." The constitution, he said, was based on natural law and derived from the basic units of the family and the municipality. Finally, Dr. Boden noted, in a way that must have been somewhat disturbing to Left-Wing readers, the constitution had been approved by the bishops of Cologne, Trier, Mainz, Speyer, and Limburg, that is, by every bishop whose jurisdiction extended over Rheinland-Pfalz.[39]

The final election results were extremely close. Although both the constitution and the confessional school referendum were passed, they received only the barest margin of consent. Of those voting, 53 per cent voted for acceptance of the constitution and 47 per cent against. Worst of all, both the constitution and the school referendum were rejected by clear margins in the Socialist-dominated Pfalz and in Rheinhessen. The Landtag election gave the Christian Democrats a firm majority, although considerably less than that they had enjoyed in the Kreis elections of October 1946 (see Table 15).

TABLE 15

LANDTAG ELECTION, RHEINLAND-PFALZ[40]
(May 18, 1947)

Party	Number of Members in Landtag	Percentage of Vote in Land Election May 18, 1947	Percentage of Vote in Kreis Election October 13, 1946
CDU	47	47	54.4
SPD	34	34.5	30.5
KPD	8	8.7	7.5
DPD	11	9.8	7.5

The election results led to even more embittered party strife. Although many felt that one good sign in the campaign had been the end of the apathy and resignation which had been obvious for months, the corollary was less satisfactory. The *Rheinischer Merkur* expressed its fears on May 24, 1947. The turnout for voting was 10 per cent higher in Rheinland-Pfalz than in Baden and Württemberg, the paper noted, but in the latter two Länder the constitution had been adopted by over two-thirds of those voting. In Rheinland-Pfalz, however, Trier and Koblenz had accepted the constitution with strong majorities and Rheinhessen and the Pfalz had rejected it. The blame for this, it concluded rather unjustly, must lie only in the "senselessness of the [Socialist] leadership and in the blind docility of the electors, whom the Social Democratic party of Rheinland-Pfalz (unlike that of both other Länder of this zone) has led into a pointless 'No.' "[41] With such emotions at play, the political future of the Land looked stormy.

In Baden, the Christian Democrats possessed an absolute majority in the Consultative Assembly. At any point, they could force through their own views against the wishes of all other parties. That in the end they did not do so, but compromised on certain key issues, speaks well for their statesmanship.

From the very beginning of the debate, the separatism of Baden was a major issue. The first storm blew up over Otto Feger's book, *Swabian-Allemanian Democracy*, published in Konstanz in 1946, which stated outright the demands of the extreme upholders of separatist views. The problem was compounded by the fact that the American military government had united both north Baden and north Württemberg into the one Land of Württemberg-Baden, so that the reunion of north and south Baden was endangered. Great annoyance was expressed in south Baden when the president of the Consultative Assembly of Württemberg-Baden wrote to Minister-President Wohleb, looking to the future reunion of north and south Baden and suggesting at the same time union with Württemberg. This issue, however, was to remain largely dormant during the constitutional campaign, except where it was raised to justify the adoption of a constitution which would be similar to that of Württemberg-Baden in order to ease the future union with that Land.[42]

The draft constitution for Baden was worked out by the Provisional Government and was ready by March 1947. It was in many ways similar to that of Württemberg-Baden. When brought before the committee of the assembly, the Christian Democrats demanded several amendments, including provisions for setting up a second house to be called a *Ständerat* or Diet and for naming the schools "Christian Community schools" instead of "simultaneous schools." Socialist demands for planned economy, socialization, and agrarian reform were rejected by an alliance of the Christian Democrats and the Democrats.

Debate in the assembly itself opened on April 10, 1947. The leading Communist spokesman, Erwin Eckert, demanded that the state be called South Baden, to prepare the way for future unification, and objected to the religious phrases in the preamble. On April 14 the Communists raised further objections to the setting up of a supreme court to decide on the constitutionality of laws, and demanded that judges be elected. Little attention was paid to these demands. The Socialists joined with the Democrats and Communists to demand the rejection of the second house, but the Christian Democrats voted it through. When the Socialists demanded nationalization of certain key industries, or at least a popular referendum on this question, they were again refused.[43]

The Christian Democrats were the sole supporters of the draft in the first vote, and it passed by only 35 to 22. They thereupon compromised with the Socialists, giving up their desire for a second house and accepting the name "simultaneous school," and when the second ballot was taken on April 21, 1947, the Christian Democrats and Democrats voted for the constitution, carrying it this time by 40 to 12.

In the election campaign the Socialists and the Communists both attacked the constitution, claiming that it was a capitalist document. In rural Baden this opposition was of little effect, and in the vote on May 18 the constitution was accepted by a comfortable 67.9 per cent of those voting.[44] Table 16 gives comparative figures for the several parties in this election and the Kreis election of the previous autumn.

TABLE 16

LANDTAG ELECTION, BADEN[45]

(May 18, 1947)

Party	Number of Members in Landtag	Percentage of Vote in Land Election, May 18, 1947	Percentage of Vote in Kreis Election, October 13, 1946
CDU (BCSV) ..	34	55.94	60.38
SPD	13	22.40	17.58
KPD	4	7.41	7.66
DPD	9	14.25	14.38

The early constitutional debates in Württemberg also hinged upon the attitude to be adopted to the constitution of Württemberg-Baden in the American zone. What made the issue more poignant in this case, however, was that the constitution of Württemberg-Baden had been drafted in large part by the president of the State Secretariat of Württemberg-Hohenzollern, Professor Carlo Schmid. He and his Socialist colleagues could be expected to look with some partiality upon the adoption of that constitution in his own Land. A special cogency was added to the argument from the Socialist point of view by their desire to avoid the fragmentation of Germany and especially that of Württemberg.[46]

The *Schwäbisches Tagblatt,* which was to take a large part in this campaign, demanded in November 1946 that Württemberg accept the constitution of Württemberg-Baden as it stood so that the reunification of Württemberg would be facilitated.[47] Carlo Schmid himself, speaking at the second meeting of the Consultative Assembly on December 2, spoke at length on the nature of constitutions and hinted that it would be wise to adopt the constitution of Württemberg-Baden.[48] The next day, however, the Christian Democrats, who were the majority party in the Assembly, gave notice that they had no intention of going along with this pressure. Lorenz Bock, speaking as leader of the party, stated once more the views which had roused so much dispute in Rheinland-Pfalz. The rights of the Land against the state must be protected, he said. His party demanded a head of state separate from the minister-president, a second chamber, and confessional schools. In spite of the demand of the three other parties that the constitution of Württemberg-Baden be taken as the basis for discussion, the Christian Democrats forced the setting up of a committee of eighteen members which asked Bock himself to supervise the drafting of a constitution.[49]

There the matter rested. By the end of January 1947 nothing seemed to have been done, and the Socialists again demanded the acceptance of the Württemberg-Baden constitution and the dismissal of the committee. In March 1947 the *Schwäbisches Tagblatt* asked the various parties to state their positions on the various constitutional questions then being debated. What were the attitudes of the parties, the paper asked, to bicameralism, the relations of church and state, the position of state president, and the confessional school? On March 7 the Communists replied that they wanted one assembly only, opposed any link of church and state, and believed that a little state like south Württemberg had no need of a state president, especially since he would become the basis for a particularist movement. They wanted community schools which would give moral instruction in humanity and socialism. They did not want the constitution of Württemberg-Baden, or any constitution at all. At this time, a simple statute was all that was necessary, they felt. Most urgent, they concluded, was agrarian reform, since the real need was to help the small peasant by breaking up the great estates and expropriating "criminals, war profiteers, and great landholders."

The Democrats were, ironically enough, in agreement with the Communists in many ways. They did not want a second house, a state president, or confessional schools. They did, however, favor the constitution of Württemberg-Baden, and they did not want agrarian reform. The Socialist party wanted a one-house legislature, since they believed that all other methods tended to take power from the people and lead to authoritarianism and dictatorship. The church should have legal rights but should not be permitted to escape its share in the bankruptcy of the Third Reich. As for confessional schools, the party felt that they were not necessary for a Christian upbringing but merely existed to give the churches power. They favored the Württemberg-Baden constitution as the best compromise between the parties. In agrarian reform they wanted the great estates broken up and divided between the small and medium farmers.

On March 14, 1947, Bock himself replied in the *Schwäbisches Tagblatt*. The center of gravity in his draft, he said, was "in the separation of powers. . . . All the power of the temporal authority comes from God. The different holders of this authority are only depositaries, to whom God has confided the exercise of power. The organs of the state have to give account in the first and last place to God." Moreover, he continued, he did not intend to introduce a parliamentary system. "The government does not rely upon the confidence of the Landtag. . . . The Landtag has legislative power and the government executive power." He proposed that there should be a state president who would at the same time be president of the council of ministers, a council of state, and confessional schools or Christian community schools in areas of mixed religious faith. In short, Bock had gone straight down the Christian Democratic party line on every detail, and it was hardly surprising that his statement aroused bitter opposition among the Socialists.[50]

Bishop Wurm, Evangelical bishop of Württemberg, came to the constitutional committee to give his views on the school question. The right of parents to have teachers of their own faith he considered vital. Where confessions were mixed, he believed that the teachers should be of both confessions. In general, he approved of the Bock draft.[51] The Christian Democrats remained firm in favor of a slightly amended version of the original draft, now known as the Bock-Niethammer constitution. At this point, however, the Socialists decided that strong action was called for and resigned from the committee. They were followed by the Democrats. The effect was all that could have been hoped for on their part. The French military government, fearing complete shipwreck of the proceedings, put pressure on the Land government to bring the parties together again. The effect was a startling turnover in which the Bock constitution was dropped and the Württemberg-Baden constitution again taken as the basis for discussion. Finally, in April 1947, the draft was debated in the Assembly, passionately and at length, and many amendments made. Only on the third reading did Carlo Schmid accept for the Socialists, and it was not until three o'clock on the morning of April 22, 1947, that the final count gave 43 votes for the draft (Socialists and Christian Democrats) and 11 votes against it (Communists and Democrats).[52]

The electoral campaign was very different from that in either Baden or Rheinland-Pfalz. Since both the Socialists and the Christian Democrats had supported the constitution, they were reduced to disputing the question of who was responsible for the best sections of it. The final result was a firm acceptance of the constitution by 69.8 per cent of those voting. However, the Socialists and Christian Democrats together obtained 82 per cent of the votes in the Landtag election, which proved that not all supporters of these parties were satisfied with the compromise constitution.

The Landtag elections, as Table 17 indicates, did not show any appreciable difference in the political strength of the various parties from that of the Kreis elections of October 1946; this was in contrast to the situation in Baden and Rheinland-Pfalz, where in each case the Christian Democrats lost support to the Socialists.

TABLE 17

LANDTAG ELECTION, WÜRTTEMBERG-HOHENZOLLERN[53]
(May 18, 1947)

Party	Number of Members in Landtag	Percentage of Vote in Land Election, May 18, 1947	Percentage of Vote in Kreis Election, October 13, 1946
CDU	32	62.8	63.2
SPD	12	19.9	19.9
KPD	5	6.9	6.5
DPD	11	10.4	10.3

The elections of May 18, 1947, marked a vitally important stage in the revival of democratic life in the French zone. As General Koenig pointed out, in the message to the opening session of the new assemblies, "The German authorities of the Länder are invested with the powers which are conferred on them by the constitutions."[54] In short, the German governments owed their powers not to the military government, but to the German people themselves. Although the constant intervention of the military government in the actions of the German governments was to make this statement seem at times little more than an amiable fiction, legal steps had been taken to give German democracy a basis in the will of the people. Each Land now had at its head a popularly elected Landtag and a responsible government which, if not always empowered to carry out the people's will, could at least complain in the people's name.

CHAPTER X

German Political Life, 1947-1949
From Landtag to Bundestag

BETWEEN 1945 and 1947 the French had slowly—and some thought, unwillingly—created a framework of democratic government throughout their zone. Their policy of localizing political administration had been made possible by the paralysis of central government in Germany, which followed the French and later the Russian refusal to make the Control Council a workable governmental organ for the whole country. From 1947 on, however, the development of a divided Germany was radically reversed. Great international pressure was exerted on France to side with Britain and the United States in the Cold War, and, as a corollary, to permit the fusion of its zone in Germany with the Bizone, thereby making possible the creation of a sound economic unit in West Germany. This change of policy had vital bearing on the revival of political life in the French zone. The two years following the elections of May 18, 1947, by which popularly elected assemblies were chosen and constitutions ratified in each of the three Länder, were dominated by the growing German responsibility for the administration of their own Länder, by increasing and largely successful pressures by the German governments on the French military government for changes in its policy, and by the cooperation of the French zone in preparations for the founding of the West German Republic.

The powers which the governments of the Länder were to wield were laid down in Ordonnance No. 95 of June 9, 1947, and Arrêté

No. 218 of June 10, 1947. These military government orders were read in an extremely terse message to the first sessions of the Landtage by the military governors of each Land. The Germans were appalled by the number of powers reserved to the French, since they included all rules relating to Control Council decisions and all matters concerning restitution and reparations, displacement of population, international penal law, plans of production, distribution of material between Länder, planning of agriculture, food, forestry, rationing of foodstuffs and essential industrial products, post and telecommunications, disarmament, decartelization, democratization, and public order.[1] It was not surprising that the Socialist paper, *Die Freiheit,* in an outspoken article entitled "It Is Time," should have demanded that greater trust be put in the Germans. "We know," the paper said, "that the hesitant attitude of France is dictated by the desire to avoid for as long as possible an exaggerated regrouping of forces on the European continent. We know, understandably, that we can expect no help from France."[2]

But it became clear as the months progressed that certain very important changes had in fact taken place in the political situation. The Land governments exerted considerable powers of administration in the day-to-day life of Germany, over such matters as schools, health care, transport, public works, justice, police, and even over such disputed matters as denazification and agrarian reform. Moreover, these governments found themselves in an increasingly strong position to make their opinions known, and in many cases respected, by the military government and the central government of France. During these two years the German governments came to be treated as equals by the French government, by the political parties in France, and even by the military government of the zone. Finally, with the all-important decisions of the London conference of 1948, the Land governments found themselves entrusted with the work of preparing for the foundation of a republic of West Germany, and in this work the representatives of the French zone played a significant part.

THE LAND GOVERNMENTS TAKE OFFICE, MAY–JULY 1947

In Rheinland-Pfalz the bitter constitutional conflict, in which the Socialists had finally demanded rejection of the constitution itself, left behind a sharp legacy of distrust between the parties. The scapegoat for the conflict was found in the president of the Provisional Government. Dr. Boden had headed the government of Rheinland-

Pfalz since its inception in August 1946, and he had often been in conflict with the opposition parties during that time, especially for his uncompromising Catholicism and his federalist sympathies. He now reaped the harvest of these disagreements. Although on June 13, 1947, he was given authority to form a government by a vote of 54 (Christian Democrats and Democrats) to 38 (Socialists and Communists), he found that the parties of the Left were unwilling to enter into a coalition government of which he was head. As a temporary caretaker government, he set up a homogeneous cabinet of Christian Democrats, with Dr. Adolf Süsterhenn as minister of justice, education, and public worship; Oskar Stübinger for food, agriculture, and finances; and Hans Junglas for work, reconstruction, communications, and social security.[3]

At the end of three weeks, Boden admitted that he could not overcome the opposition of the Socialists, and handed in the resignation of his government. Though remaining a member of the Landtag, Boden withdrew from the center of the political stage and accepted the position of the director of the Land Bank in Kaiserslautern. On July 9, Peter Altmeier (CDU) was given a unanimous vote of confidence as minister-president, and he at once formed a cabinet consisting of four Christian Democrats, three Socialists, one Democrat, and one Communist. There was an important continuity between this cabinet and that of the Provisional Government set up under Dr. Boden in October 1946, since six ministers out of nine retained their positions. The cabinet membership was as follows:[4]

Minister-President: Peter Altmeier (CDU)
Justice, Education, and Public Worship: Dr. A. Süsterhenn (CDU)
Interior: Jakob Steffan (SPD)
Finances: Dr. Hans Hoffmann (SPD)
Economy and Transport: Fritz Neumayer (DPD)
Work: Wilhelm Bockenkruger (SPD)
Agriculture and Food: Dr. Oskar Stübinger (CDU)
Reconstruction: Willy Feller (KPD)
Health and Social Security: Dr. Hans Junglas (CDU)
Chief of the Ministry of State: Dr. Hans Haberer (CDU)

The formation of this coalition cabinet was made possible by a rather unusual agreement among the political parties known as the Toleration Agreement (*Toleranzabkommen*) of July 8, 1947. The four party chiefs, Dr. Alois Zimmer for the Christian Democrats, Emil Bettgenhäuser for the Socialists, Fritz Neumayer for the Democrats, and Herbert Müller for the Communists, signed an agreement to form a four-party government, promised to refrain from personal calumny and purely political disagreements and accepted "the obligation not to suggest in the Landtag any bill which is absolutely impractical in view of the true situation of the country." They agreed on ten aims that all wished to achieve: increased agricultural production and better sharing of products, agrarian reform, struggle against the black market, increase of industrial production to satisfy German needs, increased power for German authorities, reorganization of economic councils, social insurance, denazification, respect for the constitution, and economies through administrative reform.[5]

Perhaps most important of all, the agreement at once put pressure on the French military government. It noted that "the dismantling of all factories which could be turned to peaceful use, as well as the confiscation of machinery, which has already begun, must be stopped immediately if production is not to break down completely." It stated that economic exchanges between the French zone and other zones and also with foreign countries ought to be organized by the Land governments. The amount of financial obligation owed to the occupier ought to be known. And finally, the agreement stated, "the elected representatives of the people of Rheinland-Pfalz, without distinction of party, address the French military government and ask that in this decisive hour of our destiny all efforts be made to preserve our people from the threatening fall into the abyss." These demands were to be sounded with increasing acerbity throughout the zone in the coming months. The Toleration Agreement lasted until April 8, 1948, when the other parties forced the resignation of Willy Feller, the Communist minister, because of his party's refusal to approve of the Marshall Plan. The Democrats announced that they considered the agreement to be ended by this resignation, and Fritz Neumayer resigned at the same time. The coalition of Socialists and Christian Democrats continued in power.[6]

In Baden, the Christian Democrats had won a very convincing victory in the Landtag election, in spite of the opposition of the Socialists and Communists. However, when on July 24 the Landtag chose Leo Wohleb as minister-president by 39 votes, with 17 abstentions, there was no clear way to the formation of a coalition government. Once again, as in Rheinland-Pfalz, the incumbent minister-president ran into considerable opposition to himself personally as well as to his party. Wohleb himself, writing in the *Südwestdeutsche Volkszeitung* on May 20, noted that the campaign had been unusually bitter and expressed his pleasure that the Badeners had stayed faithful to the Christian Democrats, in spite of their opponents' virulence.[7] Wohleb found, in approaching the other parties, that he would have considerable difficulty in allotting the ministerial positions. Both the Christian Democrats and the Socialists wanted the Ministry of the Interior, while the Democrats refused to have anyone as minister of the economy who had not voted for the constitution, thereby excluding both the Socialists and the Communists. Finally, the Christian Democrats entered into a coalition with the Socialists, and presented the following cabinet on July 30:

> State President, Education and Public Worship (and interim, Finances): Dr. Leo Wohleb (CDU)
> Economy and Work: Dr. Friedrich Leibbrandt (SPD)
> Justice: Dr. Marcell Nordmann (SPD)
> Interior: Dr. Alfred Schuly (CDU)
> Agriculture and Food: Lambert Schill (SPD)

When the final vote on this cabinet came on August 5, 1947, the Landtag insisted upon adopting a very curious method of approving the cabinet members. Instead of voting on the cabinet as a whole, as was customary, the Landtag demanded that they give the vote of confidence minister by minister. The purpose was to protest the appointment of Leibbrandt as minister of economy, an appointment to which the Communists and Democrats, as well as certain members of the Christian Democratic party, objected.[8]

Wohleb's ministry was destined to lead a very shaky life, since it was opposed by both Democrats and Communists, who were not admitted to the coalition, and criticized both by certain Socialists who wanted to see a four-party coalition and by certain Christian Democrats who objected to its severe measures of taxation. The final crisis came in January 1948, when the Socialist party asked their members to resign from the government because the coalition had not been broadened to include representation of all parties and because the agrarian reform was not satisfactory. As a result, Wohleb finally gave up trying to form a coalition government and formed the first one-party government in the French zone; his cabinet, announced on January 23, 1948, was as follows:[9]

State President, Education and Public Worship: Dr. Leo Wohleb
Justice: Dr. Wilhelm Eckert
Interior: Dr. Alfred Schuly
Economy and Work: Dr. Eduard Lais
Agriculture and Food: Lambert Schill (resigned Jan. 29, 1948)
Chief of State Chancellery: Clemens von Brentano

In Württemberg, the victory of the Christian Democrats in the elections of May 1947 had the immediate effect of forcing the resignation of Carlo Schmid as head of the Land government. On July 8, 1947, Lorenz Bock was chosen as state president by a vote of 43 to 17, the Socialists and Communists voting against him. Nevertheless, he was at once able to set up a coalition cabinet of all parties except the Communists, with considerable continuity from the Schmid cabinet of 1946. Only two members of the cabinet were new, Bock himself and Eugen Wirsching, minister of work. The Württemberg cabinet thus formed contained the following members:[10]

State President and Finances: Dr. Lorenz Bock (CDU)
Justice: Dr. Carlo Schmid (SPD)
Interior: Viktor Renner (SPD)
Education and Public Worship: Dr. Albert Sauer (CDU)
Economy: Eberhard Wildermuth (DPD)
Work: Eugen Wirsching (CDU)
Agriculture and Food: Dr. Frank Weiss (CDU)

On July 22, Bock presented his cabinet and his program for approval. He hoped soon, he said, to see both parts of Württemberg reunited. Germany, however, must not be a *Machtstaat*, but rather a *Kulturstaat*; "We reject every form of centralist state," he said. After mentioning the specific parts of his program, he ended with a firm demand that the French government define clearly the areas of competence between German and French authorities. When the vote came on July 23, the cabinet was approved by a vote of 42 out of 52 present, the four Communists voting against the cabinet and the six ministers abstaining. In Württemberg at least, the cabinet rested on a firm basis of consent.[11]

THE LANDTAGE AT WORK

The major work of the Landtage and of the Land governments was, of course, the details of administration that the French wished to assign to them. The military government did not intend that the policy of the occupying power should be greatly influenced by the wishes of the occupied, but rather that the policy of the French military government should be carried out by the Germans themselves. The Landtage were to find that they were able to influence French policy, but their main work remained the detailed administration of government.

Although the field of their competence was greatly limited, the German governments and the Landtage to which they held themselves responsible were determined to fulfill their duties with the greatest possible efficiency. Many speakers stressed that Germany had at last the chance to show itself a true democracy, and warned that the learning process would be hard. The more mundane tasks of government, however, hardly lent themselves to this rhetoric. The main tasks of the Landtage and the Land governments were to maintain the food supply and to supervise the rationing, to attempt to ease the housing shortage, to aid industrial production by planning in cooperation with the military government, to draw up the Land budget, and to supply the occupying power with its financial and material requirements as occupation costs. Debate on these subjects occupied the major portion of each Landtag session. There were nevertheless certain subjects that opened the way to lively political party conflict, the most important being denazification, the school question, and agrarian reform. The first two topics were considered in Chapter Nine. Like them, the question of agrarian reform was raised many times during the occupation, since it concerned the nature of the Germany that would emerge from the occupation period.

The progress of agrarian reform in the French zone illustrates perfectly the workings of occupation government, in the relationship between the French military government and the elected German governments on the one hand, and between the different German parties themselves on the other. The Soviet zone had already set the

example of large-scale agrarian reform in 1945 by expropriating without compensation 3 million hectares of land. On September 25, 1946,
the French military government first put pressure on the German
ministers to undertake agrarian reform in the French zone. Since little
action had been taken during the next twelve months by the Germans,
the French issued Ordonnance No. 116 on October 18, 1947, in which
they declared that no agricultural property should exceed 150 hectares,
although the Länder would be permitted to lower this maximum.
Those whose land was expropriated were to be indemnified.[12]

The Germans had made a first attempt to regulate the reform in
the Land constitutions themselves. In Württemberg the constitution
laid down that expropriations could only take place when urgently
needed for public use, such as colonization, and indemnification must
be paid. In Baden the constitution provided that the state must supervise the sharing and exploitation of these lands expropriated, and that
the whole process was to be regulated by a state law. In Rheinland-
Pfalz, the constitution permitted the owners of large properties to
divide them themselves but otherwise stated that holdings above a
certain maximum could be expropriated on advice of the Land agricultural chamber. But nothing more had been done when the French
Ordonnance of October 18, 1947, pushed the Landtage to take action
again, and when General Koenig announced that action had to be taken
by December 31.[13]

The struggle over agrarian reform then became a source of party
dissension among the Germans themselves. The French zone, however, unlike the Russian zone, possessed very few owners of large estates. In the entire zone, there were only 967 properties of more than
100 hectares, and of these 500 had no agricultural land. The real
problem in the French zone was quite the contrary, namely, that the
holdings were too small. The average size of holdings in Baden, for
example, was 2.5 hectares. Out of 450,000 holdings in the zone,
350,000 were less than 5 hectares. Nevertheless, since the problem
had been thrust upon the Germans as part of the democratization
process, agrarian reform was treated by the parties as almost entirely
a matter of whether or not to expropriate the large land holders.[14]

The Landtage proceeded to draw up laws for agrarian reform in
the winter of 1947. In Rheinland-Pfalz, the first reading took place
on February 25, 1948, with further debate on March 2–3. A clear
division at once became apparent between the Christian Democrats and

the Democrats, who wished to keep the reform as mild as possible, and the Socialists and Communists, who saw the reform as a first measure in the founding of a new socialized society. The Christian Democrats and Democrats in the Rheinland-Pfalz, said the Socialist Otto Schmidt, have the maxim, "Wash my fur, but don't get me wet." They had no desire for genuine reform, he felt. The Communist party paper, *Neues Leben,* announced, "Reactionary agrarian law passed." The law, as passed on March 4, set a ceiling of 150 hectares to individual properties, and introduced a progressive scale for expropriating the excess properties. The text of the agrarian reform law in Rheinland-Pfalz was the only one in the French zone which received the assent of the military government, since it was the only one which included forests in the property to be expropriated.[15]

In Baden and Württemberg, where the great slopes of the Black Forest and Swabian Alps were the main stronghold of the large proprietors, the struggle was waged much more furiously. In Baden the conflict was between the Christian Democrats, who wanted a ceiling set at 150 hectares, and the Socialists and Communists, who wanted it to be 100 hectares. After much squabbling, the limit was set at 100 hectares, but this limit was made meaningless by the fact that the progressive tariff above that limit never exceeded 90 per cent, with the result that properties would be well above 100 hectares. The forest lands were left virtually untouched.[16] In Württemberg disagreements between the Socialists and the Christian Democrats forced the revision of the law in January and February, 1948; especially important was the Socialist demand that the forest lands be included in the area for expropriation. On February 4, 1948, an impassioned debate in the Landtag took place. Speaking for the Christian Democrats, Dr. Frank Weiss, minister of agriculture and food, quoted figures to show that only 2.5 per cent of the agricultural land in Württemberg was held in properties of over 100 hectares, and he pointed out that the yield per hectare was greater on a large farm than on a small. Dr. Dieter Roser replied for the Socialists, giving a long list of the proprietors of the large holdings. The list included such historic names as the Fürst von Hohenzollern-Sigmaringen, who owned 14,500 hectares in Württemberg, of which 2,900 were agricultural, and another 2,200 in Bavaria and 500 in Baden. Roser concluded that, according to his figures, 8.5 per cent of the land of south Württemberg was owned by forty-eight people, and 7.8 per cent by only twenty-five people. Carlo

Schmid summed up the Socialist argument against the nobility in a picturesque way. "Certainly," he said, "I have an understanding—yes, I can feel it myself—of this charming scene, as the nobleman on his white horse, his hunting horn by his side, throws a kiss to a country maid, and shoots his stag. That is a lovely picture. I like to get carried away thinking about such scenes. We have them here on the wall, as if one didn't want us to forget them . . . but there is no room for such feelings at a time when all our great cities are piles of rubble, when 12 or 13 million of our people, guiltless, wander through our land with the white staff of the expellees."[17] The bill was passed on March 23, 1948, by a vote of 51 to 6.

The laws of Baden and Württemberg failed to satisfy the French military government, since neither made more than a token provision for expropriation of forest lands. After consultation with the Paris government, however, the military government gave the order for the German authorities to begin application of the laws as they had been voted in the Landtage. In Rheinland-Pfalz, a colonization society was founded and a study made of the territories which would be freed for redistribution. A census of property was begun in Baden, and the first methods of application were being studied in Württemberg in 1949. But, by the time of the founding of the West German Republic, very little had been achieved.[18] Agrarian reform, which had roused so much passion, was allowed to pass away unnoticed.

Thus, during the two years 1947–49, the Landtage were occupied with the details of local administration, and with party conflicts over certain measures, such as denazification or agrarian reform, which were to be applied in the Länder themselves. Yet, the Landtage served an even more important function during these years. They became the mouthpiece of German opinion and instruments by which the Germans could apply pressure upon the military governments. This function took two forms: the Landtage influenced the French military government in certain aspects of its occupation policy, and they expressed German opinion on the international negotiations which affected the future of Germany.

GROWING PROTESTS BY LAND GOVERNMENTS

Not all Germans were willing to show the patience with occupation rule that Carlo Schmid had counseled in 1946. By the middle of 1947, a growing disenchantment with the occupying power was showing. Most of all, annoyance centered on the low food supply which the French maintained, the economic exploitation which was felt to be carried on in the secret offices of the Oficomex, and on the dismantlings, which were reaching an ever greater number instead of passing with the first sharp pains of the invasion.

Speaking to the Landtag of Baden on August 5, 1947, Minister-President Wohleb painted a gloomy picture of the prospects of increasing the food supply and concluded that there was little hope of spreading democracy among hungry people.[19] The situation was so bad in September that it made news when it could be announced in the Rheinland-Pfalz Landtag that the amount of potatoes to be taken by the military government would be reduced. The Socialist newspaper, *Die Freiheit,* finally passed the point of tolerable criticism and was suspended when it published on April 23, 1948, a graph purportedly showing that a concentration camp inmate in Buchenwald in 1944-45 received a better food supply (1,675 calories a day) than the average consumer in the French zone in 1947 (805 calories a day). In its next issue, the paper retracted slightly by admitting that perhaps it had shown the food situation in the concentration camp in too favorable a light in view of the small number of survivors.[20] However, this point was revived in a celebrated incident a month later. Dr. Neubronner (DPD), speaking about the food supply, rather unwisely claimed: "After all the privations endured during the war years, we are living now, three years later, in a state of famine no concentration camp in the world has known." At this point, Colonel Magniez, a French officer in civilian clothes, jumped to his feet shouting, "It's not true. I'm leaving. You have never been in a concentration camp." The session was suspended, and the presidents of the parties in the Landtag were called to Baden-Baden to see Koenig. Finally, they dissociated themselves and their parties from the speech; and Dr. Neubronner decided that he had not intended to make that particular remark.[21]

The incident, however, was all the more striking in that it followed a series of food strikes which had threatened to close down the vast industrial complex of Ludwigshafen. *Die Freiheit,* on July 11, 1948, claimed that workmen were at the end of their strength. In the Pfalz, it noted, men were sitting by their machines without the strength to work. At a great strike meeting, the workers met Franz Bögler, Socialist Oberregierungspräsident of the Pfalz, Jakob Steffan, Socialist minister of the interior, Wilhelm Bockenkruger, minister of work, and Hans Junglas, minister of health and social security. After a tense meeting, the workers were with great difficulty persuaded to go back to their jobs.[22]

This was the background to the growing discontent felt in all the Länder with the continuing dismantling. The Toleration Agreement in Rheinland-Pfalz had already demanded that the French cease dismantling factories that could be turned to peaceful uses. The publication on October 16, 1947, of the list of factories to be dismantled in the Bizone, and on October 20 of the factories in the French zone, provoked a great reaction. *Rheinpfalz,* in an editorial on October 22 on "dismantling and democracy," pointed out that the confidence raised by the Marshall Plan was already being shaken. *Rheinischer Merkur* showed the ironic fact that the publication of the former list was due to the bizonal administration's desire to know from where it would start, when it received Marshall aid. *Schwabenecho* felt that dismantling of the Persil factory could hardly be considered removal of war production. *Die Freiheit* asked, "Whom is dismantling helping?" and decided that no one was being helped.[23]

The effect of dismantling was far greater in Baden and Württemberg than in Rheinland-Pfalz, since in those Länder, the lack of alternative employment for the workers of dismantled factories caused sharp regional unemployment. As a result, the protests in the southern triangle of the zone were even more vociferous than those in the north. On May 23, 1947, *Südkurier* put its finger on the heart of the matter. Dismantling, it said, is useless, since Germany's economic production is needed in the world's economy and since dismantling is more expensive than it is worth. Moreover, it added, "it is also showing little sense to take away from Germany now the means of production which are not completely new, to be obliged one day to supply it with new ones in order to permit it to pay its debts."[24] After the IARA had designated twenty-seven more factories in the French zone for dismantling, the presidents of the four parties wrote a joint letter to the minister-president of Baden, saying that dismantling "strikes industrial production working for exportation at its very center and makes it impossible to establish a plan of exportation which would have beneficial effects on the supply and feeding of the people of Baden. . . . It is the most obvious task of the government of Baden to prevent such results by all possible means and to make a request to the military government at once, listing the dangers and demanding a revision of the dismantling plan."[25] On November 28, 1947, the Landtag went into secret session to hear a government declaration on dismantling; and a group of parliamentary leaders went to see the military governor, Pène, who promised to pass their request on to higher authorities.

In 1948 the protests redoubled in violence. When Pierre Schneiter, commissioner general for German and Austrian affairs, visited Freiburg on January 25, 1948, Wohleb spoke openly about his worries over dismantling. In a particularly bitter session on May 12, 1948, the anger of the Landtag boiled over. Wohleb had just returned from Paris, where Schneiter had made more promises, one being to increase the food ration to 1,600 calories. But the Landtag was not satisfied with this. Hermann Schneider, speaking for the Christian Democrats, raised every objection at once. The French must stop taking cattle, he said, since the Germans need more meat: "The period of vegetarianism of our people must be finally ended." The French must stop taking the wood from the forests and machinery from the factories. Denazification must be stopped. In this bitter and sarcastic speech, Schneider mirrored the mood of the assembly. Finally, all parties joined together to vote a resolution which demanded greater power for the Landtag, an occupation statute, a share in the administration of the external commerce of the Land, reduction in the felling in the forests, raising of the German share of production, faster denazification, and 40 per cent reduction in cattle taken. With its fury expressed, the Landtag adjourned.[26]

On June 16, Wohleb was able to announce that their protest had brought some results. Denazification would be accelerated. The French would take a smaller share of the meat supply. The powers of the Landtag would be increased.[27] But this was only the calm before the second and greater storm. Dismantling remained at the root of all disagreements. In a momentous session on August 26, 1948, the Landtag again broached the question of dismantling. The session began with Dr. Lais, minister of economy, reading his correspondence with the military government to show how unsatisfactory their relations remained. "These dismantlings," he continued, "strike directly against the aims of the Marshall Plan for reconstruction of the Euro-

pean economy with the inclusion of Germany. The American tax-
payer may well concern himself with this question." And the lack of
power which a freely elected government has in this zone, he concluded, will end up by discouraging young people from believing in
the value of democracy at all.[28]

Dr. Wohleb summed up the attitude of his government. "Since
it has not been possible," he said, "in spite of all the efforts of the
Land government of Baden, to bring the negotiations in the dismantling question, which is vital to the life of the people of Baden, to a
favorable conclusion in agreement with the unanimous motion of the
Baden Landtag, the State President and the Land government no
longer find themselves in a position of being able to continue to hold
governmental responsibility. . . . The lessening of our export capacity through dismantling immediately endangers the imports necessary for the existence of the people of Baden and the livelihood of a
section of our highly qualified skilled workers." With that he handed
in the resignation of his government.[29]

His action was at once approved by the other parties. Speaking for
the Democrats, Dr. Wäldin pointed out that "it is quite incomprehensible that, at the moment when the London recommendations are
being put into force, total or partial dismantling of further factories
should be demanded." As for finding other employment for the skilled
workers from the precision industries, "Should they go into tobacco,
for example?" he asked.[30] Dr. Haas, for the Socialists, looked sorrow-
fully at the lost opportunity for Franco-German understanding. "One
must consider," he said, "what an infinitely great opportunity for mutual understanding France has had in the last three years, an opportunity of which, unfortunately—and we greatly regret this—no use
has been made. . . . The people see the assembly today as a stage
and the government as mere marionettes."[31]

The government did not give up its work but continued in office
as a provisional government. This somewhat curious procedure undoubtedly took away most of the effect of the resignation. The Landtag remained, however, the official sounding board for criticism, which
reached a last flurry in the debate on November 23, 1948, following
General de Gaulle's outspoken press conference of November 17, 1948.
De Gaulle had said that the British and the Americans wanted to re-
establish the Reich whereas he wanted the traditional German organi-

zation of a federation of states. If the Allies did not agree to this, he had continued, we have "guarantees. . . . It was I who took them. They are the Saar, the left bank of the Rhine, Baden, part of Württemberg. We must use them. Why permit the French zone to be united with the others? People will say to me that the Marshall plan would be threatened. But we have lived for centuries without the Marshall plan."[32] Wohleb saw in this speech of de Gaulle's a symbol of the failure of the occupation. He looked back on the visit of de Gaulle to Freiburg in October 1945. "The words which General de Gaulle spoke to us were based on high responsibility, humanity, and the will to reconciliation," he said. Now his attitude had changed. "All clear-sighted Germans," he continued, "understand that the memories of the invasion of the year 1940, of the German occupation and of the many sufferings and sacrifices of the French people are still vivid memories in France. But, I must be permitted to say, [it can be] shown that the population of the French zone has had to endure years of privations and sacrifices, which I will not compare with those the French people suffered in the war, but which have been hard on us in the same way."[33] It was only on February 21, 1949, that the Baden Landtag re-elected Wohleb State President with full legal powers.

In Württemberg, too, the protests followed a similar pattern. Here, with a few exceptions, the dismantling hit the precision industries of the small towns. On October 1, 1947, the Landtag voted a resolution claiming that the military government's aim of dismantling 2,700 industrial machines would put 10,000 people out of work, and asking the government to do everything it could to change this order. In November the Landtag again faced the problem. Assembly President Gengler noted that "the publication of the dismantling list has struck us a terrible blow. Our most pessimistic estimates have been exceeded. . . . Our very existence is in question. If these dismantlings were to be carried out, all our work, all our hopes for the future, our democratic reform, would be gravely weakened."[34]

As in Baden, representatives were sent to the military governor, and a note was sent to Koenig. *Das Volk*, the Socialist paper in Württemberg, published the full text of the note, which began by stating that the dismantling hit Württemberg-Hohenzollern harder than it did the Bizone. "If after the confiscations of the years 1945–46 and of 1947, these dismantlings were to be carried out, the reconstruction of a peacetime industry in Württemberg-Hohenzollern would become impossible"; and moreover, the note continued, the government had tried hard to work loyally with the French. These actions, however, would take away the very modest life the Germans then had, and would make the position of the government untenable.[35] *Schwaben-echo* added the hysterical claim that industrial productivity would be reduced to 40 per cent of 1938 capacity.[36]

In April 1948 the storm broke in Württemberg as well. On April 29 the Landtag was informed that the military government had ordered it not to discuss deforestation in Württemberg. This deliberate attempt to prevent them from airing one of their favorite grievances drove the assembly into another passionate debate, at the end of which it decided to adjourn *sine die*. All agreed to the motion of Gebhard Müller, president of the CDU: "The military government has reserved to itself legal power in certain fields. But this does not mean that the Landtag, in order to represent the interests of the people, should not discuss deforestation, and especially so since these burdens can no longer be endured. Moreover, if these restrictions on democratic discussions are maintained, the people will no longer believe in democracy."[37]

After five weeks, the Landtag was called together by Minister-President Bock to hear that in this particular instance at least they were victorious. The military government had agreed to the right of the Landtag to question this policy. In June the food situation looked a little brighter when the French announced that 50 per cent of their needs in meat would be met from France.[38] The next day, Wildermuth, the minister of economy, showed a certain understanding for France's position on dismantling when, in reply to a Socialist question, he admitted that France could not stop dismantling unilaterally.[39]

In August 1948, however, the untimely death of Minister-President Lorenz Bock coincided in a dramatic way with a new outburst of indignation at the continuance of dismantling. It was rumored that the disputes with the military government over dismantling had, if not caused, at least hastened Bock's death. Speaking at the opening of the Landtag session of August 6, in memory of the minister-president, Gebhard Müller compared Bock's position to that of "a man carrying a cross up a hill and knowing that he himself will be nailed to it. . . . He fought to the end against dismantling."[40] After such an introduction, the session could hardly fail to be stormy. Dr. Wildermuth, minister of economy, stated that he was uncertain now of the relationship between the IARA in Brussels and the French military government, but that he was sure that "the confiscation of machinery has succeeded to the benefit of France." He noted that better relations had been promised by Pierre Schneiter, that the European Recovery Program had begun, and that a hard currency reform had laid the foundations for industry, but that "execution of dismantling in the way intended cannot be combined with these aims and plans."[41]

Carlo Schmid, who had taken over the presidency in the interim following the death of Bock, then handed in the resignation of the government, stating that "the cooperation of a German government in measures which must forcibly drag down the living standards of our people to an intolerable degree and whose results will not be repaired in many years would be a betrayal on the part of the government, towards the people, of its constitutionally assumed powers. Since the government, in spite of its understanding with the military government, . . . has not succeeded in bringing about a real change in the situation, it finds itself no longer able to bear the political responsibility for the fate of the Land. It announces its resignation."[42] The resignation was unanimously supported. As in Baden, however, this did not mean that the government went out of office. At the session of August 13, 1948, by a vote of 53 out of 59 present, Gebhard Müller was chosen as minister-president to replace Bock, on a provisional basis only, since the resignation of the government was still officially in force.[43] This strange situation lasted until May 12, 1949, when provisional Minister-President Müller announced that changes in the situation made it possible to reconsider the resignation of the government. First, he said, twenty-seven factories had been removed from the dismantling list and another six would be partly rather than totally dismantled. General Koenig and other officials had shown great understanding of the problems of Württemberg, which was evident in the freeing of buildings, the reduction of felling in the forests, and the near-cessation of requisitioning of private homes. On June 24 Müller announced that a new government had been formed, in which he himself would take the Ministry of Finance.[44]

Thus German demands, combined with the pressure of changes at the international level, led, curiously enough, to the development of better relations between the German governments and the French military government. Here again the decisive moment came when the London conference determined that the three western zones of Germany should be invited to create a West German state. From that moment on, the French military government found itself forced to admit the German governments to greater power and to put an end to the situation which had so annoyed the newly elected governments in 1947. The new era was symbolized in the trip which Premier Robert Schuman made through the zone in October 1948. Schuman succeeded in convincing the Germans (and incidentally General Clay) that in him the Germans had found a friend who was determined that Germany should again be in a position to play an independent role in world affairs. The *Rheinischer Merkur* expressed the pleasure of many Germans in his openness and his desire to bring the Germans closer to the rest of the world.[45] On November 10, following this happy omen, General Koenig called the three minister-presidents of the zone to his Villa Maria Halder in Baden-Baden, and announced that he would meet them on the fourteenth and twenty-ninth of every month to coordinate their views, before he went to the fortnightly meetings in Frankfurt with the other commanders-in-chief for the discussion of the founding of the Trizone.[46]

On November 10, he discussed with them the dismantling question, occupation costs, and the collaboration of German and French administrators. At the meeting of November 29, André François-Poncet, the former French ambassador in Berlin and future high commissioner, was also present. On that day, occupation costs were reduced 25 per cent, and it was decided that the German authorities of the Länder would set up a bureau of liaison in Frankfurt for preparing links with the bizonal organization and with the French representative in Frankfurt. From this point on, each of the meetings granted some demand of the Germans. On February 14, 1949, Koenig told them that the dismantling list of October 30, 1947, was the last and would not be increased. On March 11 he indicated that there was no question of the French annexation of the town of Kehl, the opposite end of the bridgehead from Strasbourg.[47]

Thus the period between the Landtag elections of May 18, 1947, and the Bundestag election of August 14, 1949, was a period of growing competence of the German administration at the Land level and of the development of the Land as an efficient unit of government. Greatly influenced by international developments, the German governments reached a pitch of indignation in the summer of 1948, when they believed nothing good of their French occupiers. Finally, with the development of greater trust between occupier and occupied, a period of moderate reconciliation ushered in the founding of the new republic.

German political circles were, however, by no means unanimous in their attitude toward the international events which were changing their internal situation. German political life found its first major division of principle in the attitudes adopted by the political parties to the international decisions affecting Germany during these years.

THE LANDTAGE TAKE THEIR STAND ON POLICY

After May 1947 the French zone was increasingly influenced by changes at the international level. The great turnabout in American opinion, heralded by Byrnes's Stuttgart speech of 1946, was followed the next year by Secretary Marshall's offer of economic aid. From this point, the French zone became a major source of concern to the other Western powers, and as a result, the German authorities found that they were increasingly able and willing to express their wishes on the policy they wanted to see carried out by the occupying power in the French zone.

The full significance of the Marshall Plan was grasped almost immediately by the German political parties in the zone. F. A. Kramer noted in July 1947, in an editorial in the *Rheinischer Merkur,* that in the shortest international conference since 1945 the illusion of combining with Russia had been cast off, and he welcomed Marshall aid as the economic counterpart of the political federation of Europe for which he had been campaigning.[48] It was only when the London conference of February–June 1948 decided in its early sessions that Germany should be included in the Marshall Plan that the changed situation made its full impact on German politics. Then, the knowledge that the three western zones of Germany would receive economic aid from the United States was linked with two other issues. First, it was obvious, and in fact was determined by the second session of the London conference, that the union of the French zone with the Bizone was an inevitable consequence of the receipt of Marshall aid. Second, it followed that the formation of a Trizone would involve the creation of a government for western Germany, with the consequent need to decide such thorny questions as the amount of power to be exercised by the federal government and on the boundaries of the Länder within the new West German state. All of these three problems—the acceptance or rejection of Marshall aid and all that it implied in terms of the political division of Germany, the nature of the new West German constitution, and the boundaries of the Länder within the new state—were to provoke bitter political conflicts in the French zone.

The summer of 1947 was thus a period of both hope and despair for Germans. The failure of the Moscow conference of March–April 1947, from which so much had been expected, made it clear that Germany was going to remain for much longer a pawn in the Cold War. Its hopes of reunification were indefinitely postponed. On the other hand, the reverses of the Moscow conference brought as an immediate aftereffect Secretary of State Marshall's offer of economic aid to Europe. When Soviet Russia and the satellites refused to accept this aid, it became obvious that the Iron Curtain that split Germany in two would become an ever greater reality. And Marshall aid, which emphasized the division of Germany, seemed to offer the one great hope of economic recovery for an increasingly impoverished land. It became necessary at this point for the different German parties to take their stand regarding acceptance of the aid.

In Rheinland-Pfalz, the debate over the Marshall Plan led to a cabinet crisis. The Communist party throughout Germany had made it clear that it completely disapproved of the Marshall Plan. The only Communist minister in the three Länder of the French zone was Willy Feller, an outspoken syndicalist and militant Communist, who held the position of minister of reconstruction in Rheinland-Pfalz. On April 7, 1948, the other parties determined that the minister in charge of a reconstruction which must be carried out with the aid of Marshall Plan funds could hardly be someone who was opposed to the acceptance of Marshall aid. The Christian Democrats therefore proposed a motion of no confidence in Feller, which was passed by the CDU, the SPD, and the Democrats. Feller resigned and was replaced by a Socialist, Otto Schmidt. Speaking in that debate, Minister-President Altmeier made a firm statement of his party's position with regard to the Communists, both in the zone and in the whole of Europe. "This new nationalism," he said, "in contrast with that of the years after 1918, represents no internal German reaction to the lost war, but rather is consciously using all our present difficulties to bring our people under the political forces of the East. When we can always hear the loud cry, 'One People, one Reich, one Unity Party,' then every one of us knows what the hour is sounding. A new imperialism from the East threatens to flow over our western zone of Germany and over all Europe." The London conference has made clear the world situation, he said, breaking open the carefully bound-up rift between East and West. The Marshall Plan, the Dunkirk treaty, and other signs were proving that the old nationalisms were giving way. This extremely important speech of Altmeier's was the parting of the ways. It had its counterpart a month later in the great debate on the London conference in the French National Assembly. Both France and West Germany from this point on realized that they had entered a new era, which demanded an entirely different frame of mind.

For the Socialists, the problem was somewhat harder. They had demanded, from the beginning of the occupation, the reunification of Germany and the re-establishment of a central government for the whole of Germany. Now they found themselves faced with the prospect of accepting aid which they felt was vitally needed, yet of paying the price in the perpetuation of the disunity of Germany. Following Altmeier in the Landtag debate, Franz Bögler, secretary of the Socialist party, attempted to have the best of both worlds. "This economic help for the world must be the basis for a united Germany," he said. "This world aid must be the beginning of European unity. . . . Our economic aim, socialization, will in no way be affected by the Marshall plan. We expect that, in connection with this receipt of aid, our own German legal administrative organizations will be created."

The Democrats were more enthusiastic. But Dr. Neubronner, speaking for the Democrats, voiced a warning. "We are of the opinion that the restoration of the German economy to health and life . . . through the Marshall plan will be carried out," he said. "But if this Marshall plan is not linked with the creation of the economic unity of the three western zones and with the creation of a corresponding central authority for these German areas, then it will . . . end in failure."[49] In October the Democratic party went even further, and in its paper, *Rheinisch-Pfälzische Rundschau,* published a series of

approving articles by an unwisely chosen commentator, Hjalmar
Schacht.[50]

The debate on April 7, 1948, was closed by the Communist speaker,
Herbert Müller. The Marshall Plan, he said, had the task of serving
American business interests. It had the job of finding a market for the
products of the mammoth American industry which developed during
the war. This outlet would be Germany and Europe. ("Would that
it were already," called a voice from the assembly.) Moreover,
Müller continued, disregarding the interruption, the Marshall Plan
would set aside the decisions of Yalta and Potsdam, which could have
given Germans the opportunity to build a free and independent nation.
It sapped the political and economic strength of Germany. It prevented the democratization of industry and made impossible Germany's independence. The Communist paper, *Neues Leben,* reporting the speech, heralded its views with the headline: "Those who accept the Marshall plan, choose the road to catastrophe."[51]

The Landtag finally voted a resolution approving Germany's inclusion in the Marshall Plan. "The Landtag welcomes," the motion read,
"the inclusion of Germany in the organization and economic reconstruction program of the Marshall plan. The Landtag expects that
the economic cooperation begun here will make it possible to overcome
the German people's shortages of goods and food and to prevent any
tendency toward totalitarianism."

The final decisions of the London conference were announced on
June 7, 1948, and on July 1, the minister-presidents of the three western zones were called to Frankfurt to meet with the three commanders-
in-chief and to be given the three "London documents." The Germans
were being asked to write a constitution for a new German state composed of the three western zones, to reconsider the question of the
boundaries of the Länder within the new German state, but above all
to consider the greatest question of all, whether they were willing to
create this West German state. That problem had to be faced before
they could proceed to the more detailed questions of the nature of the
new state itself.

The Landtag of Rheinland-Pfalz approached this question in a
long and extremely important debate on June 16, 1948. As Minister-
President Altmeier said at the time, so long as there was no central
government of Germany, the Landtag had a duty to consider the

wider questions of world policy, as well as looking after the special interests of the Land. He went on to state the position of the Christian Democratic party of Rheinland-Pfalz. One must recognize, he said, that Germany had now become the place where the fields of power of West and East, or rather of the United States and Russia, meet. It was correct, he said, to speak of an Iron Curtain. Even though the Germans could not influence Allied policy, they had to speak out, to say that they would never accept the splitting of their territory: "Every great *Kulturvolk* claims the recognized natural right to live in political unity." However, he continued, the coming of the Marshall Plan would be greatly endangered if the blows against the German economy continued to be made by the occupying powers. "The taking by the Allies of raw materials and foodstuffs, the delivery of livestock, the felling of timber, the dismantling of factories, the seizure of machinery, the confiscations from industrial production, the requisitions and occupation costs, mean a further weakening of the German economy already shattered by the war and postwar times," he concluded. In short, although welcoming the London decisions, he had drawn a practical conclusion from them—that the occupation regime must change its nature, and quickly.

Friedrich Wagner, in a fascinating, rhetorical speech in behalf of the Socialist party, opened with a quotation from Hoffmann von Fallersleben: "Over our Fatherland lies a dark night, / And our own disgrace and shame have brought this night upon us." This night, he said, was the product of fascism, of Hitlerism, and of circumstances beyond German control. And, he went on, "this night is not only a night over Germany, and not only a night for Germany. It is a night over Europe. It is a night which surrounds the whole world, and it is not only a material, an economic night. It is a spiritual night." The war, he felt, ceased to be a war against fascism, but gradually became a war against Germany itself. Finally, he felt, the new situation demanded above all a new understanding between France and Germany. He was opposed to both extreme parties in France, the Gaullists and "the other nationalists, the French Communists," who both acted as though a band of militarists and nationalists still held power in Germany.[52]

These views were echoed in Baden and Württemberg with only slight variations. The Landtage themselves, occupied as they were with the growing conflict over dismantling, did not devote much time to debating the wider significance of the London conference, and it was largely in party meetings that the attitudes of the parties were made known. Minister-President Bock, speaking at the CDU party congress in Ravensburg, Württemberg, noted with satisfaction that the states of western Germany were included in the European community through the Marshall Plan, and, like Altmeier, he drew the practical conclusion that the moment had come to stop dismantling, to give the Germans freedom of economic relations, and to lessen occupation costs. He, too, felt that the need was for a greater rapport with France.[53] The Democrats, meeting on June 5 and 6, echoed this view, emphasizing that Franco-German collaboration should be within a European Union. The Socialist party attitude was expressed by Carlo Schmid at the monthly meeting of the SPD in Tübingen in November 1947. While the Socialists still felt that "German unity is the only guarantee of world unity," Schmid said, they were willing to accept the Marshall Plan as the only way to revive the European economy, in spite of their misgivings that they were thereby reinforcing those elements that opposed Socialism.[54]

In Baden the Landtag examined the meaning of the London conference and the Frankfurt meeting of the minister-presidents, in their debate of July 5. Leo Wohleb opened the debate by reporting on the Frankfurt meeting, which to him had immense significance for the future of Germany. "The meeting in Frankfurt," he said, "must in any circumstances be regarded as a milestone in the political development of West Germany, and, I venture to add, for all Germany. One may well say that with the Frankfurt conference, a period of history came to an end and a new period began for the West German Länder."[55] Speaking for the Socialists, Richard Jäckle was much less enthusiastic. "The enemy of Europe," he said, "is the opposition of the two present world giants, Russia and America. The task of Europe is to put an end to this situation." The London agreements left much to be desired, he felt, since no Germans had been present, Germany had been divided, and only a provisional sovereignty had been given to Germany. What the Socialist party desired, he added, was a "unified administration" of the three western zones, not a new state.[56]

It was clear by July 1948 that German political parties accepted the Marshall Plan, although with varying degrees of enthusiasm, and that they endorsed the London agreements. It now became the task of the representatives of the Länder, in accordance with the three London documents handed to the minister-presidents on July 1, to make preparations for the founding of the West German Republic. This involved writing a constitution and establishing the boundaries of the Länder which would compose the new German state.

THE FOUNDING OF THE BUNDESREPUBLIK

There was one matter on which all parties, again with the sole exception of the Communists, had agreed for some time—namely, that the French zone should be united with the Bizone as soon as possible. In October 1947 Minister-President Altmeier, writing in the *Rheinischer Merkur* "on the German question," had pointed out that the time had come to think beyond the Gemeinde, the Kreis, and the Land. Germany needed a federalist state, he felt.[57] By the end of 1947 demands for the formation of a Trizone were widespread. *Die Freiheit*, the Socialist paper of Rheinland-Pfalz, noted that only the Communists opposed this unification, and that the Socialist party agreed with the Christian Democrats in this instance, that the Trizone should be based on an economic rather than a political orientation.[58] This demand was even more encouraged by the failure of the Foreign Ministers' Conference of December 1947, which brought to a definitive break the deadlock which had developed in Moscow in the spring. The Landtag of Rheinland-Pfalz decided that the moment had come to take action.

On January 21, 1948, during the debate on the budget of the Ministry of Economy, the Landtag adopted unanimously (with the exception of the seven Communists) a motion asking for the union of the French zone with the Bizone. The motion, presented by Dr. Würmeling of the Christian Democrats, stated:

> The deadlock at the conference of foreign ministers in London has created for the Land of Rheinland-Pfalz, as well as for all German Länder, a situation which makes necessary rapid provisional measures with the aim of guaranteeing the survival of German economic life.
>
> The economic unity of all the zones, desired in principle by all the occupying powers, has not been realized at the moment, to the great detriment of the German people. Thus, the union of the French zone of occupation with the British and American zones . . . has now become imperative.

This will create, at least, an essential basis for the restoration of acceptable conditions of life and work for the great mass of the population and will permit the collaboration of our Land in the common reconstruction of Germany.

The Landtag therefore asks the Land government to put pressure on the Military Government, underlining the vital needs of the Rheinland-Pfalz population and economy, in order to bring about the union of the French zone with the Bizone.[59]

As might have been expected, there was a violent Communist reaction. Willy Feller, the Communist minister for reconstruction, had already denounced the idea of a Trizone in December 1947 with the aphorism, "We love our country and we hate all separatists and reactionaries who sell their opinions for CARE packages."[60] On January 9, 1948, Feller again returned to the danger of the new separatism. "The KPD leadership in Rheinland-Pfalz opposes all federalist and openly separatist plans for the splitting of Germany," he wrote. "Seeds for spring, immediate help for the victims of flooding, these are the cares of the little man in Rheinland-Pfalz."[61] And in reporting the debate of the Landtag, *Neues Leben* gave great play to the speech of the Communist deputy Ernst Buschmann, denouncing Marshall aid as "delivering our industry over to monopoly capitalism."[62]

Although the Christian Democrats, the Socialists, and the Democrats found themselves in agreement that the French zone should be united with the Bizone, they were not agreed on the form the new Trizone should take. The London documents, of course, had laid down to a large extent the principal lines the constitutional planning should take—namely, that the Trizone should have the form of a state, that it should have a constitution written by the Germans but approved by the occupying powers, and that this constitution should be federalist in form. This had been made clear to the minister-presidents at the Frankfurt meeting of July 1.

The only action the Landtage were called upon to take in this constitutional process was to elect the members who would represent them in the "Parliamentary Council" which would write the "Basic Law," as the constitution was euphemistically called. It is interesting to note that in the preliminary negotiations which the minister-presidents carried on with the military governors throughout July and August, General Koenig was the only military governor sympathetic with the German view that they should not write a constitution but merely an administrative statute for the Trizone. It is ironic that whereas the German attitude was determined by the desire to advance the future unification of Germany, Koenig's sympathy probably sprang from a desire to avoid it.

Several representatives of the French zone sent to Bonn were already experienced in the writing of constitutions, since they had taken a large part in the writing of the constitutions of their own Länder. Rheinland-Pfalz chose as one of its representatives Dr. Adolf Süsterhenn, the minister of justice and principal author of the first draft of the constitution of Rheinland-Pfalz, a convinced federalist who was to play an important part in the deliberations of the Council of Elders and of the Main Committee, and as deputy member of the Committees on General Organization and Basic Rights; its other representatives were Dr. Albert Fink, Friedrich Wagner, and Karl Kuhn. On August 1, 1948, the Württemberg Landtag chose Dr. Carlo Schmid, minister of justice, a very obvious and indeed inevitable choice, and Dr. Paul Binder, former minister of finance (CDU). In Baden, Dr. Hermann Fecht was chosen for the Christian Democrats and Friedrich Maier for the Socialists.

During the deliberations of the Parliamentary Council, resemblances to the controversies which arose during the writing of the constitutions of the Länder of the French zone could be seen. For example, Dr. Süsterhenn was one of the principal proponents of writing a list of natural rights into the Basic Law. "There are . . . rights prior to and superior to the State," he said, rights resulting from the nature and being of man and his various associations, which the state has to respect. Every power of the state was limited by these natural, God-given rights of the individual, the family, the local communities of town and country, and the occupational groups.[63] And it was Carlo Schmid who replied, "I recall that the amazing Burke, in his reactions to the French Revolution, said that, in general, men appear to have no concrete rights arising from nature, that their rights evolve historically. . . . To erect natural law as an absolute is a dangerous business."[64]

Meanwhile, the politicians in the various Länder were contenting themselves with an occasional howl of protest at the length of time it was taking to get a constitution written and with quarreling among themselves over the one problem which fell clearly in their jurisdiction—the boundaries of the Länder in the coming state. The London documents had recognized that the boundaries of the Länder, as they had been laid down by the exigencies of the invasion and early occupation period, were unsatisfactory. The prospect of changing them at once opened the way to bitter strife, particularly in the French zone, which had been the most curious product of all the boundary agreements.

In Rheinland-Pfalz the problem took several forms. In the first place, there was the question whether Rheinland-Pfalz should be enlarged. In the early days of the occupation, the Christian Democrats had been strong proponents of a Rhine state. As early as July 1946, the *Rheinischer Merkur*'s editor, Dr. F. A. Kramer, had pondered "the destiny of the Rhineland," especially since Prussia, "unregretted and without renown, has passed into history."[65] One of Dr. Süsterhenn's first contributions was a series of articles on the life of Benedikt Schmittmann, a Rhenish federalist.[66] In August of the next year, G. Markscheffel, editor of the Socialist paper *Die Freiheit*, outspokenly attacked the idea of the Rhineland as a unity, a passion that was flamed by the thought that the Socialist nucleus in the Pfalz would be even further swamped if it were linked to the predominantly Christian Democrat domain of Minister-President Adenauer in Nordrhein-Westfalen.[67]

Adenauer himself became the focus of a further quarrel in February 1948, when the *Rheinischer Merkur* published the report of a communication from him that pointed out the need to build the future of Germany upon the historical affinity of the German Länder, and especially upon the affinity existing between Nordrhein-Westfalen and Rheinland-Pfalz.[68] Adenauer wanted the west of Germany to become a stabilizing element in a federalized Germany, holding the balance between the centralist north and the particularist south. In reply, *Die Freiheit* took an opposite position by publishing a communiqué from Dr. Schumacher, in which he took a strong stand against Adenauer's project. "The temptation to create a Catholic Rhenish Prussia is too strong," he wrote. In his opinion, Adenauer wanted to create a great bloc which would inevitably be particularist, which would lead to the internationalization of the Ruhr and would be under strong French influence.[69] Altmeier added a conciliatory word on March 13, in the

Rheinischer Merkur, saying that the boundaries of the Länder were far from settled, but adding that any modification of the borders should wait until the final political powers of these Länder were settled. Then, any decision would be made by the people themselves. It was clear what a difficult postion Altmeier was in. The quarrel had been brought in from the outside and was not really stirring Rheinland-Pfalz at all, but Altmeier was forced to support his CDU chief by mouthing platitudes and waiting for the crisis to blow over.[70]

At the same time, the Communist paper *Neues Leben* proclaimed a plague on both their houses. In an article on "clerical federalism in the South-West," W. Prinz noted that federalism was strong where Catholicism was strong, namely in the southwest and west, and especially around Aachen, Koblenz, and Munich. The Christian Democrats, he went on, were divided between the worst federalists of all, such as Schäfer, Adenauer, Kramer, and Süsterhenn; the liberal federalists such as Altmeier and Müller; and the evangelical group which was Prussian junker in orientation. As for the Socialists, he added, the party, and especially its leader Schumacher, was completely federalist. Only the Communist party, he decided, wanted the unity of Germany.[71]

The second major boundary problem facing Rheinland-Pfalz was the dispute over the position of the Pfalz. This dispute flared up in October and November. The Catholic Church seemed to be in favor of returning the Pfalz to Bavaria, especially because of the close relationship between Cardinal Faulhaber of Munich and Bishop Wendel of Speyer. The Christian Democrats continued to play for time by avoiding a decision. Altmeier demanded a complete maintenance of the status quo. Dr. Hans Haberer, head of the Christian Democratic party in the Pfalz, suggested linking the Pfalz with the territories on the right bank of the Rhine. For the Socialists, however, this seemed the ideal opportunity to get the Pfalz free from the Christian Democrat dominance in Rheinland-Pfalz, and they proposed to join the Pfalz to Württemberg-Baden. Not content with that, they proposed the further mutilation of Rheinland-Pfalz, by giving Rheinhessen and Montabaur to Hessen, and Trier and Koblenz to Nordrhein-Westfalen. *Die Freiheit*, proposing this on July 10 and 14, pointed out that the major aim was to avoid the creation of a state on the left bank of the Rhine. The Democrats proposed yet another solution, the union of Pfalz with Hessen. Such widely differing opinions could hardly be reconciled or compromised, and *faute de mieux* Altmeier's opinion finally carried the day.[72]

The boundary dispute in Baden and Württemberg took a more passionate form. The problem was complicated by the fact that the reunion of north and south Baden and of north and south Württemberg could only be carried out by splitting up the Land of Württemberg-Baden, which the American military government had created in 1945. This Land had proved to be a successful unit, and there was no pressure from the government of Württemberg-Baden for its dissolution. It appeared to many that the obvious solution to the whole question was to unite the three Länder of south Baden, south Württemberg, Württemberg-Baden into one Land, which even then would scarcely be larger than Rheinland-Pfalz and which would have the dual purpose of reuniting both Baden and Württemberg without splitting Württemberg-Baden. This scheme was highly satisfactory to Dr. Reinhold Maier, minister-president of Württemberg-Baden and was acceptable to Gebhard Müller, of Württemberg-Hohenzollern. But it aroused the vehement opposition of Leo Wohleb of Baden. Wohleb told the *Allgemeine Zeitung* that it was unthinkable that Baden and Württemberg should be united.[73] When Adenauer came out for three large states in the southwest and west, Wohleb indignantly opposed him. He was now fighting with his back to the wall, since he was opposed by the other parties in Baden, by all parties in Württemberg and in Württemberg-Baden, and even by some Christian Democrats in south Baden. He continued to fight a delaying action, however. Throughout the boundary discussions in August, he fought against the fusion, forcing the military governors to attempt to mediate the question. Finally, in a meeting in Bebenhausen in south Württemberg, the three minister-presidents discussed what should be done if the people were to reject fusion. Wohleb and Müller wanted them to have a choice of reconstructing Baden and Württemberg, while Maier, intent on preserving the identity of his new Land, wanted them only to have the choice of creating a state of south Baden and a united state of Württemberg-Hohenzollern and Württemberg-Baden, or a unification of all three.[74]

Gebhard Müller, reporting on the results of the conferences to the Württemberg Landtag on October 7, 1948, said that the decisive point was that the people of north Baden and north Württemberg no longer wanted to be separated. As a result, he was willing to accept fusion. He found the attitude of Freiburg, he said, "not incomprehensible, but unjustified."[75] Wohleb put his own case to the Landtag of Baden on September 7, 1948. He was almost defeated, however, when the Socialists demanded an immediate vote on the ratification of the union of Baden and Württemberg. The Socialist motion was rejected by only 25 votes to 22, with 3 abstentions.[76] The final effect of Wohleb's opposition was that the problem of the future status of Baden and Württemberg was postponed, and in fact was only settled in 1952, when the people of the three Länder voted for fusion, after the federal parliament had passed a law ordering the referendum and laying down the form in which it was to be held. In the final vote, only the people of south Baden rejected the fusion, which was upheld in north and south Württemberg and in north Baden.[77]

The early months of 1949 were relatively quiet on the political scene. While the minister-presidents were slowly gaining more of the attributes of political equals, through their conferences with Koenig and through several visits to Paris to confer with the premier, Robert Schuman, all were waiting for the results of the debates of the Parliamentary Council to be made known. Occasional reports of the disputes that were consuming so many months drifted through. In February 1949 the *Rheinischer Merkur* noted that Süsterhenn was again cast in the role of supporting the rights of the church schools against the other parties.[78] In March there came a great crisis when the military governors handed to the Parliamentary Council a long list of objections to the electoral law which had only finally been passed by the Council on February 24. This action raised a great outburst of ill-feeling against the military governors. Carlo Schmid, writing in *Die Welt* on March 17, 1949, blamed the governors for waiting so long before presenting their objections.[79] What was worse, in Socialist eyes, the objections of the military governors seemed a deliberate attempt, instigated by General Koenig, to change the final draft in a way more acceptable to the Christian Democrats and the French. However, this disagreement was finally compromised when the decisions of the Washington conference of April 1949 were made known. On April 25, 1949, the military governors accepted the Basic Law.[80]

The disputes continued during the discussion of the electoral law.

Already, in March, the military governors had interfered to demand that the Landtage make their own electoral laws, and in May to ask for changes in the method of weighting adopted between proportional and party list representation. On the latter occasion, the Socialists again claimed collusion between the French and the Christian Democrats; and Dr. Schumacher accused the "CDU politicians of working behind the scenes with the French."[81] The military governors finally took upon themselves the onus of ordering the changes they wanted, and these were immediately accepted by the Germans.

After the Basic Law had been accepted by the Parliamentary Council, it remained for the Landtage to take a position on it. The Landtag of Rheinland-Pfalz met on May 18, 1949. The only major speech was by Minister-President Altmeier, in which he recommended the immediate ratification of the constitution. In the final vote, the Basic Law was accepted by 91 votes to 8, the Communists alone voting against it.[82]

In Baden there was only a very short debate. Friedrich Maier, the Socialist representative at the Parliamentary Council, gave a brief historical review of the events leading to the writing of the Basic Law, and noted the importance of the Cold War. The only long or passionate speech was Erwin Eckert's denunciation, as Communist spokesman, of the whole procedure of writing a constitution for West Germany. The final vote was an overwhelming acceptance by 49 to 2.[83]

In Württemberg, on the contrary, the session gave rise to a full and interesting debate. Opening the debate on May 21 for the Christian Democrats, Gebhard Müller regretted the small part played by the minister-presidents in writing the law, the long delay before the law was completed, and the Allied note of April 23, which he felt made the Germans accept a more centralized constitution. He welcomed the direct participation of Germany in European affairs, however, and praised the Länder for their work since 1945. Paul Binder, the Christian Democratic representative on the Parliamentary Council, reproached the Allies for delaying progress and for their failure to state at the beginning their understanding of the term federalism. As a result, he said, there was less federalism in the law than there was in the first compromise between the CDU and the SPD. Nonetheless, he felt that the constitution had the "spirit of liberal rationalism" and did give important powers to the Länder, especially through the Bundesrat. Carlo Schmid again gave a full and reasoned account of the Socialist position. He began by congratulating the Länder upon their achievements during the past years. They had, he said, "succeeded in maintaining peace and order, in laying somewhat of a groundwork for reconstruction of the state, and in securing the food supply—that has been, God knows, great work by the Länder." He was not entirely happy about the federalism in the constitution, since he did not believe that federalism could solve the problems of the refugees, of the destroyed cities, or economic organization, or power in industry, of transport or food supply. But it was a compromise. The final vote, however, was 34 for and 16 against, with one abstention.[84]

The ratification of the constitution by south Württemberg gave the two-thirds majority needed for its promulgation, and it was declared officially in force the same afternoon. It was then possible to proceed to the federal elections which would bring to an end the separate existence of the French zone. In November of the previous year, the Germans in the French zone had gone to the polls again, for the second election of the Gemeinde and Kreis assemblies. As Table 18 shows, this time there was little of the flurry and excitement and widespread participation which had greeted the return of the ballot box in September and October of 1946.

The campaign for the Bundestag elections was held in the summer of 1949, and it did not provoke much greater excitement in the French

TABLE 18

GEMEINDE AND KREIS ELECTIONS IN THE FRENCH ZONE[85]
(Gemeinde: November 14, 1948)
(Kreis: December 5, 1948)

	RHEINLAND-PFALZ		BADEN		WÜRTTEMBERG		LINDAU	
	Gemeinde	Kreis	Gemeinde	Kreis	Gemeinde	Kreis	Gemeinde	Kreis
Per cent voting....	74.1	74.7	66.4	65.7	66.9	74.0		
CDU	28.2	47.6	43.0	49.3	20.0	40.8	34.7	52.4
SPD	25.4	32.9	20.9	25.6	10.5	15.2	13.4	10.9
KPD	5.4	5.7	4.5	6.0	3.3	3.9	1.5	
DPD	5.3	10.0	13.6	19.0	6.1	8.8	3.2	
Independents	19.1	3.8			60.1	36.9	42.6	12.1

zone than had been shown in the earlier regional elections. The percentage of those voting in Baden and Rheinland-Pfalz was very little higher than it had been in the local elections the previous winter, and in Württemberg it was even lower. The final results of the election of August 1949 (see Table 19) showed that the Christian Democratic party had maintained its hold on the French zone and would have a majority in the Bundestag. As shown in Table 20, however, the union of the French and American zones, which were largely Christian Democrat, with the British zone with its majority of Socialists, greatly reduced the preponderance of the CDU as compared with the majorities it had enjoyed in the French zone.

The French zone as a separate entity ceased to exist on September 21, 1949. With the inauguration of the new government of the West

TABLE 19

BUNDESTAG ELECTION IN THE FRENCH ZONE[86]
(August 14, 1949)

	Rheinland-Pfalz	Baden	Württemberg
Per cent voting......	79.6	70.0	64.6
CDU	49.1	49.6	59.1
SPD	28.6	24.0	18.9
KPD	6.2	3.8	5.3
DPD	15.8	19.3	15.3

TABLE 20

BUNDESTAG ELECTION: FRENCH, AMERICAN, AND BRITISH ZONES[87]
(August 14, 1949)

Party	French Zone	American Zone	British Zone	All Zones	Number of Members in Bundestag
CDU	51.4	27.6	29.6	31.1	139
SPD	25.7	26.3	32.2	29.4	131
KPD	5.6	5.6	5.9	5.7	15
DPD	16.1	16.1	7.9	11.8	52
Bavarian Party		4.1		4.1	17
German Party				3.8	17

German Republic, the replacement of the military governors by the civilian high commissioners, and the final ceremony by which the tri-zone was officially created, the period of military occupation came to an end. These four years had been of great importance for political life in the French zone. Although the French had lagged behind the Bizone in the speed with which they had permitted German politicians to take over responsibility for administration of their own affairs, they had created a workable administration in a complicated administrative area. They had encouraged a new generation of German politicians to gain experience in the workings of democracy in the Gemeinde, the Kreis, and the Land, and to develop administrative skills. They had furthered the development of constitutional thought and its practical application, at the Land level, with wholly beneficial results when the time came to apply that experience at the national level. They had given the people of the French zone—and particularly the young people, who had never witnessed the democratic process in action—the time to grow up politically and to gain familiarity with the processes of democratic life. The ease with which the politicians of the French zone were able to step into national responsibilities speaks highly for the results of the occupation period. Most important of all, the men who rose to prominence during the occupation period were in no sense regarded as collaborationists when West Germany regained its inde-pendence. This major fact is perhaps the best testimony to the political acumen and good faith of those men, and also of the military govern-ment which permitted them to rise to power.[88]

CHAPTER XI

Conclusions

THE policy of the French in their zone of occupation in Germany had three aims—security, economic exploitation, and Franco-German *rapprochement*. These aims were obviously contradictory. The criticism that was lavished on the French military government during these years was due to French attempts to guarantee the security and the economic revival of France, and much of this criticism was valid. The critics failed to take into account, however, the surprising success of the French policy of encouraging the growth of understanding between the two countries. The achievements of the French in this sphere justify calling the occupation a success.

In 1944 General de Gaulle had made it clear that France intended to guarantee its own security and that possession of a zone of occupation in Germany was an integral part of his policy. He intended particularly that France should occupy most of the left bank of the Rhine. The French thesis that the Rhineland should be detached from Germany, the Ruhr internationalized, and the Saar placed under French occupation, was France's answer to the problem of guaranteeing its security against German aggression. Moreover, de Gaulle was determined that the re-created army of France should play as large a part as possible in 1945 in ensuring that France be granted its demands.

Between March and May 1945, in the invasion of Germany, the French army was used to take for France the "gages" of her future security. By constant pressure on the American commanders, both at the divisional level and at supreme headquarters, the French were able to take over increasingly large parts of the invasion front. As General de Gaulle has written, "whatever the manner, our troops had to seize, on the right bank, a French zone of occupation."[1] In March the French First Army established itself along some forty kilometers of the left bank of the Rhine. By May, after campaigns undertaken in certain cases for political rather than military motives, the French had crossed the Rhine, captured the major part of the Länder of Baden and Württemberg, including their capital cities of Karlsruhe and Stuttgart, and taken the Vorarlberg in Austria. This military campaign was conducted while negotiations proceeded in the European Advisory Commission and between heads of state on the boundaries of the zone to be assigned to France, a zone which, according to the Yalta agreement, was to consist of sections of the British and American zones. It is clear that the French military actions during the invasion were intended to exercise a direct influence upon the boundary negotiations taking place at the same time. The delay of two months after the end of hostilities before the boundary settlement was reached was due to French demands for territory which its Western allies were not willing to give up.

The zone which France finally agreed to accept was of considerable value. French troops were stationed along the whole course of the Rhine from Switzerland to Remagen, assuring in the most direct sense the security of France. Occupation of the zone gave France, through the Allied Control Council, a share in the governing of Germany as a whole and at the same time the power to block any attempts to re-create a strong, centralized Germany which might again endanger France. Early American attempts to implement the Potsdam agreement by creating a central economic administration were vetoed by the French, and French opposition to any steps toward unification of Germany was maintained just long enough for the growing animosity of the Soviet Union and the United States to become a guarantee of the future maintenance of German disunity.

Security, then, was the first aim of the French occupation. A further aim, which gradually became predominant from 1946 onward, was to use the zone to speed the economic recovery of France. Exploitation of the zone's resources took many forms. The most obvious were the restitution of goods removed from France during the German occupation, the collection of reparations in kind from the zone by the dismantling of industrial equipment, and the use of the zone's resources to maintain an important section of the French army, a large military government staff and numerous bands of dependents brought from France. Finally, the industrial production and foreign trade of the zone were developed for the benefit of France.

Throughout the period of the occupation, no charges for the occupation fell to the French treasury, beyond a minimal nine billion francs yearly in support of the French army. For the first three years of the occupation, the value of exports from the zone exceeded the cost of imports. Only when it became obvious that the United States would cover the cost of any deficit through the grant of Marshall aid was the zone permitted to import more than it exported. The favorable balance of trade was maintained by permitting the Germans only a very low standard of living, especially of food supply, by making the fullest use of stocks of raw materials and natural resources without replenishing them by the re-investment of capital, and by developing export industries, such as coal, rather than industries useful for home consumption, such as leather goods.

France itself took the majority of the zone's exports, and for that reason industrial production was geared to the manufacture of those goods most needed in French reconstruction. France obtained much needed sources of power from German coal and electricity; it bought scarce chemicals and metal goods; and it cut heavily into the zone's forests to provide the wood needed for French rebuilding. And in all French commercial transactions with Germany, the French military government not only fixed the price of goods to be sold but also enjoyed a 20 per cent discount on all goods purchased, as a form of reparation.

Much of the criticism by foreign observers of France's policy of seeking security and its own economic recovery seems justified. At the same time, much of the criticism made by French observers also seems valid. During the months immediately following the invasion of Germany, the military government of the French zone did become the refuge of many former adherents of the Vichy regime. Moreover, the great reduction in strength of the army after the end of hostilities was undoubtedly used by officers of the regular army to eliminate some of the members of the Resistance who had received commissions after the Liberation. Many representatives of French business firms did find employment in the zone, and some of them were able to use their positions to aid the companies they represented.

Nevertheless, the critics presented a very one-sided picture of the French occupation. In the final analysis, the policy pursued by France in the zone was more to be justified than condemned. The German invasion and occupation had bled France white. The French economy had been ruthlessly exploited; over two million French workers had been sent to Germany; the border provinces had been stripped of their industrial and agricultural equipment. France's sufferings during the war explain, and perhaps justify, the French government's determination to secure guarantees of the future security of France and economic recompense for the losses France had suffered.

The maintenance of French troops in Germany gave both the French and German people several years in which to readjust their attitudes toward each other in relation to the new power struggle of the postwar era. Furthermore, the economic policy pursued in the zone proved of great benefit in rehabilitating the French economy, and it provided only a temporary drag on German economic recovery.

The most persuasive argument, however, that can be made in defense of the French occupation in Germany lay in the undeniable *rapprochement* between the two peoples which the occupation fostered. The policy of re-educating the German people proved to be an immense success because it was carried out so broadly and so intelligently. The officers of the French military government charged with the educational program set as their main aim bringing the Germans back into the mainstream of European culture. They saw the isolation of the German mind as the greatest danger. The false nationalism which they believed lay at the root of the aggressive militarism of the past century could only be displaced, they believed, by truer ideals. In the first place, the Germans were encouraged to return to the worthy traditions in their own past, to "the true humanist tradition represented with such glory by a Goethe, a Kant, or a Beethoven."[2] But above all the French were determined to introduce the Germans to the achievements of French civilization, to show them, as one observer put it, the French sense of the dignity of man and "that universalism which is the vocation of the French spirit."[3]

Hence, it is in the educational sphere that the French zone stood as an example to the other zones. In the French zone, the schools and

universities were the first to open. The French published almost twice
as many school textbooks per child as the British, and seven times as
many as the Americans. Several hundred young French instructors
taught the French language in German schools. The University of
Mainz, founded on French initiative, rapidly became one of Germany's
great institutions of learning. Above all, the French military government had the courage to organize personal contacts in ever growing
numbers between French and German students, writers, artists, workers, and administrators. They brought French painting, music, sculpture, drama, and literature within the reach of all the Germans in the
zone. And they never frowned upon personal contacts with the Germans. There was no policy of nonfraternization in the French zone,
and Germans were permitted to go on living in the same houses as
the French. Even the much criticized band of dependents encouraged
the development of personal acquaintance between the occupiers and
occupied, with surprising results in the legacy of good will left behind.
The popularity of the "twinning" of German and French cities and
provinces is a result of many of these contacts.

Even the storms of the early days of German self-government have
left a favorable balance. It is true, of course, that in the very first
months of the occupation, an attempt was made, especially in the Pfalz
and the Saar, to use Germans who were separatists, but from the winter
of 1945 on the French were satisfied to nominate Germans to political
office who were proven democrats. A very large number of these
Germans, who worked as well as they could with the French administration, first as nominated administrators and then as popularly elected
representatives, have remained in the forefront of political life at both
the regional and the national level. Their disagreements with the
French over such matters as dismantling and denazification proved
that the French, although refusing to share as much political power
with the Germans as, for example, the Americans were willing to do,
had permitted the election of genuinely representational bodies, and
were even, at times, swayed by the wishes of those bodies.

Thus the French zone presented the paradox of a military government pursuing two conflicting policies. On the one hand, Germany was treated as a traditional enemy against whom military guarantees had to be assured and as a criminal nation whose duty it was
to repair, in part at least, the damage done during the occupation of

France. But on the other hand—and this policy has been more lasting in its effects—the Germans of the French zone were being treated as welcome partners in a common cultural inheritance. An observer traveling through the zone today is struck by the lack of bitterness toward France felt by the older people and the friendliness shown by the younger generation. Such attitudes are the best testimony to the success of France's policy in its zone of occupation in Germany.

Notes

CHAPTER I

1. Cordell Hull, *Memoirs* (New York, 1948), II, 788.
2. James F. Byrnes, *Speaking Frankly* (New York, 1947), p. 25; Edward R. Stettinius, *Roosevelt and the Russians: The Yalta Conference* (New York, 1950), p. 127; Robert E. Sherwood, *Roosevelt and Hopkins* (2nd ed. rev., New York, 1950), p. 777.
3. Charles de Gaulle, *Vers l'armée de métier* (Paris, 1934).
4. Charles de Gaulle, *Mémoires de guerre* (Paris: Librairie Plon, 1954–59), I, 267–68.
5. Royal Institute of International Affairs, Arnold and Veronica M. Toynbee (eds.), *Survey of International Affairs, 1939–1946: Hitler's Europe* (London, 1954) [hereafter referred to as R.I.I.A., *Hitler's Europe*], pp. 457–58. The Free French forces operated almost exclusively under British control until May 1943, since until then they were largely British-trained and British-equipped. Roosevelt declared them eligible to receive lend-lease equipment in mid-November of 1941, but with the proviso that they be supplied indirectly through the British. In this way Roosevelt postponed a decision on the problem of the political status of the Free French movement. For a full account of American relations with the French armed forces throughout the war, see Marcel Vigneras's excellent study, *Rearming the French* (United States Army in World War II: Special Studies, Washington, 1957).
6. Winston S. Churchill, *The Second World War* (Boston, 1948–53), II, 182, 215.
7. Royal Institute of International Affairs, Margaret Carlisle (ed.), *Documents on International Affairs, 1939–1946*, Vol. II, *Hitler's Europe* (London, 1954), 167–70.
8. Georges Catroux, *Dans la bataille de Méditerranée: Égypte-Levant-Afrique du Nord, 1940–1944: témoignages et commentaires* (Paris, 1949), p. 30; R.I.I.A., *Hitler's Europe*, p. 359.
9. Hull, *Memoirs*, I, 860; R.I.I.A., *Hitler's Europe*, p. 362; William D. Leahy, *I Was There: The Personal Story of the Chief of Staff to Presidents Roosevelt and Truman Based on His Notes and Diaries Made at the Time* (New York, 1950), p. 6.
10. Churchill, *Second World War*, II, 508.

11. De Gaulle, *Mémoires*, I, 472, 506.

12. William L. Langer gives a full, documented account of American policy toward the Vichy regime in *Our Vichy Gamble* (New York, 1947).

13. Henry L. Stimson and McGeorge Bundy, *On Active Service in Peace and War* (New York, 1950), p. 551.

14. For a detailed account of the St. Pierre–Miquelon incident, see Sherwood, *Roosevelt and Hopkins*, pp. 479–86.

15. Jacques Soustelle, *Envers et contre tout* (Paris, 1947), I, 328; de Gaulle, *Mémoires*, II, 23.

16. *Ibid.*, II, 81. Details of Giraud's relations with the Americans are given in Vigneras, *Rearming the French*, pp. 16–44.

17. Churchill, *Second World War*, IV, 644–45.

18. De Gaulle, *Mémoires*, II, 79. Accounts of this dramatic meeting at Casablanca are given in de Gaulle, *Mémoires*, II, 79–81; Sherwood, *Roosevelt and Hopkins*, pp. 675–85; Churchill, *Second World War*, IV, 680–82, 693; Elliott Roosevelt, *As He Saw It* (New York, 1946), pp. 68–120. Churchill took great exception to this account by President Roosevelt's son, especially to the imputation that Churchill was trying to stop de Gaulle from going to Casablanca.

19. Jean de Lattre de Tassigny, *The History of the French First Army*, translated by Malcolm Barnes (London: George Allen & Unwin Ltd., 1952), p. 28.

20. Stimson and Bundy, *On Active Service*, pp. 545–46.

21. Hull, *Memoirs*, II, 1431.

22. Leahy, *I Was There*, p. 244; Hull, *Memoirs*, II, 1433.

23. De Gaulle, *Mémoires*, III, 44, 302–10; Churchill, *Second World War*, VI, 247.

24. De Gaulle, *Mémoires*, II, 237–39.

25. *Ibid.*, II, 240.

26. Churchill, *Second World War*, V, 179.

27. De Lattre, *French First Army*, p. 180.

28. Stimson and Bundy, *On Active Service*, pp. 575–76.

29. *New York Times*, August 15, 1944. This, and other evidence on the development of de Gaulle's views, is given in Joachim Joesten, *The Rhineland Question* (Elmhurst, N.Y., 1945), p. 19.

30. Contre-Amiral Pierre Barjot, "Le Problème militaire du Rhin," in Jean Dumont (ed.), *Le Rhin: Nil de l'Occident* (Paris, 1946), pp. 197–98, and map facing p. 193.

31. Sherwood, *Roosevelt and Hopkins*, p. 844. The discussions on the possibility of granting France a zone of occupation in Germany and a seat on the Control Council are given at length in most accounts of the conference. See especially, United States, Department of State, *Foreign Relations of the United States, Diplomatic Papers: The Conferences at Malta and Yalta, 1945* (Washington, 1955) [hereafter referred to as Dept. of State, *Conferences at Malta and Yalta*]; Sherwood, *Roosevelt and Hopkins*, pp. 870–90; Stettinius, *Roosevelt and the Russians*; Byrnes, *Speaking Frankly*, pp. 21–45; Churchill, *Second World War*, VI, 346–64; Leahy, *I Was There*, pp. 291–323. Good secondary accounts are given in John L.

Snell, *Wartime Origins of the East-West Dilemma Over Germany* (New Orleans, 1959), pp. 139–68, and in his chapter "What to Do with Germany?" in John L. Snell (ed.), *The Meaning of Yalta: Big Three Diplomacy and the New Balance of Power* (Baton Rouge, 1956), pp. 67–70; and in Ernst Deuerlein, *Die Einheit Deutschlands: Ihre Erörterungen und Behandlung auf den Kriegs- und Nachkriegskonferenzen 1941–1949* (Frankfurt, 1957).

32. Stettinius, *Roosevelt and the Russians*, p. 128; Churchill, *Second World War*, VI, 253, 259; Sherwood, *Roosevelt and Hopkins*, pp. 845–46. De Gaulle himself states in his memoirs that although the British and the Russians were far from enthusiastic about having France represented at the conference, they made it clear to him that "among the 'Three,' one only opposed our presence. . . . I could not doubt that the explicit refusal came from President Roosevelt." De Gaulle, *Mémoires*, III, 81.

33. Churchill, *Second World War*, VI, 258.

34. Dept. of State, *Conferences at Malta and Yalta*, pp. 283–87.

35. Philip E. Mosely, "The Occupation of Germany: New Light on How the Zones Were Drawn," *Foreign Affairs*, XXVIII (July 1950), 589–97.

36. On the Quebec Conference, see Hull, *Memoirs*, II, 1603–22; Stimson and Bundy, *On Active Service*, pp. 560–83; Sherwood, *Roosevelt and Hopkins*, pp. 818–32; Byrnes, *Speaking Frankly*, pp. 183–87; Churchill, *Second World War*, VI, 146–61; Snell, *Dilemma over Germany*, pp. 75–76, 88.

37. Dept. of State, *Conferences at Malta and Yalta*, pp. 293–94, 300–301.

38. Stettinius, *Roosevelt and the Russians*, p. 63.

39. *Ibid.*, pp. 101–2.

40. Dept. of State, *Conferences at Malta and Yalta*, p. 572.

41. *Ibid.*, p. 628.

42. Stettinius, *Roosevelt and the Russians*, p. 89.

43. Churchill, *Second World War*, VI, 353.

44. Stettinius, *Roosevelt and the Russians*, pp. 126–29.

45. Dept. of State, *Conferences at Malta and Yalta*, pp. 617–19, 629–30.

46. Stettinius, *Roosevelt and the Russians*, p. 170.

47. Sherwood, *Roosevelt and Hopkins*, pp. 858–59, 861.

48. Dept. of State, *Conferences at Malta and Yalta*, pp. 899–900, 948.

49. Sherwood, *Roosevelt and Hopkins*, p. 861.

50. *Le Figaro*, February 21, 1945. In his memoirs, de Gaulle claims that there was no point in his going to Algiers since the decisions at Yalta had already been made. He ignores the fact that the important question of the boundaries of the French zone was still undecided. De Gaulle, *Mémoires*, III, 87.

51. Mosely, "Occupation of Germany," *Foreign Affairs*, XXVIII (July 1950), 588.

52. Dumont, *Le Rhin*, pp. 197–98.

53. *New York Times*, August 14, 1944.

54. Dept. of State, *Conferences at Malta and Yalta*, pp. 284, 288–89.

55. De Gaulle, *Mémoires*, III, 68.

56. Dept. of State, *Conferences at Malta and Yalta*, pp. 293–94, 572.

57. *Le Figaro*, February 6, 1945.

58. De Gaulle, *Mémoires*, III, 131–32, 152–53.

59. De Lattre, *French First Army*, p. 407.

60. *Ibid.*, p. 410.

61. *Ibid.*, p. 421; de Gaulle, *Mémoires*, III, 155–56, 490.

62. De Lattre, *French First Army*, p. 422; *Revue historique de l'armée*, No. 2 (October 1945), 292; No. 2 (April–June 1947), 92.

63. De Lattre, *French First Army*, pp. 482–83.

64. "West of Laufen without change, then the Heilbronn-Stuttgart railway as far as Asperg, the autobahn crossroad north of Leonberg, and the autobahn Karlsruhe-Augsburg to Bernhausen, Metzingen, Dettingen, Ehingen, Rheinstetten (to the 1st Army), Kempten and Hofen (to the 7th Army)." *Ibid.*, p. 489.

65. *Ibid.*, p. 490.

66. Dwight D. Eisenhower, *Crusade in Europe* (New York, 1950), p. 412. Eisenhower's letter and de Gaulle's reply are printed in de Gaulle, *Mémoires*, III, 491–94.

67. Harry S. Truman, *Memoirs* (New York, 1955–56), I, 238–39.

68. De Lattre, *French First Army*, p. 492.

69. Mosely, "Occupation of Germany," *Foreign Affairs*, XXVIII (July 1950), 600.

70. *Ibid.*

71. Lucius D. Clay, *Decision in Germany* (New York, 1950), p. 13.

72. *New York Times*, May 26, 1945; June 8, 1945; June 14, 1945. De Gaulle was occupied in May by another conflict with the United States over French seizure of certain enclaves of Italian territory on the Alpine frontier of France, as well as with a quarrel with Britain over France's desire to extend the French zone to include Cologne. Truman, *Memoirs*, I, 102, 215, 240–41; de Gaulle, *Mémoires*, III, 179–84; Leahy, *I Was There*, pp. 373–74; Churchill, *Second World War*, VI, 566–68.

73. Germany (Territory under Allied occupation, 1945——, French zone), Commandement en chef français en Allemagne, *Notice sur le gouvernement militaire* (Baden-Baden, 1945), p. 16.

74. *New York Times*, July 28, 1945.

75. *Notice sur le gouvernement militaire*, p. 16. Excellent maps showing the different plans for the division of Germany proposed during the war are given in Deuerlein, *Die Einheit Deutschlands*, pp. 25, 41, 47, 49.

CHAPTER II

1. De Gaulle, *Mémoires*, III, 305.

2. United States, Department of State, *Bulletin*, V, 112 (August 16, 1941), 125–26. Alfred Grosser, in *L'Allemagne de l'Occident, 1945–1952* (Paris, 1953), p. 35, remarks that the Atlantic Charter "is now neglected everywhere in the world except in Germany, where it is constantly quoted to prove that the allies'

policy and behavior toward the Germans are a betrayal of their principles." An official account of the organization by which postwar policy was planned in Washington during the war is given in United States, Department of State, *Postwar Foreign Policy Preparation, 1939–1945* (Washington, 1949).

3. Sherwood, *Roosevelt and Hopkins*, p. 797.

4. Mosely, "Occupation of Germany," *Foreign Affairs*, XXVIII (July 1950), 588–89, 594. A defense of the War Department, which, according to Mosely, caused great difficulties in the negotiations, is made by Alfred G. Warner in "Our Secret Deal over Germany," *Saturday Evening Post*, August 2, 1950, pp. 30, 66–68. See also Walter L. Dorn, "The Debate over American Occupation Policy in Germany in 1944–1945," *Political Science Quarterly*, LXXII (December 1957), 487–88, for an explanation of the motives of the War Department.

5. Details of the conflict over the Morgenthau plan are given in Stimson and Bundy, *On Active Service*, p. 150; Hull, *Memoirs*, II, 1603–22; Byrnes, *Speaking Frankly*, pp. 183–87; Sherwood, *Roosevelt and Hopkins*, pp. 818–32; Churchill, *Second World War*, VI, 156–57; Dept. of State, *Conferences at Malta and Yalta*, pp. 137–38; E. F. Penrose, *Economic Planning for the Peace* (Princeton, N.J., 1953), pp. 243–58; Snell, *Dilemma Over Germany*, pp. 64–93; Carl J. Friedrich *et al.*, *American Experiences in Military Government in World War II* (New York, 1948), pp. 36–38. Morgenthau's own views are expressed in Henry Morgenthau, Jr., *Germany Is Our Problem* (New York, 1945).

6. Mosely, "Occupation of Germany," *Foreign Affairs*, XXVIII (July 1950), 598; Lord Strang, *Home and Abroad* (London, 1956), p. 220; Hajo Holborn, *American Military Government: Its Organization and Policies* (New York, 1947), pp. 22–26, 44. The lack of more detailed information on the work of the European Advisory Commission makes it difficult to describe fully the negotiations over the boundaries of the French zone of occupation and the pressures being exerted by the French government.

7. Royal Institute of International Affairs, Beate Ruhm von Oppen (ed.), *Documents on Germany under Occupation, 1945–1954* (London, 1955) [hereafter referred to as R.I.I.A., *Documents on Germany*], pp. 29–35.

8. R.I.I.A., *Documents on Germany*, pp. 35–37.

9. Philip E. Mosely, "Dismemberment of Germany: The Allied Negotiations from Yalta to Potsdam," *Foreign Affairs*, XXVIII (April 1950), 487–98; Deuerlein, *Die Einheit Deutschlands*, p. 101.

10. André Siegfried (ed.), *L'Année politique, 1944–1945* (Paris, 1946), p. 130.

11. *L'Aube*, February 21, 1945.

12. *L'Humanité*, February 14, 1945; February 17, 1945.

13. R.I.I.A., *Documents on Germany*, pp. 42–45.

14. Clay, *Decision in Germany*, pp. 108–9.

15. Germany (Territory under allied occupation, 1945———), Allied Control Council, *Official Gazette*, No. 1 (October 29, 1945), 6–23.

16. Germany (Territory under allied occupation, 1945———, French zone),

Commandement en chef français en Allemagne, Direction de l'information, *Revue de la zone française,* No. 2 (December 15, 1945), 10.

17. "Le représentant français au Conseil de Contrôle interallié de Berlin ne sera pas autorisé à souscrire à une mesure préjugeant le sort particulier de la région rhéno-westphalienne avant que la question posée à Londres ait été débattue par les cinq ministres et ait fait l'objet d'une décision." France, Ministère des affaires étrangères, *Documents français relatifs à l'Allemagne, 1945–1947* (Paris, 1947) [hereafter referred to as *Documents français relatifs à l'Allemagne*], p. 16.

18. Clay, *Decision in Germany,* p. 110.

19. *Ibid.,* p. 121.

20. Control Council, *Official Gazette,* No. 3 (January 31, 1946), 43–46; No. 5 (March 31, 1946), 98–115; No. 9 (July 31, 1946), 166–69.

21. Basil Davidson, *Germany, What Now? Potsdam, 1945—Partition, 1946* (London, 1950), p. 64; Holborn, *American Military Government,* pp. 66–68.

22. *Revue de la zone française,* No. 2 (January, 1946), 10.

23. *The Times* (London), November 30, 1945.

24. *Ibid.,* April 8, 1946. See also Bidault's own statement of the French thesis in his article "Agreement on Germany: Key to World Peace," *Foreign Affairs,* XXIV (July 1946), 571–78, and the good summary of French aims in Dorothy Pickles, *France: The Fourth Republic* (London, 1955), pp. 187–93.

25. *L'Année politique, 1944–1945,* pp. 65, 67.

26. *L'Aube,* January 26, 1945.

27. *Ibid.,* May 4, 1945; *Le Figaro,* May 4, 1945.

28. *Documents français relatifs à l'Allemagne,* pp. 8–9.

29. *The Times* (London), September 10, 1945. De Gaulle followed up this idea on several occasions during the next month. Speaking in the French zone of occupation, he pointed to the "ties which formerly brought together the French and the south Germans." In Strasbourg, he proclaimed the "great French Rhenish task," which was to make the river a link with the west. In Brussels he spoke of "a western grouping, having for arteries: the Rhine, the Channel, the Mediterranean." De Gaulle, *Mémoires,* III, 218–22. According to Jacques Daubry, in his article, "Le Rhin, la Ruhr et l'Europe Occidentale," *Cahiers du Monde Nouveau,* II (1945), No. 6, "the Rhenish policy of France is entirely new. . . . The French government is no longer working toward a policy of assimilation and annexation. France intends to safeguard its security within the framework of international institutions."

30. *L'Humanité,* May 30, 1945.

31. *Revue de la zone française,* No. 1 (November 15, 1945), 9–10.

32. *Documents français relatifs à l'Allemagne,* pp. 13–16.

33. *Ibid.,* pp. 17–19.

34. *L'Année politique, 1946,* pp. 595–96.

35. *Documents français relatifs à l'Allemagne,* pp. 25–26.

36. *L'Humanité,* September 28, 1945.

37. *Ibid.,* October 20, 1945.

38. *L'Année politique, 1944–1945,* p. 486.

39. *L'Aube*, September 11, 1945.
40. *Ibid.*, February 21, 1945.
41. *La Nation*, September 11, 1945.
42. *Ibid.*, September 28, 1945.
43. *Le Populaire*, September 11, 1945.
44. *Ibid.*, March 14, 1946; March 26, 1946; March 31–April 1, 1946.
45. *The Times* (London), April 3, 1946.
46. *France-Soir*, April 6, 1946.
47. *Le Populaire*, July 28, 1946. Blum developed his views even further in *Le Populaire* on July 21–22, 1946, and July 24, 1946.
48. *Ibid.*, July 17, 1946.
49. *The Times* (London), January 14, 1947.
50. *Documents français relatifs à l'Allemagne*, pp. 42–45.
51. *Ibid.*, pp. 46–56.
52. *Ibid.*, pp. 57–64.
53. *Le Populaire*, April 22, 1947.

CHAPTER III

1. *L'Année politique, 1947*, p. 88. Bidault was referring to the coal agreement signed by the three Western foreign ministers in Moscow on April 21, which announced that if the Saar were integrated into the French economy, all Saar coal would be removed from the pool of the European Coal Organization, and a greater proportion of the coal from the other German mines would be made available for export.
2. *Ibid.*, p. 144.
3. France, Assemblée nationale, *Débats parlementaires; compte rendu in extenso des séances de l'Assemblée nationale et du Conseil de la République, 28 novembre, 1946—décembre, 1950* (Paris, 1946–51) [hereafter referred to as France, Assemblée nationale, *Débats*], Novembre 14, 1947, pp. 5024–41.
4. In 1946, Britain spent £40,000,000 on its zone of Germany. In 1947, even after bizonal fusion, Britain's share of the bizonal costs was £80,000,000. See Royal Institute of International Affairs, Peter Calvocoressi, *Survey of International Affairs, 1947–1948* (London, 1952), p. 64.
5. R.I.I.A., *Documents on Germany*, p. 196.
6. "It is the view of the American government that the German people throughout Germany, under proper safeguards, should now be given the primary responsibility for the running of their own affairs." United States, Department of State, *Germany, 1947–1949: The Story in Documents* (Washington, 1950) [hereafter referred to as *Germany, 1947–1949*], p. 7. Byrnes gives his own view of the motives which led him to make this speech in his *Speaking Frankly*, p. 187. Otto Butz gives a good, short account of this "phase of defensive improvisation" in American policy in his book, *Germany: Dilemma for American Foreign Policy* (New York, 1954).

7. Clay, *Decision in Germany*, p. 175.

8. *L'Année politique, 1947*, pp. 145–46.

9. France, Secrétariat d'état, Direction de la documentation, *Notes documentaires et études* [hereafter referred to as *Notes documentaires*], No. 737, p. 3.

10. R.I.I.A., *Documents on Germany*, pp. 238–39.

11. *Ibid.*, pp. 239–45. A summary of economic measures taken in the Bizone, with an annotated collection of documents, is given in James K. Pollock, James H. Meisel, and Henry L. Bretton (eds.), *Germany under Occupation: Illustrative Material and Documents* (rev. ed., Ann Arbor, Mich., 1949), pp. 222–63.

12. *New York Times*, January 3, 1948; Germany (Federal Republic, 1949——), Press and Information Office of the Federal German Government, *Germany Reports* (Bonn, 1955), p. 283.

13. *L'Année politique, 1947*, p. 215; Philip Williams, *Politics in Post-War France* (2nd ed., London, 1958), p. 32.

14. *Notes documentaires*, No. 789, p. 1.

15. *Le Monde*, December 6, 1947; *Notes documentaires*, No. 868, pp. 15–16.

16. *Ibid.*, No. 789, p. 4.

17. *The Times* (London), December 17, 1947; Clay, *Decision in Germany*, p. 176.

18. R.I.I.A., *Documents on Germany*, pp. 268–79. The new measures included a doubling of the number of members in the Economic Council and the creation of a Länderrat, or second house, and of a German High Court. See the diagram facing p. 466 in *Germany, 1947–1949.*

19. Clay, *Decision in Germany*, p. 179.

20. *Le Figaro*, January 22, 1948.

21. Clay, *Decision in Germany*, pp. 178–79; *The Times* (London), February 21, 1948.

22. France, Assemblée nationale, *Débats*, February 13, 1948, pp. 741–47.

23. *Germany, 1947–1949*, pp. 75–76.

24. Clay, *Decision in Germany*, pp. 397–400; Elmer Plischke, *The Allied Commission for Germany* (Bad Godesberg/Mehlem, 1953), p. 8.

25. R.I.I.A., *Documents on Germany*, p. 284.

26. R.I.I.A., *Survey of International Affairs, 1947–1948*, pp. 84–87. Congress later reduced the amount of aid to $5,000,000,000. Text of the Foreign Assistance Act is given in Royal Institute of International Affairs, Margaret Carlisle (ed.), *Documents on International Affairs, 1947–1948* (London, 1952) [hereafter referred to as R.I.I.A., *Documents, 1947–1948*], pp. 76–115. On the significance of French acceptance of the aid, see André Fontaine, "La Fin de l'histoire de la France," *La Nef*, Cahier No. 1 (December 1952), 142. The whole of this extremely useful issue of *La Nef* is devoted to the "German Problem."

27. *Germany, 1947–1949*, pp. 76–80.

28. R.I.I.A., *Documents, 1947–1948*, pp. 646–48.

29. This decision was taken at a meeting of the Foreign Affairs Committee of the National Assembly, the committee stating that the London agreements "ne répondent que dans une certaine mesure, sur des points importants, aux vues et

requêtes constamment soutenues par la France. . . ." *Le Monde*, June 11, 1948.

30. France, Assemblée nationale, *Débats*, March 5, 1948. On the background of the moves to force the Communists from Ramadier's government, see Alexander Werth, *France, 1940–1955* (New York, 1956), pp. 348–56.

31. *L'Humanité*, July 1, 1947.

32. *Ibid.*, July 4, 1947.

33. At this time, the Communist party indulged in a major campaign against General Koenig, with the intention of proving that he was instigator of the "complot bleu," a minor military plot for a *coup d'état*, which was discovered in May 1947. *Ibid.*, July 14, 1947.

34. *Ibid.*, June 5, 1948.

35. France, Assemblée nationale, *Débats*, June 11, 1948, pp. 3467–75; June 12, 1948, pp. 3484–88.

36. *L'Humanité*, June 19, 1948.

37. *Le Monde*, April 9, 1947.

38. The full text of the declaration is given in *L'Année politique, 1948*, pp. 334–35. Of the Right Wing papers, *Ce Matin* printed a full report but without editorial comment. *L'Ordre* reported his views on Germany approvingly, but ignored his offer to take over power. *Ce Matin*, June 10, 1948; *L'Ordre*, June 11, 1948.

39. *The Economist* (London), June 12, 1948, p. 955.

40. *Le Populaire*, June 9, 1948; June 10, 1948.

41. France, Assemblée nationale, *Débats*, June 12, 1948, pp. 3491–97.

42. *Ibid.*, June 15, 1948, pp. 3529–32.

43. *Ibid.*, June 12, 1948, pp. 3527–29.

44. The MRP's views on foreign policy were linked with their doctrinal basis in the Catholic conception of history. This prepared them for acceptance of a European rather than a nationalist foreign policy. After Bidault's fall from power, it was Robert Schuman, another member of the MRP, who was to carry further the plans for a united Europe, through the Schuman plan. See Mario Einaudi and François Goguel, *Christian Democracy in Italy and France* (Notre Dame, Ind., 1952), pp. 123–32, 149–52.

45. France, Assemblée nationale, *Debats*, June 1, 1948, pp. 3454–61.

46. *Ibid.*, June 1, 1948, pp. 3579–81.

47. Text of the Assembly motion is given in *L'Année politique, 1948*, pp. 335–36.

48. The next major decision in relations with Germany faced the French political parties in 1951–52, during the long discussions over the Schuman plan for the establishment of a European Coal and Steel Community. It is interesting to see that the attitudes adopted by the various parties to the London agreements were taken again with regard to this measure. A useful summary of the attitudes of the French political parties on this question and with regard to European integration, as of 1952 and 1957, may be found in Ernst B. Haas, *The Uniting of Europe: Political, Social and Economic Forces, 1950–1957* (Stanford, Calif., 1958), pp. 115–27. A modern German study of the French attitude toward European inte-

gration and especially toward Germany, is Walther E. Schmitt, *Zwischenrufe von der Seine* (Stuttgart, 1958).

49. France, Assemblée nationale, *Débats*, June 11, 1948, p. 3461. Bidault was not correct in his inference that the zone was no longer economically viable *because* the Saar had been detached from it. In fact, the Saar had been the only section of the zone which had shown a deficit in its trade balance during the first three years of the occupation.

50. The result, Clay later wrote, was that the French referred almost every measure of importance to their government, and, in negotiations at that level, almost always received satisfaction. Clay, *Decision in Germany*, p. 407.

51. Clay described a "fantastic midnight negotiation" between Noiret and himself in Berlin, and Koenig in Baden-Baden, while Noiret's aides kept calling Paris to learn the result of the vote in the Assembly, which was expected hourly. *Ibid.*, p. 213.

52. Details of these protracted, inconclusive negotiations will be found in Plischke, *Allied High Commission*, pp. 18–22.

53. Clay, *Decision in Germany*, pp. 413–16.

54. *Ibid.*, pp. 425–27.

55. Text of Law No. 75 is given in R.I.I.A., *Documents on Germany*, pp. 335–43.

56. *L'Année politique, 1948*, p. 218; *Le Monde*, November 19, 1948; R.I.I.A., *Documents, 1947–1948*, p. 645. Many books and articles appeared in France dealing with the problem of the Ruhr. Two thoroughly documented studies, published by the Fondation nationale des sciences politiques and the Centre d'études de politique étrangère, respectively, are Jean Weydert, "La Ruhr et l'avenir de l'Europe," in *Études économiques allemandes* (Paris, 1951), pp. 1–66, and Louis F. Aubert *et al.*, *Contrôle de l'Allemagne* (Paris, 1949). An earlier study by Louis F. Aubert is also of interest, as documenting the stand taken by Bidault in 1946. See Louis F. Aubert, *Sécurité de l'Occident: Ruhr-Rhin* (Paris, 1946). The statistical background is studied in France, Institut national de la statistique et des études économiques, *L'Économie de la Ruhr* (Paris, 1947).

57. R.I.I.A., *Documents on Germany*, pp. 446–59. A German text and study of the new legal position of Germany is given in Dr. Gustav von Schmoller's *Die Befugnisse der Besatzungsmächte in der Bundesrepublik: Die wichtigste Dokumente mit einer Einführung* (Dokumente und Berichte des Europa-Archivs No. 8, Oberursel, 1950).

58. R.I.I.A., *Documents on Germany*, pp. 37, 375–77.

59. *Germany, 1947–1949*, pp. 92–97.

CHAPTER IV

1. Title given to the French First Army by General de Lattre in Order of the Day No. 8 of April 24, 1945.

2. De Lattre, *French First Army*, p. 30.

3. *Ibid.*, pp. 169–73. (FFI was the abbreviation of *Forces Françaises de l'Intérieur*, the French Forces of the Interior, or Resistance forces.) The rearming of the Resistance forces presented great problems, particularly because the American government was very suspicious of the political complexion of many of these troops. The success of the German offensive in the Ardennes in December 1944, however, persuaded Eisenhower to support two programs for the rearming of the French metropolitan forces—the so-called "Metropolitan Program" and the "Liberated Manpower Program." This rearming came to an end after the Stuttgart incident and the Italian frontier dispute, when it seemed almost as though French troops might fight American forces. Vigneras, *Rearming the French*, pp. 299–361; de Gaulle, *Mémoires*, III, 30–32.

4. Marcel Cachin, "Il faut lier l'armée au peuple," *L'Humanité*, September 15, 1944; André Marty, "Il faut constituer une grande armée nationale," *ibid.*, September 19, 1944; Marcel Cachin, "Faisons le point," *ibid.*, September 27, 1944; Marcel Cachin, "Pour l'armée du peuple," *ibid.*, October 18, 1944.

5. See the Socialist attack on military credits in the 1946 budget in France, Assemblée nationale constituante, *Débats; compte rendu in extenso des séances, 6 novembre, 1945—6 novembre, 1946* (Paris, 1945–47) [hereafter referred to as France, Assemblée constituante, *Débats*], December 31, 1945, pp. 695–96; and *Le Populaire*, November 8, 1946; November 9, 1946; November 15, 1946.

6. *L'Année politique, 1944–1945*, p. 485.

7. Jean Capdeville, speaking for the Socialist party, noted that "les Allemands de notre zone, après avoir tendu le dos et redouté de justes représailles, se sont rassurés d'abord, ont souri ensuite, et maintenant ont tendance à mépriser quelque peu les forces françaises d'occupation." France, Assemblée constituante, *Débats*, December 31, 1945, p. 695.

8. James de Coquet, *Nous sommes les occupants* (Paris, 1945), p. 107. For a short account of this division of Algerian infantry during the campaign, see Pierre Lyautey, *Carnets d'un goumier: campagne d'Allemagne 1945* (Paris, 1945), or the pamphlet *L'Épopée de la 3ᵉ division d'infanterie algérienne* (Montrouge, 1945).

9. Germany (Territory under allied occupation, 1945——, French zone), Commandement en chef français en Allemagne, Cabinet du général commandant les troupes d'occupation, *Revue d'information des troupes d'occupation en Allemagne*, No. 2 (November 1945), 8.

10. De Coquet, *Nous sommes les occupants*, p. 107.

11. *Revue d'information*, No. 1 (October 1945), 6–7; No. 2 (November 1945), 2–3. The 9th Division had been "whitened" in the winter of 1944, by replacing the Senegalese troops with soldiers from the Resistance. On the "whitening," see Eisenhower, *Crusade in Europe*, pp. 413–14, and de Lattre, *French First Army*, p. 177. The tank divisions are described in *Revue historique de l'armée*, No. 2 (June 1947), 93, and in *Revue d'information*, No. 3 (December 1945), 4–5.

12. *Ibid.*, No. 8 (May 1946), 10–15; *New York Times*, May 20, 1945, for map on p. 19.

13. France, Assemblée nationale constituante, *Documents de l'Assemblée nationale constituante élue le 21 octobre, 1945; annexes aux procès-verbaux des séances* (No. 1–1236: 6 novembre, 1945—25 avril, 1946, Paris, 1946) [hereafter referred to as France, Assemblée constituante, *Annexes*], No. 920 (April 8, 1946), 906.

14. De Coquet, *Nous sommes les occupants*, p. 47.

15. *New York Times*, May 21, 1945; May 26, 1945; June 3, 1945; June 4, 1945. A pamphlet on the occupation published in Paris at this time showed a picture of several little old men standing outside the military government office in Speyer, the captain noting that as hostages they must "rester au garde à vous, tête nue, pendant plusieurs heures devant l'immeuble du Gouvernement Militaire." "Anon.," *Images de vérité sur l'occupation: De Baden-Baden à Berlin* (Paris, 1945), p. 1.

16. Jean Botrot, *Une Allemagne toute neuve* (Paris, 1957), p. 60; Claude-Albert Moreau and R. Jouanneau-Irriera, *Présence française en Allemagne* (Paris, 1949), pp. 66–67; and Claude-Albert Moreau, "1945—nous voulions tout casser," *France-Illustration*, September 17, 1949, pp. 8–9.

17. *Notice sur le gouvernement militaire*, p. 16.

18. Edgar Morin, *Allemagne, notre souci* (Paris, 1947), pp. 28–34. This book gives much interesting information but leans heavily to a Left Wing point of view. General Koeltz described the recruitment of military government teams in an interview with *Le Monde*, published on June 28, 1945. The instructions given to the military government officers are summarized in the AMFA handbook: France, Mission militaire pour les affaires allemandes, *Mémento pour les officiers des détachements de gouvernement militaire* (Paris, 1945), which was based upon the American military government handbook. The planning of the American military government units, by which the French were strongly influenced, is described in Oliver J. Frederiksen's *The American Military Occupation of Germany, 1945–1953* (Historical Division, Headquarters, United States Army, Europe, 1953), pp. 1–13.

19. France, Secrétariat d'état, Direction de la documentation, *Cahiers français*, No. 77 (February 1, 1947), 11. This extremely useful issue is devoted almost entirely to the French zone of occupation in Germany.

20. Eisenhower, *Crusade in Europe*, pp. 431–32.

21. *Notice sur le gouvernement militaire*, p. 14; *Le Monde*, June 28, 1945. The term "adjoint" was to cause considerable difficulty when the generals came to define their areas of authority.

22. Jean de Lattre de Tassigny, *Histoire de la première armée française: Rhin et Danube* (Paris, 1949), p. 618. The last chapter is not included in the English translation. De Lattre's character is interestingly described in a biography by Major General Sir Guy Salisbury-Jones, *So Full a Glory: A Biography of Marshal de Lattre de Tassigny* (London, 1954); and in Genêt's "Letter from Lake Constance," in the *New Yorker*, July 7, 1945, pp. 38–44.

23. An attempt has been made to give the impression that he had received a promotion. De Lattre's biographers are agreed, however, that he regarded his

career as ended. See Pierre Croidys, *Jean de Lattre de Tassigny: Maréchal de France* (Paris, 1952), pp. 183–85, and Louis Chaigne, *Jean de Lattre, Maréchal de France* (Paris, 1952), pp. 153–54.

24. De Lattre, *Première armée française*, p. 615.

25. De Coquet, *Nous sommes les occupants*, p. 155. This discipline became almost a fetish. Officers repeated that a button left unfastened would mean two months in jail, according to Jean Fayard, "L'Allemagne sous la Croix de Lorraine," *Les Œuvres libres*, No. 5 (1945), 45–72. There was even a story current that a soldier was sent up into a church tower which de Lattre passed daily, to keep the hands of the broken clock moving while the general drove by.

26. Paul Garcin, *Au pays des vaincus* (Lyon, 1947), p. 28.

27. Général du Souzy, "Jean de Lattre: 'Grand de France,'" in Commandant Storelli *et al.*, *Jean de Lattre, Maréchal de France. Le soldat—l'homme—le politique* (Paris, 1953), p. 227.

28. He explained these ideas in one of his long midnight conversations with a visitor to Lindau in August, 1945. See Jean Tharaud, "Les Nouvelles épîtres," No. 7, présentées par *Le Monde illustré*, August 1945.

29. Carl Burckhardt, *Begegnungen* (Zürich, 1954), pp. 45–46.

30. Du Souzy, "Jean de Lattre: 'Grand de France,'" in Storelli, *Jean de Lattre*, p. 81; *Le Monde*, May 20–21, 1945.

31. René Thomasset, *La Vie exaltante de Jean de Lattre de Tassigny, Maréchal de France* (Paris, 1952), p. 87. Jean Fayard tells the story of the toast made by General Devers at that time, recalling his past disagreements with de Lattre. "I lift my glass in the honor of my brother-in-arms, General de Lattre," he said, "with whom I have fought for so long—for the most part against the Germans." Fayard, "L'Allemagne," *Les Œuvres libres*, No. 5 (1945), 56.

32. De Coquet, *Nous sommes les occupants*, p. 160; Robert Rey, "Une 'Villa Médicis' en terre allemande," in Storelli, *Jean de Lattre*, pp. 213–15; de Lattre, *Première armée française*, pp. 619–20; *L'Aube*, July 26, 1945; September 20–21, 1945.

33. France, Assemblée constituante, *Annexes*, No. 926 (April 8, 1946), 615.

34. Garcin, *Au pays des vaincus*, p. 54.

35. Croidys, *Jean de Lattre*, p. 183; Werth, *France, 1940–1955*, p. 254. De Gaulle himself speaks very highly of de Lattre's personal characteristics as a military leader and especially of his loyalty. The faults with which he had been reproached were, de Gaulle thought, the "excesses of his qualities." As for the dismissal, or rather the promotion, de Gaulle remarks rather laconically in his memoirs, that "General de Lattre, whatever annoyance he may have felt, gave up his command at this moment, called as he was to the highest post in the army, that of the chief of the general staff." De Gaulle, *Mémoires*, III, 207.

36. Werth, *France, 1940–1955*, p. 234; *France d'abord*, May 26, 1947. The latter was a weekly Resistance paper, under the direction of the Communist R. Roucaute. It maintained a continual attack on the officer corps of the army of occupation.

It should also be remembered that the British had a similar attachment to the spa of Bad Oeynhausen, and that the Americans were pleasantly installed in Wiesbaden.

37. Morin, *Allemagne, notre souci*, p. 36.

38. *Revue de la zone française*, No. 2 (December 15, 1945), 5; No. 5 (March 1946), 3.

39. General Pierre Koenig, "Bilan de quatre années d'occupation," *France-Illustration*, September 17, 1949, pp. 1–2.

40. *Cahiers français*, No. 77 (February 1, 1947), 4.

41. Clay, *Decision in Germany*, pp. 413–16. See also the analysis of French policy in the book by Drew Middleton, the *New York Times*' Berlin correspondent, *The Struggle for Germany* (Indianapolis, 1949), especially pp. 146–47.

42. *Le Populaire*, November 7, 1946; France, Assemblée nationale, *Débats*, June 12, 1948, p. 3496. *L'Humanité*, July 4, 1947, noted that "à la veille de la Conférence de Moscou, un motocycliste quitta Baden-Baden pour Colombey-les-deux-Églises, afin de recevoir ses dernières instructions."

43. He was compulsorily retired on account of his age on June 15, 1946, and was replaced in Berlin by General Noiret. *L'Année politique, 1946*, p. 485. For attacks on him by the Left Wing, see Morin, *Allemagne, notre souci*, pp. 31–32; Georges Rul, *Le Quatrième Reich ou la guerre qui vient* (Paris, 1946), pp. 122–23.

44. *Revue d'information*, No. 2 (November 1945), 1.

45. *Cahiers français*, No. 77 (February 1, 1947), 6.

46. *France d'abord*, September 4, 1946; June 5, 1947; Morin, *Allemagne, notre souci*, pp. 38–39.

47. France, Assemblée constituante, *Annexes*, No. 956 (April 9, 1946).

48. Germany (Territory under allied occupation, 1945———, French zone), Commandement en chef français en Allemagne, *Journal officiel du commandement en chef français en Allemagne* (Baden-Baden, 1945–49) [hereafter referred to as Commandement en chef, *Journal officiel*], No. 1 (September 3, 1945), 4; *Notice sur le gouvernement militaire*, p. 7.

49. *The Times* (London), November 30, 1945.

50. France, Assemblée constituante, *Débats*, December 21, 1945, p. 291.

51. See Royal Institute of International Affairs, Arnold and Veronica M. Toynbee (eds.), *Survey of International Affairs, 1939–1946: The Realignment of Europe* (London, 1955) [hereafter referred to as R.I.I.A., *Realignment of Europe*], pp. 481–86; Werth, *France, 1940–1955*, pp. 101–6; Gordon Wright, *The Reshaping of French Democracy* (New York, 1948), pp. 58–60.

52. Édouard Herriot raised the question of this grant of decorations in the Assembly on January 16, 1946. De Gaulle himself replied, defending his action on the ground of the need for national reconciliation. The incident is described in *L'Année politique, 1946*, p. 2. See also France, Assemblée constituante, *Débats*, January 16, 1946, pp. 39–42; de Gaulle, *Mémoires*, III, 284–85.

53. Albert Vallet, *Le Problème militaire de la quatrième république* (Lyon, 1947), pp. 47–48.

54. France, Assemblée constituante, *Débats*, April 3, 1946, p. 1397.

55. France, Assemblée constituante, *Annexes*, No. 959 (April 9, 1946), 924-44.

56. *Le Populaire*, November 7, 1946; November 8, 1946; November 9, 1946; November 15, 1946.

57. *Ibid.*, July 1, 1947; *L'Humanité*, July 3, 1947; *France d'abord*, May 29, 1947; July 10, 1947.

58. France, Assemblée constituante, *Débats*, January 16, 1946, p. 38.

59. *Ibid.*, March 29, 1946, p. 1239.

60. France, Assemblée constituante, *Annexes*, No. 959 (April 9, 1946), 942-44.

61. France, Assemblée consultative provisoire, *Débats de l'Assemblée consultative provisoire* (Paris, 1944–45) [hereafter referred to as France, Assemblée consultative, *Débats*], June 28, 1945, p. 1242; France, Assemblée constituante, *Débats*, December 31, 1945, p. 693; Garcin, *Au pays des vaincus*, pp. 61–62. Botrot points out that the French occupation cost 163 marks per head of the German population compared with 120 per head in the British zone. Botrot, *Allemagne toute neuve*, pp. 61–62. A British observer noted with some surprise that on entering the French zone, one would hardly believe himself not in France, so many French people crowded the streets. Stefan Schimanski, *Vain Victory* (London, 1946), pp. 68–69.

62. Jean Planchais, *Le Malaise de l'armée* (Tribune libre, No. 16; Paris, 1958), p. 24.

63. *Le Populaire*, January 5, 1946; France, Assemblée constituante, *Débats*, December 31, 1945, p. 693.

64. France, Ministère des armées, *Vers les armées de demain: six mois d'efforts au ministère des armées, novembre, 1945–mai, 1946* (Paris, 1946), pp. 3–4.

65. *Notes documentaires*, No. 629, pp. 2–3; No. 941, pp. 5–6.

66. France, Assemblée constituante, *Annexes*, No. 926 (April 8, 1946), 915.

67. *The Times* (London), December 20, 1946.

68. France, Assemblée constituante, *Débats*, March 26, 1946, p. 1242. It should be remembered that this plethora of administrators was not a universal phenomenon in the zone, since, for example, the University of Freiburg had only one Germanist to supervise all teaching. Interview with Professor Gerhard Ritter, Freiburg, 1958.

69. France, Assemblée constituante, *Annexes*, No. 926 (April 8, 1946), 915.

70. Clay, *Decision in Germany*, p. 105; *Cahiers français*, No. 77 (February 1, 1947), 6.

71. Colonel de Tarragon, *Le Gouvernement militaire en Allemagne* (Paris, 1945).

72. Marshall Knappen, *And Call It Peace* (Chicago, 1947), p. 144.

73. Grosser, *L'Allemagne de l'Occident*, pp. 294–95.

74. *Le Monde*, November 16–17, 1947.

75. *Le Figaro*, November 15, 1947; *Le Populaire*, November 18, 1947.

76. The administrative reform was officially approved in Paris when Pierre Schneiter returned after his tour of the zone in January 1948. The cabinet ap-

proved the reorganization on March 26, and it was made official by an *arrêté* of the secretary of state for German and Austrian affairs published in the *Journal officiel* on April 11, 1948. The application of the law was brought into force in Germany by the "decision" of the commander-in-chief No. 419, of April 12, 1948, by which the office of secretary general to the commander-in-chief was created. The secretary general was to supervise the work of the central services, which were to be divided into a Division of Administrative, Cultural and Social Affairs, a Division of Public Education, a Division of General Economy and Finance, a Division of Industrial Production, a Division of Agricultural Production and Food, a Division of Communications, Radio, and Post, and a Service of Restitution and Reparations. These services were grouped into four divisions—a Political Division, an Information Division, a Security Division, and a Division of General Inspection of Disarmament. On April 18, 1948, Roger Gromand was named secretary general. See Germany (Territory under allied occupation, 1945——, French zone), Commandement en chef français en Allemagne, Direction de l'information, *La France en Allemagne*, No. 9 (June 1948), 96–97; *Europa-Archiv* (January 1948), p. 1061; Stephen Simmons, "The French Zone of Germany," *The Contemporary Review*, No. 990 (June 1948), 338; Maurice Sabatier, "Que ce qui est juste soit fort," *France-Illustration*, September 17, 1949, pp. 14–17.

77. Clay, *Decision in Germany*, pp. 413–14; Harold Zink, *The United States in Germany, 1944–1955* (New York, 1957), p. 119.

78. France, Assemblée constituante, *Débats*, March 29, 1946, p. 1240.

CHAPTER V

1. Hermann Karl Weinert, "Das Bild des Deutschen in der französischen Nachkriegsliteratur," in Deutsch-Französisches Institut, *Deutschland-Frankreich: Ludwigsburger Beiträge zum Problem der deutsch-französischen Beziehungen* (Stuttgart, 1954–57), I, 255–69.

2. To cite only a few, Franck Delage, *Oradour, ville martyre* (Paris, 1945); Jean Pereck, *La Montagne des sept douleurs: Vercors* (Paris, 1945); Marcel Conversy, *Quinze mois à Buchenwald* (Paris, 1945). A full list, with commentary, is given in Henri Berr, *Allemagne: le contre et le pour* (Paris, 1950).

3. Rul, *Le Quatrième Reich.*

4. Léon Daudet, *Connaissance de l'Allemagne* (Paris, 1947).

5. Edmond Vermeil, *Les Doctrinaires de la révolution allemande (1918–1938)* (Paris, 1938); *L'Allemagne: essai d'explication* (2nd ed., Paris, 1945); *L'Allemagne contemporaine: sociale, politique et culturelle, 1890–1950* (Paris, 1952–53).

6. France, Mission militaire pour les affaires allemandes, *AMFA: Bulletin d'information*, No. 1 (March 1945), 3.

7. Pierre Benaerts, *Partage de l'Allemagne* (Paris, 1945), pp. 11–15.

8. *Sondages*, February 16, 1947.

9. Robert Minder, *Allemagnes et allemands* (Paris, 1948).

10. Benaerts, *Partage de l'Allemagne*, p. 22.

11. Paul Olagnier, *Les Trois Allemagnes* (Paris, 1946).

12. Wladimir d'Ormesson, *L'Éternel problème allemand* (Paris, 1945), p. 54.

13. *Sondages*, September 1–16, 1945.

14. Weinert, "Das Bild des Deutschen," *Deutschland-Frankreich*, p. 266. Weinert cites as proof of this contact two novels—J. Perret, *Le Caporal épinglé* (Paris, 1947), and Nicole Védrès, *Les Cordes rouges* (Paris, 1952). Other novels illustrating aspects of the occupation period are Jean-Louis Curtis, *Siegfried* (Paris, 1946); Georges Auclair, *Un Amour allemand* (Paris, 1950); Michel Boutron, *Hans* (Paris, 1951); Pierre Fisson, *Voyages aux horizons* (Paris, 1948); Pierre Frédérix, *Mort à Berlin* (Paris, 1948); Roger Nimier, *Le Hussard bleu* (Paris, 1950); and Elsa Triolet, *Inspecteur des ruines* (Paris, 1948).

15. Byrnes, *Speaking Frankly*, p. 25; Stettinius, *Roosevelt and the Russians*, p. 127.

16. Contre-Amiral Pierre Barjot, "Le Problème militaire du Rhin," in Dumont, *Le Rhin: Nil de l'Occident*, pp. 197–99; *The Times* (London), September 10, 1945.

17. Mosely, "Occupation of Germany," *Foreign Affairs*, XXVIII (July 1950), 600. De Gaulle had told British Ambassador Duff Cooper on April 27, 1945, that he wanted French occupation of Germany from Switzerland to Cologne, and he had asked, "Why refuse us the occupation of Cologne, which is not part of the Ruhr?" De Gaulle, *Mémoires*, III, 503–4.

18. Foundation for Foreign Affairs, Washington, D.C., *Field Report on the French Zone in Germany* (Foundation Information Pamphlet No. 1, Washington, 1946) [hereafter referred to as *Field Report on French Zone*], p. 1.

19. "Les districts de Trèves et de Coblence sont séparés du reste de la province rhénane où ils trouvent cependant leur complément. Par contre, étudiés dans leur ensemble, ils possèdent une certaine unité." *Notes documentaires*, No. 255, p. 3.

20. James Kerr Pollock, *Germany in Power and Eclipse* (New York, 1952), pp. 407–21, gives a thorough analysis of the racial, linguistic, agricultural, and industrial differences of the two sections of the Rheinprovinz. See also "La zone d'occupation française en Allemagne," *Notes documentaires*, No. 255, pp. 4–5; "Esquisse d'une géographie politique de la zone d'occupation française en Allemagne," *Notes documentaires*, No. 497, pp. 29–30.

21. Description compiled from Pollock, *Germany in Power*, pp. 441–59; and *Notes documentaires*, No. 255, pp. 4–5; No. 467, pp. 28–29; "Les problèmes historiques de la Hesse et du Nassau," *Notes documentaires*, No. 1065, p. 9.

22. *New York Times*, July 28, 1945. The American section of Hessen-Nassau had fallen deeply under Nazi influence, thus providing a further problem for the American authorities. See *Notes documentaires*, No. 1065, p. 9.

23. Pollock, *Germany in Power*, pp. 451, 456; *Notes documentaires*, No. 467, p. 27; Arthur D. Kahn, *Betrayal: Our Occupation of Germany* (Warsaw, 1947), pp. 30–42. Kahn believed the people of Mainz had regarded the Allies as liberators and were greatly disappointed at the treatment they received.

24. "L'industrie chimique en zone française d'occupation: Ludwigshafen," *France en Allemagne,* No. 1 (July 1946), 33–38. William Friedmann in his book *The Allied Military Government of Germany* (London, 1947), p. 73, holds that the Pfalz's natural economic tie was with north Baden. This view was also put forward later by the government of Baden-Württemberg. See Walter Siebler, "Kann die Pfalz abseits stehen," in Karl Hook (ed.), *Lebensraum: Südwest Staat* (Mannheim, 1950), p. 16. See also Pollock, *Germany in Power,* pp. 553, 569–70; and *Notes documentaires,* No. 255, pp. 8–9, and No. 467, pp. 26–27.

The separatist movement in the Pfalz between 1920 and 1923 is described in "Problèmes historiques des pays rhénans," *Notes documentaires,* No. 1051, p. 36. The aim of French officials to create a new separatism in the Pfalz after 1945 was denounced in the Landtag of Rheinland-Pfalz by Franz Bögler, Oberregierungspräsident of the Pfalz, in a fiery speech on November 6, 1947. "This movement in the Pfalz," cried Bögler, "has been led by a numerically unimportant group, whose strength is just as big as the size of the French forces which they hope to win for the support of their plans." The whole Landtag joined in voting a motion of disapproval of all separatist tendencies. See Germany (Territory under allied occupation, 1945——, French zone, Rheinland-Pfalz), Landtag, *Stenographischer Bericht, Landtag Rheinland-Pfalz, 1947——, 1. Wahlperiode* (Koblenz, 1947——) [hereafter referred to as Rheinland-Pfalz, Landtag, *Verhandlung*], November 6, 1947, pp. 188–92.

A well-documented account of developments in the Pfalz under the French occupation is given in the official report of the local military government office in 1948. See Germany (Territory under allied occupation, 1945——, French zone), Commandement en chef français en Allemagne, Délégation de la province du Palatinat, *Le Palatinat en 1948* (Neustadt, 1948).

25. Hermann Overbeck and Georg W. Sante, *Saar-Atlas* (Gotha, 1934), Map 6. This atlas is a valuable reference work on all economic aspects of the Saar. See also *Notes documentaires,* No. 255, pp. 5–8, and France, Institut national de la statistique et des études économiques, *L'Économie de la Sarre* (Paris, 1947).

26. Fred H. Sanderson, "Germany's Economic Situation and Prospects," in Gabriel A. Almond (ed.), *The Struggle for Democracy in Germany* (Chapel Hill, N.C., 1949), p. 167.

27. By the Treaty of Versailles, France was granted absolute possession of the Saar mines, but government of the area was vested in the League of Nations. After fifteen years, the inhabitants were to decide by plebiscite whether they wished to become part of Germany or of France. See Treaty of Versailles, Section IV, Articles 45–50, and Annex; and "Le Statut de la Sarre depuis le Traité de Versailles," *Notes documentaires,* No. 506, and Jean Chardonnet, *La Sarre* (Paris, 1945). The view that the plebiscite of 1935 was invalid is put by G. André-Fribourg, in "La Sarre et la France," *Fait du Jour,* No. 7 (May 21, 1946); "Anon.," *La Sarre fut vendue* (Toulouse, 1945); and *Notes documentaires,* No. 326, pp. 13–14. Other writers, however, consider that the French had already lost the sympathy of the Saarlanders by the occupation of the Ruhr in 1923 and that the result of the plebiscite in 1935 was expected by most Frenchmen. See Laing Gray Cowan, *France*

and the Saar, 1680–1948 (New York, 1950), pp. 151–67; Pollock, *Germany in Power*, p. 464. The findings of a recent study carried out by a team of political scientists are given in Jacques Freymond, *The Saar Conflict, 1945–1955* (New York, 1960).

28. *Notes documentaires*, No. 255, p. 9; No. 467, pp. 19–20; Pollock, *Germany in Power*, pp. 617–18.

29. *Notes documentaires*, No. 255, pp. 9–11; No. 467, pp. 24–25; Pollock, *Germany in Power*, pp. 586–606.

30. Compiled from *Notes documentaires*, No. 255, pp. 3–11, and Germany (Territory under allied occupation, 1945——, French zone), Commandement en chef français en Allemagne, Direction générale de l'économie et des finances, *Bulletin statistique*, No. 3 (February 1947), Chart 1.

31. *Bulletin statistique*, No. 4 (October 1947), 52.

32. *Cahiers français*, No. 77 (February 1, 1947), 16.

33. Statistical sources on the French zone of occupation are Klaus Mehnert and Heinrich Schulte (eds.), *Deutschland Jahrbuch, 1949* (Essen, 1949); Wilhelm Cornides (ed.), "Wirtschaftsstatistik der deutschen Besatzungszonen, 1945–1948," *Europa-Archiv* (Oberursel, 1948); "La zone française d'occupation," *Cahiers français*, No. 77 (February 1, 1947); United States, Economic Cooperation Administration, *Western Germany: Country Study* (Washington, 1948); Organisation for European Economic Co-operation, *Report to the Economic Co-operation Administration on the First Annual Programme, July 1st, 1948—June 30th, 1949* (Paris, 1948); Organisation for European Economic Co-operation, *Report to the Economic Co-operation Administration on the 1949–1950 Programme, July 1st, 1949—June 30th, 1950* (Paris, 1949); United Nations, Department of Economic Affairs, *Economic Survey of Europe since the War* (Geneva, 1948); United Nations, Economic Commission for Europe, *Economic Survey of Europe in 1948* (Geneva, 1949); and three major statistical reports of the Direction générale de l'économie et des finances, *Bulletin statistique*, *Statistique industrielle*, and *Statistique industrielle mensuelle* (Baden-Baden, 1947——). The sources are synthesized in André Piettre, *L'Économie allemande contemporaine (Allemagne Occidentale), 1945–1952* (Paris, 1952), and in Royal Institute of International Affairs, Michael Balfour and John Mair, *Four-Power Control in Germany and Austria, 1945–1946* (London, 1956) [hereafter referred to as R.I.I.A., *Four-Power Control*], pp. 8–14. On the situation prevailing in the first year of the occupation, see Edgar Morin's highly critical book, *L'An zéro de l'Allemagne* (Paris, 1946), and Pierre Grappin's *Que faire de l'Allemagne?* (Paris, 1945).

34. R.I.I.A., *Four-Power Control*, p. 16; Piettre, *L'Économie allemande*, p. 65; *L'Économie de la Sarre*, pp. 31–32.

35. *Cahiers français*, No. 77 (February 1, 1947), 15–16; *Revue de la zone française*, No. 2 (December 15, 1945), 30.

36. *Bulletin statistique*, No. 3 (February, 1947), Chart 32, which gives comparative yields for 1938, 1944/45, and 1945/46.

37. *Notes documentaires*, No. 255, p. 3; *Bulletin statistique*, No. 3 (February 1947), Chart 1; Piettre, *L'Économie allemande*, p. 57; *Revue de la zone française*,

No. 2 (December 15, 1945), 32. The most authoritative description of the treatment of displaced persons in the French zone is the account by the Service des personnes déplacées of the Haut commissariat de la république française en Allemagne, *Sept ans d'activité en faveur des personnes déplacées en zone française d'occupation, 1945–1952* (Baden-Baden, 1952). An excellent account of the legal, financial, and economic significance of the displaced-person problem in the whole of western Germany is given by the Institut für Besatzungsfragen in *Das DP-Problem: Eine Studie über die ausländischen Flüchtlinge in Deutschland* (Tübingen, 1950).

38. Compiled from *Bulletin statistique*, No. 3 (February 1947), Chart 2.

CHAPTER VI

1. R.I.I.A., *Documents on Germany*, p. 46.

2. *Notes documentaires*, No. 255, pp. 13–14. It is not surprising that France profited from the 20 per cent discount, which was an indirect form of reparation, to buy goods worth $57,000,000 from the zone between August 1945 and December 1946, since this represented a saving of $14,250,000 on world prices. Moreover, the French themselves set the price of goods for sale, to the Germans' annoyance. Export figures in *Deutschland Jahrbuch, 1949*, p. 218.

3. *Notes documentaires*, No. 255, p. 13.

4. Piettre, *L'Économie allemande*, p. 104. A fuller account is given in Richard Castillon, *Les Réparations allemandes: deux expériences, 1919–1932; 1945–1952* (Paris, 1953), pp. 80–81.

5. A full account of the spoliation question is given in "Spoliations et restitutions: 1re partie, les spoliations," *Notes documentaires*, No. 1107. The juridical basis for the return of the spoliations is described in "Spoliations et restitutions: 2me partie, les restitutions," *Notes documentaires*, No. 1108, pp. 4–9. The same issue gives a thorough study of the method by which restitution was carried out by the Office of Private Goods and Interests in Paris and by the central French Office of Restitution in Berlin and the Reparations-Restitution Directorate in Baden-Baden.

6. Germany (Territory under allied occupation, 1945———, French zone), Commandement en chef français en Allemagne, *La Zone française d'occupation* (Baden-Baden, 1948) [hereafter referred to as Commandement en chef, *Zone française*], p. 112.

7. *Ibid.*, p. 113; *Cahiers français*, No. 77 (February 1, 1947), 19.

8. See Piettre, *L'Économie allemande*, pp. 104, 125. The figure for restitution includes monetary gold recovered. A further class of spoliations was of precious objects and art treasures. French art treasures in large numbers were found in the American zone. In the French zone, however, only a few were discovered; five convoys were sufficient to take them back to France. *Notes documentaires*, No. 1109.

9. *Cahiers français*, No. 77 (February 1, 1947), 16; Inter-Allied Reparations Agency, *First Report to the Secretary-General for the Year 1946* (Brussels,

1947), pp. 3–10; B. U. Ratchford and W. D. Ross, *Berlin Reparations Assignment: Round One of the German Peace Settlement* (Chapel Hill, N.C., 1947), pp. 86–130; R.I.I.A., *Documents on Germany*, pp. 113–18; Castillon, *Réparations allemandes*, pp. 115–18.

10. R.I.I.A., *Documents on Germany*, p. 13.

11. Commandement en chef, *Zone française*, p. 111.

12. *Ibid.*; *Notes documentaires*, No. 1523, p. 10; IARA, *Report, 1947*, p. 7.

13. *Cahiers français*, No. 77 (February 1, 1947), 18–19.

14. Commandement en chef, *Zone française*, p. 112; *Notes documentaires*, No. 893, pp. 6–10.

15. The communiqué issued by the conference is given in R.I.I.A., *Documents on Germany*, pp. 238–39, and the text of the plan on pp. 239–45.

16. Clay, *Decision in Germany*, p. 122; *New York Times*, November 15, 1947. See also Christopher Emmett and Fritz Baade, *Destruction at Our Expense* (New York, 1947); Karl Brandt, *Germany: Key to Peace in Europe* (Claremont, Calif., 1949), pp. 44–50; Gustav Stolper, *German Realities* (New York, 1948), pp. 135–52; Sanderson, "Germany's economic situation," in Almond, *Struggle for Democracy*, pp. 145–48. The first French criticism was made by René Lauret in *Faites travailler l'Allemagne* (Paris, 1948).

17. Jacques Rueff, "Les nouvelles réparations allemandes," in Louis F. Aubert *et al.*, *Nouveaux aspects du problème allemand* (Centre d'études de politique étrangère, Section d'information, Publication No. 17, Paris, 1947), pp. 193–213; IARA, *Report, 1948*, p. 8; Piettre, *L'Économie allemande*, p. 113.

18. *L'Année politique, 1947*, p. 205; *L'Année politique, 1948*, p. 145. The actions of the Land governments of the French zone in opposition to dismantling are described in detail in Chapter Ten.

19. *Ibid.*, p. 414. The British reaffirmed their position on dismantling in even stronger terms. See R.I.I.A., *Documents on Germany*, p. 331.

20. Piettre, *L'Économie allemande*, p. 120.

21. Compiled from Inter-Allied Reparations Agency, *Report of the Assembly of the Inter-Allied Reparations Agency to Its Member Governments* (Brussels, 1951), Annex 19.

22. Stolper, *German Realities*, p. 71. In 1946, for example, 1,400 machines from the Bosch factory in Reutlingen were taken to Homburg in the Saar, on the pretext that workers were not available to operate the factory in Reutlingen. The factory was later considered removed under the provisions of the decartelization law, and the Homburg factory paid RM9.5 million for the machines. See Institut für Besatzungsfragen, *Einwirkungen der Besatzungsmächte auf die westdeutsche Wirtschaft* (Tübingen, 1949), p. 52; Richard Tüngel and Hans Rudolf Berndorff, *Auf dem Bauche sollst du kriechen: Deutschland unter den Besatzungsmächten* (Hamburg, 1958), pp. 278–79.

23. G. W. Harmssen, *Am Abend der Demontage: 6 Jahre Reparations-Politik* (Bremen, 1951), cited in Piettre, *L'Économie allemande*, pp. 129–30.

24. *L'Année politique, 1947*, p. 55; *L'Année politique, 1948*, p. 32; Economic Commission for Europe, *Economic Survey, 1948*, pp. 157–58.

25. On the legal aspect of the powers exercised by the occupying regime, see Institut für Besatzungsfragen, *Sechs Jahre Besatzungslasten: Eine Untersuchung des Problems der Besatzungskosten in den drei Westzonen und in Westberlin 1945–1950* (Tübingen, 1951), pp. 38–69; Institut für Besatzungsfragen, *Das Besatzungsregime auf dem Gebiet der Rechtspflege* (Tübingen, 1949. Roneotyped); G. von Schmoller, H. Maier, and A. Tobler, *Handbuch des Besatzungsrechts* (Tübingen, 1951———); Michel Virally, *L'Administration internationale de l'Allemagne du 8 mai 1945 au 24 avril 1947* (Paris, 1948). The two views, that unconditional surrender extinguished Germany's existence as a state under international law and that Germany was only a subjugated state, are discussed in M. E. Bathurst and J. L. Simpson, *Germany and the North Atlantic Community: A Legal Survey* (London, 1956), pp. 30–41. The legal rights of a German citizen during the occupation are discussed in Institut für Besatzungsfragen, *Bürgerrechte und Besatzungsmacht: Eine Übersicht* ("Kleine Schriften für den Staatsbürger," Heft 12, Institut zur Förderung öffentlicher Angelegenheiten, Frankfurt am Main, 1951).

26. Institut für Besatzungsfragen, *Sechs Jahre Besatzungslasten*, p. 3; Institut für Besatzungsfragen, *Besatzungskosten—ein Verteidigungsbeitrag?* (Tübingen, 1950), which is published in English as *Occupation Costs: Are They a Defence Contribution?* (Tübingen, 1951). The figures used by the institute in compiling this table are based upon contemporary statistics prepared by the Land governments of the zone in preparation for the end of the occupation, when a precise reckoning would be needed. A very detailed account of the legal and economic implications of the demands of the occupying power is given in Dr. Wilhelm Rentrop *et al.*, *Requisitionen, Besatzungsschäden und ihre Bezahlung* (Stuttgart, 1950).

27. Institut für Besatzungsfragen, *Sechs Jahre Besatzungslasten*, p. 187.

28. *Ibid.*, Anlage 1.

29. *Ibid.*, pp. 108–9. The regulations concerning requisitioning in the French zone were laid down in a long, very detailed book, which explained even the number of chairs, bedsheets, and so on which each rank could expect. Unmarried captains and lieutenants, for example, were to have a bedroom and bathroom and the use of the living room. The commander-in-chief was to have twenty-five servants for his quarters in Baden-Baden. See Germany (Territory under allied occupation, 1945———, French zone), Commandement en chef français en Allemagne, *Circulaire portant réglementation du droit de réquisition en zone française d'occupation et de l'affectation entre les diverses parties prenantes des prestations de logement, cantonnement et accessoires* (Baden-Baden, 1947).

30. Compiled from Institut für Besatzungsfragen, *Sechs Jahre Besatzungslasten*, pp. 6, 8.

31. France, Assemblée nationale, *Débats*, December 23, 1946, pp. 343–44.

32. Germany (Federal Republic, 1949———), Bundestag, *Verhandlungen. Stenographische Berichte, 1. Wahlperiode: Sept. 7, 1949——* (Bonn, 1949———), January 18, 1951, pp. 4210–13.

33. Auclair, *Un Amour allemand*, p. 67. Another form of pillaging in the early days was the "wild dismantling" (*wilde Demontagen*), machinery being dis-

mantled and sent to France without agreement from the reparations commission. Institut für Besatzungsfragen, *Bürgerrechte*, p. 21.

34. Bundestag, *Verhandlungen*, April 26, 1951, pp. 5526–32.

35. *Ibid.*, July 2, 1953, p. 13950; Germany (Federal Republic 1949——), Bundestag, *Anlagen zu den stenographischen Berichten. Drucksachen. 1. Wahlperiode*: Nr. 1 (Bonn, 1950——), Anlage 6b, No. 4260, pp. 206–8.

36. *Notes documentaires*, No. 1523; IARA, *Report, 1951*, Schedules 1 and 2.

CHAPTER VII

1. "De remettre l'Allemagne au travail en orientant son activité dans un sens conforme à nos intérêts." *Notes documentaires*, No. 255, p. 14. An extremely useful German study is Deutsches Institut für Wirtschaftsforschung, *Wirtschaftsprobleme der Besatzungszonen* (Berlin, 1948). The French zone is studied on pages 179–87.

2. Figures cited by Jacques Rueff in Aubert, *Nouveaux aspects du problème allemand*, pp. 205–6.

3. Account compiled from "Le Plan Monnet, réalisation et perspectives," *L'Année politique, 1949*, pp. 235–44.

4. *Cahiers français*, No. 77 (February 1, 1947), 25. Cf. Jean Chardonnet, *Crise du Charbon en France* (Paris, 1945).

5. *Sondages*, December 16, 1944; *L'Humanité*, October 20, 1945; *Le Populaire*, March 31 – April 1, 1946; *Revue de la zone française*, No. 1 (November 15, 1945), 9.

6. France, Assemblée constituante, *Débats*, December 21, 1945, p. 291.

7. *France en Allemagne*, No. 9 (June 1948), 16–17; *Revue de la zone française*, No. 1 (November 15, 1945), 22; "Le rétablissement de la navigation rhénane et l'oeuvre du gouvernement militaire en zone française d'occupation," *France en Allemagne*, No. 1 (July 1946), 42–48.

8. See the map of the railroad network in May 1945 in "Dix-huit mois d'activité des chemins de fer en zone française d'occupation," *France en Allemagne*, No. 4 (January-February 1947), facing p. 48.

9. *Ibid.*, pp. 30, 33; *Revue de la zone française*, No. 2 (December 15, 1945), 33. The building of the Maxau bridge is described in "Le pont de Maxau sur le Rhin, trait d'union des deux parties de la zone française d'occupation," *France en Allemagne*, No. 5 (March-May 1947), 21–30.

10. Examples given include development of the Trier line to simplify the transit of Ruhr coal to France and the shipment of 27,900 carloads of wood to France in nine months. *France en Allemagne*, No. 4 (January-February 1947), 48.

11. "Bilan économique et social d'un an d'activité française en Allemagne," *France en Allemagne*, No. 2 (August-September 1946), 43–44; "Le système bancaire," *Revue de la zone française*, No. 3 (January 15, 1946), 30; No. 6–7 (April-May 1946), 40–41; Piettre, *L'Économie allemande*, pp. 231–33; Ger-

many (Territory under allied occupation, 1945——, French zone), Commandement en chef français en Allemagne, Direction générale de l'économie et des finances, *Manuel de contrôle de biens: Handbuch für Vermögenskontrolle* (Baden-Baden, 1947).

12. M. Mitzakis, *Politique monétaire: note sur les émissions de marks d'occupation* (Baden-Baden, 1945; Roneotyped); M. Mitzakis, *Le Contrôle de la monnaie du crédit et des changes dans la zone française d'occupation en Allemagne de 1945 à 1948: conférence faite le 22 avril 1948 à Baden-Baden au centre d'études germaniques de Strasbourg* (Baden-Baden, 1948; Roneotyped).

13. *Notes documentaires*, No. 255, pp. 14–15.

14. Commandement en chef, *Zone française*, p. 45.

15. *Notes documentaires*, No. 255, p. 23; *The Times* (London), December 20, 1946; *Cahiers français*, No. 77 (February 1, 1947), 19. The zone also received 15,000 tons of wheat which SHAEF had brought in 1945. Clay, *Decision in Germany*, p. 264.

16. Compiled from *Bulletin statistique*, No. 9 (April 1949), 18–19.

17. Charts of the calorie allowance in the French zone for 1946–47 are given in Commandement en chef, *Zone française*, p. 54; and for the period following, in Germany (Territory under allied occupation, 1945——, French zone), Commandement en chef français en Allemagne, *Recueil de documentation économique* (Baden-Baden, 1949), Chart 2.

18. Commandement en chef, *Zone française*, p. 106; ECA, *Western Germany*, p. 21. Total imports rose to $181,288,500 for 1948. *Bulletin statistique*, No. 9 (April 1949), 43.

19. France, Assemblée consultative, *Débats*, June 28, 1945, pp. 1239, 1245; Assemblée constituante, *Débats*, February 12, 1946, p. 267.

20. Stolper, *German Realities*, p. 70; Brandt, *Germany: Key to Peace in Europe*, p. 51. See also Freda Utley's virulent account of the French occupation in *The High Cost of Vengeance* (Chicago, 1949), especially p. 275, and James P. Warburg's accusations in *Germany—Bridge or Battleground* (New York, 1947), pp. 59–65.

21. *Le Figaro*, September 26, 1945.

22. *Cahiers français*, No. 77 (February 1, 1947), 26. The whole tobacco crop was taken for the army. The whole wine output was taken for export or for the occupation forces. *Notes documentaires*, No. 255, p. 15. The blockade of the sugar barges is reported in *France d'abord*, September 18, 1947, and *L'Aube*, October 4, 1947. A table illustrating the proportions of the foodstuffs produced by each of the three Länder of the French zone which were taken by the French occupation regime is given in Institut für Besatzungsfragen, *Sechs Jahre Besatzungslasten*, Anlage 13b.

23. France, Assemblée constituante, *Débats*, December 31, 1945, p. 693; *Notes documentaires*, No. 629, pp. 2–3; No. 941, pp. 5–6. The report of the committee of inquiry is given in France, Assemblée constituante, *Annexes*, No. 922 (April 8, 1946), 911–12. The clothing situation of the French army was apparently worse than its food supply, each soldier possessing only one uniform and

one pair of shoes. Since he often had no blanket or sleeping bag, according to the committee, presumably he slept in his clothes.

24. *The Times* (London), December 20, 1946.

25. "La pénurie de charbon," *Le Monde*, March 6–7, 1945; "Le charbon de l'Allemagne occidentale," *Notes documentaires*, No. 414, pp. 1–6.

26. *Ibid.*, p. 8. ECO consisted solely of European countries.

27. In March 1946, for example, France received 360,000 tons of German coal, of which only 100,000 came from the Saar. *L'Année politique, 1946*, p. 133.

28. *Cahiers français*, No. 77 (February 1, 1947), 20; *Notes documentaires*, No. 414, p. 6; *Bulletin statistique*, No. 4 (October 1947), 38.

29. On June 6, 1946, the British refused to allow the French to take the Saar coal produced above the level of the last quarter of 1945, as the French had proposed they should be allowed to do. *The Times* (London), June 7, 1946; *Bulletin statistique*, No. 3 (February 1947), Table 123; Economic Commission for Europe, *Economic Survey, 1948*, pp. 157–58.

30. "Charbons allemands et industrie française," *Revue de la zone française*, No. 2 (December 15, 1945), 27.

31. *Cahiers français*, No. 77 (February 1, 1947), 25.

32. "L'énergie éléctrique en zone française," *Revue de la zone française*, No. 5 (March 1946), 34–39, an account which seems, however, too optimistic in estimates of electricity production in the zone itself. A later and more credible account is given in Commandement en chef, *Recueil de documentation économique*, Charts 3, 4, and 5.

33. *Bulletin statistique*, No. 4 (October 1947), 52; *Revue de la zone française*, No. 3 (January 15, 1946), 28; No. 5 (March 1946), 24–26; "L'industrie chimique en zone française d'occupation: Ludwigshafen," *France en Allemagne*, No. 1 (July 1946), 36.

34. *Deutschland Jahrbuch, 1949*, p. 218; *Bulletin statistique*, No. 5 (January 1948), 120; ECA, *Western Germany*, pp. 17, 20.

35. *Bulletin statistique*, No. 4 (October 1947), 52; *L'Économie de la Sarre*, pp. 51–71; "La sidérurgie en zone française d'occupation," *France en Allemagne*, No. 1 (July 1946), 29–30.

36. *Deutschland Jahrbuch, 1949*, p. 218; Commandement en chef, *Recueil de documentation économique*, Chart 15; ECA, *Western Germany*, p. 17.

37. *Bulletin statistique*, No. 4 (October 1947), 52; *Cahiers français*, No. 77 (February 1, 1947), 16; "Une industrie clé de la zone: le cuir et ses dérivés," *Revue de la zone française*, No. 6-7 (April-May 1946), 30–32; France, Assemblée constituante, *Annexes*, No. 918 (April 8, 1946), 904.

38. *Revue de la zone française*, No. 6-7 (April-May 1946), 32, 53; *Deutschland Jahrbuch, 1949*, p. 218; ECA, *Western Germany*, p. 20; Commandement en chef, *Recueil de documentation économique*, Chart 27.

39. The forestry plan estimated annual forest growth at 60,000,000 cubic meters. It foresaw a yearly felling of 3,500,000 cubic meters, rising later to 6,500,000 cubic meters, with a ceiling of 9,000,000. See "L'industrie du bois en zone française," *Revue de la zone française*, No. 6-7 (April-May 1946), 36.

40. *Bulletin statistique*, No. 5 (January 1948), 120; Cornides, "Wirtschafts-statistik," *Europa-Archiv*, p. 98; ECA, *Western Germany*, pp. 16–17.

41. Freda Utley, in proof of excessive French exploitation of forest reserves, cites Hans Huth, *Report on the Present Situation of Nature Protection in the American, British, and French Occupied Zones of Germany* (Chicago, 1948). Cf. Utley, *High Cost of Vengeance*, p. 279. Interview with Ministerialdirektor Duppré, August 1960.

42. The Institut für Besatzungsfragen has shown, however, that the complaints by Germans in the French zone—that the felling of timber there was greater than in the other western zones—were unfounded. In fact, while the annual percentage of the normal felling in the American zone was 188.9, and in the French 285.0, in the British zone it was 348.4 per cent. The French methods of felling, on the other hand, were much more criticized than those of the British or Americans. Institut für Besatzungsfragen, *Einwirkungen der Besatz-ungsmächte*, pp. 104–5.

43. ECA, *Western Germany*, p. 20.

44. *The Times* (London), December 20, 1946.

45. Figures for 1945–46 and 1947 are taken from Commandement en chef, *Zone française*, p. 106; figures for 1948 from *Bulletin statistique*, No. 9 (April 1949), 42–43; and figures for 1949 from *Bulletin statistique*, No. 11 (September 1949), 28–29.

46. *Bulletin statistique*, No. 5 (January 1948), 118; No. 9 (April 1949), 43.

47. *The Times* (London), December 20, 1946; France, Assemblée nationale, *Débats*, June 11, 1948, p. 3461.

48. *Bulletin statistique*, No. 4 (October 1947).

49. Interview with René Monnier, June 1960.

50. OEEC, *Report, July 1st, 1948–June 30th, 1949*, p. 66; ECA, *Western Germany*, p. 82.

51. *Ibid.*, p. 101.

52. P. Lebée, "La réforme monétaire," in *Études économiques allemandes*, pp. 106–22; Clay, *Decision in Germany*, pp. 212–13, admits the hardships caused. The dangerous social effects were pointed out by *Le Monde*, October 24, 1948; M. Mitzakis, *Les Finances de la zone française d'occupation de 1948 à 1949: conférence faite le 14 avril 1949 à Baden-Baden au centre d'études germaniques de Strasbourg* (Baden-Baden, 1949; Roneotyped); M. Mitzakis, *Les Enseignements de la réforme monétaire en Allemagne occidentale: conférence faite le 20 juin à Paris au centre d'études supérieures de banque, fondation nationale des sciences politiques* (Paris, 1949; Roneotyped). Interview with M. Mitzakis, June 1960. The reform was followed by an unexpected inflation, which, however, had been curbed by the end of 1948. Henry C. Wallich, *Mainsprings of the German Revival* (New Haven, 1955), pp. 73–79.

53. English text is given in *Germany, 1947–1949*, pp. 492–518.

54. Piettre, *L'Économie allemande*, p. 207.

55. ECA, *Western Germany*, pp. 20, 82–83; OEEC, *Report, July 1st, 1949–June 30th, 1950*, p. 83.

CHAPTER VIII

1. Leland M. Goodrich and Marie J. Carroll (eds.), *Documents on American Foreign Relations, July, 1942 – June, 1943* (Boston, 1944), p. 44, and Leland M. Goodrich and Marie J. Carroll (eds.), *Documents on American Foreign Relations, July, 1944–June, 1945* (Princeton, N.J., 1947), p. 7, cited in R.I.I.A., *Four-Power Control*, pp. 15, 22.

2. R.I.I.A., *Documents on Germany*, p. 156.

3. R.I.I.A., *Four-Power Control*, p. 34.

4. See, for example, Victor Gollancz, *In Darkest Germany* (London, 1947), and William Peters, *In Germany Now: A Diary of Impressions in Germany, August – December, 1945* (London, 1945). Contrast these with Jean Guignebert's *A l'Écoute de l'Allemagne* (Paris, 1947).

5. Field-Marshal the Viscount Montgomery of Alamein, K.G., *Memoirs* (Cleveland, 1958), p. 331.

6. AMFA, *Bulletin d'information*, No. 1 (March 1945), 3.

7. César Santelli, "La rééducation de l'Allemagne est-elle possible?" *Fait du Jour*, No. 14 (July 16, 1946).

8. Guignebert, *A l'Écoute*, pp. 51, 57.

9. Édouard Bonnefous, *A travers l'Europe mutilée: devant et derrière le rideau de fer* (Paris, 1947), pp. 14–15.

10. Auclair, *Un Amour allemand*, p. 62.

11. See report of parliamentary committee of inquiry, France, Assemblée constituante, *Annexes*, No. 924 (April 8, 1946), 913–14; and John D. Montgomery, *Forced to Be Free: The Artificial Revolution in Germany and Japan* (Chicago, 1957), p. 117.

12. Interview with Guillaume Widmer, délégué supérieur of Württemberg, June 1960. See also Konrad F. Bieber's *L'Allemagne vue par les écrivains de la résistance française* (Geneva, 1954), pp. 33–38. This book gives an extremely useful and comprehensive view of French writing about Germany both during and immediately after the war.

13. *Revue de la zone française*, No. 3 (January 15, 1946).

14. France, Assemblée nationale, *Débats*, June 15, 1948, p. 3528.

15. Germany (Territory under allied occupation, 1945———, French zone, Württemberg-Hohenzollern), Beratende Landesversammlung, *Verhandlung der Beratenden Landesversammlung für Württemberg-Hohenzollern von 22 November 1946 bis 9 Mai 1947 und Inhaltsübersicht mit Anhang* (Tuttlingen, 1946–47) [hereafter referred to as Württemberg-Hohenzollern, Beratende Landesversammlung, *Verhandlung*], November 22, 1946, pp. 6–11.

16. R.I.I.A., *Four-Power Control*, pp. 54–56.

17. Saul K. Padover, *Psychologist in Germany: The Story of an American Intelligence Officer* (London, 1946), p. 36.

18. Karl Strölin, *Stuttgart im Endstadium des Krieges* (Stuttgart, 1950), pp. 51–52. Strölin's book gives an interesting firsthand account of how he attempted to get into touch with the French troops approaching the city from the south, and

of the actual take-over of the city. Strölin himself had taken part in the July 20 plot in 1944, having been chosen to contact Rommel to ask him to join the plot. See Hans Speidel, *We Defended Normandy* (London, 1951), pp. 126–27.

19. William Ernest Hocking, *Experiment in Education: What We Can Learn from Teaching Germany* (Chicago, 1954), p. 48.

20. Carlo Schmid, *Die Forderung des Tages, Reden und Aufsätze* (Stuttgart, 1946), pp. 24–37.

21. Hocking, *Experiment in Education*, p. 52.

22. *Schwäbisches Tagblatt*, January 15, 1946.

23. R.I.I.A., *Documents on Germany*, p. 43.

24. Germany (Territory under allied occupation, 1945———, French zone), Commandement en chef français en Allemagne, *Recueil des textes législatifs publiés par ou sous l'autorité du commandement suprême interallié en vigueur dans la zone française d'occupation en Allemagne* (Baden-Baden, 1945), pp. 8–10; Commandement en chef, *Journal officiel*, No. 11 (January 9, 1946), 74–75; Control Council, *Official Gazette*, No. 2 (November 30, 1945), 26–27.

25. Germany (Territory under allied occupation, 1945———, French zone), Commandement en chef français en Allemagne, Direction générale de la justice, *Note sur l'organisation judiciaire en Allemagne occupée par le gouvernement militaire français* (Baden-Baden, 1945; Roneotyped); Direction générale de la justice, *Exposé sur l'activité de la direction générale de la justice* (Baden-Baden, 1947; Roneotyped); Direction générale de la justice, Contrôle de la justice allemande, *Rapport à Monsieur le directeur général pour la commission parlementaire d'enquête* (Baden-Baden, 1947; Roneotyped). Interview with President Furby, June 1960. A useful handbook is Marcel Martin's *La Législation française en Allemagne* (Baden-Baden, 1947).

Two important conferences of lawyers from the occupying countries and from Germany took place in 1947, one at Konstanz and another in Bad Godesberg, giving German lawyers a chance to resume their contacts with legal developments outside Germany. See Germany (Territory under allied occupation, 1945———, French zone), Commandement en chef français en Allemagne, Direction générale de la justice, *Journées juridiques de Constance (1947, 2–5 juin): Recueil des débats* (Tübingen, 1947), and Dr. E. Ehard *et al.*, *Tagung Deutscher Juristen, Bad Godesberg, 30 September – 1 Oktober 1947: Reden und Vorträge* (Hamburg, 1947).

26. *Revue de la zone française*, No. 5 (March 1946), 56; No. 6–7 (April-May 1946), 3–4; *France en Allemagne*, No. 1 (July 1946), 16–19. See also the article "La répression des crimes de guerre" in Germany (Territory under allied occupation, 1945———, French zone), Commandement en chef français en Allemagne, Direction de l'information, *Réalités allemandes*, No. 5 (May 1949), 19–30.

27. Guenther Roth and Kurt H. Wolff, *The American Denazification of Germany: a Historical Survey and an Appraisal* (Studies in German-American Postwar Problems, No. 1; Columbus, Ohio, 1954), p. 1.

28. JCS 1067 states: "6 (*c*). All members of the Nazi party who have been more than nominal participants in its activities, all active supporters of Nazism or

militarism and all other persons hostile to Allied purposes will be removed and excluded from public office and from positions of importance in quasi-public and private enterprises such as (1) civic, economic and labor organizations, (2) corporations and other organizations in which the German government or subdivisions have a major financial interest, (3) industry, commerce, agriculture, and finance, (4) education, and (5) the press, publishing houses and other agencies disseminating news and propaganda." *Germany, 1947–1949,* p. 24. For reference to the nature of German bureaucracy, see Almond, *Struggle for Democracy,* pp. 189–90.

29. Roth and Wolff, *The American Denazification,* pp. 15–19; Montgomery, *Forced to Be Free,* pp. 21–26. Montgomery's book is particularly interesting for his parallels between procedures adopted in Japan and Germany.

30. Ernst von Salomon, *Der Fragebogen* (Hamburg, 1951), also available in an English translation by Constantine Fitzgibbon as *Fragebogen (The Questionnaire)* (New York, 1955).

31. *Revue de la zone française,* No. 2 (December 15, 1945), 31.

32. Germany, Control Council, *Official Gazette,* No. 5 (March 31, 1946), 98–115.

33. *Ibid.,* No. 11 (October 31, 1946), 184–211.

34. *France en Allemagne,* No. 8 (March 1948), 65.

35. *Rheinpfalz,* February 1, 1947.

36. Künzel's success in this difficult post is best attested by the fact that he has remained Bürgermeister of Reutlingen since the end of the occupation. Künzel's organization of the process is illustrated in a documentary collection in the Rathaus in Reutlingen. See Germany (Territory under allied occupation, 1945———, French zone, Württemberg-Hohenzollern), Staatskommissariat für die politischen Säuberung, *Grundlagen und Organisation zur politischen Säuberung* (Reutlingen, 1947).

37. Württemberg-Hohenzollern, Beratende Landesversammlung, *Verhandlung,* January 9, 1947, pp. 13–16.

38. Germany (Territory under allied occupation, 1945———, French zone, Württemberg-Hohenzollern), Staatssekretariat, *Amtsblatt des Staatssekretariats für das französisch besetzte Gebiet Württemberg und Hohenzollerns* (Tübingen, 1945–47), June 8, 1946, pp. 67–74. For the text of the American zone law, see Pollock, *Germany under Occupation,* pp. 152–74, and for detailed commentary on the working of the law by Erich Schullze, *Gesetz zur Befreiung von Nationalsozialismus und Militarismus, mit den Ausführungsvorschriften und Formularen* (Munich, 1946).

39. Interview with P. Arnal, former head of the Oficomex, June 1960.

40. *Contrôle de la justice allemande, Rapport à Monsieur le directeur.*

41. *France en Allemagne,* No. 3 (October-November-December 1946), 51. In Württemberg, at least, the French permitted the "followers" to retain their positions in the administration, and they were thus able to make use of qualified administrators in the lower ranks of government. They also left themselves open to the charge that they permitted Nazis to retain office. Horst Locher, "La fonction publique dans le Württemberg depuis 1945," in Alfred Grosser (ed.), *Administra-*

tion et politique en Allemagne Occidentale (Cahiers de la fondation nationale des sciences politiques No. 57; Paris, 1954), p. 131.

42. Germany (Territory under allied occupation, 1945——, French zone, Rheinland-Pfalz), Landesregierung, *Verordnungsblatt der Landesregierung Rhein-land-Pfalz* (Koblenz, 1946–47), April 21, 1947, pp. 121–29. *Die Freiheit* pointed out the flexibility of this law on October 3, 1947. For the debate on this law in the Consultative Assembly of Rheinland-Pfalz, see Germany (Territory under allied occupation, 1945——, French zone, Rheinland-Pfalz), Beratende Landesversammlung, *Beratende Landesversammlung Rheinland-Pfalz: Drucksachen* (Koblenz, 1946–47), February 27, 1947, pp. 13–20.

43. Württemberg-Hohenzollern, Beratende Landesversammlung, *Verhandlung*, April 1, 1947, pp. 1–2.

44. *Badener Tagblatt*, April 16, 1947. The extent to which denazification was applied varied considerably in the French zone, not only between industry and administration, but also within the ministries themselves. Montgomery shows that the highest percentage of removals was in the ministries of labor, but he believes that the extent of denazification was dependent solely upon the number of cases examined. Montgomery, *Forced to Be Free*, pp. 77–78. Montgomery goes on to show from two examples of towns in the French zone how dominance of an economically powerful clique and religious differences could affect the success of denazification (pp. 133–38).

45. Commandement en chef, *Journal officiel*, No. 69 (May 5, 1947), 700–701.

46. *Ibid.*, No. 122 (November 21, 1947), 1244–45.

47. *Badener Tagblatt*, January 9, 1946.

48. *Schwäbisches Tagblatt*, December 5, 1945.

49. *Badener Tagblatt*, April 6, 1946.

50. *Rheinischer Merkur*, October 4, 1946.

51. *New York Times*, October 21, 1945; October 24, 1945.

52. *Rheinischer Merkur*, October 8, 1946.

53. *Le Monde*, November 29, 1946.

54. *Südkurier*, February 14, 1947.

55. *Rheinpfalz*, February 1, 1947.

56. Wilfrid Schilling, *The Fear Makers* (New York, 1960), p. 6. Many Germans had in fact been afraid to join in the work of denazification because of the possibility of reprisals. Almond, *Struggle for Democracy*, p. 200. The official prosecutor of the denazification court of Freiburg, Hub, was murdered in Oehringen in the spring of 1947. (*Das Volk*, April 5, 1947.) According to Montgomery, "Nazis were still a potential force in German life for a time even after they had been discredited by defeat and embarrassed by denazification." But he felt that the lack of support of neo-Nazism showed that "formal Nazism seemed as dead as its masters." Montgomery, *Forced to Be Free*, pp. 67–70.

57. *Neues Leben*, March 5, 1948; August 10, 1948.

58. *Rheinischer Merkur*, July 16, 1949.

59. Edmond Vermeil, "Les alliés et la rééducation des allemands," in Helen

Liddell (ed.) *et al.*, *Education in Occupied Germany: L'Éducation de l'Allemagne occupée* (Paris, 1949), p. 43.

60. Joseph Rovan, "L'Allemagne de nos mérites," *Esprit*, No. 11 (October 1, 1945), pp. 531–32.

61. Hocking, *Experiment in Education*, p. 220.

62. Padover, *Psychologist in Germany*, pp. 114, 176.

63. Jules-Albert Jaeger, "La jeunesse allemande," in Aubert, *Nouveaux aspects du problème allemand*, pp. 76, 90–91.

64. *Badener Tagblatt*, April 13, 1946.

65. *Rheinischer Merkur*, May 10, 1946.

66. *Ibid.*, November 5, 1946.

67. *Trierische Volkszeitung*, January 3, 1947.

68. Germany (Territory under allied occupation, 1945———, French zone), Commandement en chef français en Allemagne, Direction de l'éducation publique, Bureau d'étude, *Enquête sur la jeunesse* (Baden-Baden, 1945).

69. Germany (Territory under allied occupation, 1945———, French zone), Commandement en chef français en Allemagne, Direction de l'éducation publique, *Sondages sur les opinions et le comportement de la jeunesse*, prepared by Bernard Lahy (Baden-Baden, 1948–49), No. 1 (January 1948).

70. Elisabeth Noelle and Erich Peter Neumann, *Jahrbuch der öffentlichen Meinung, 1947–1955* (Allensbach am Bodensee: Verlag für Demoskopie, 1956), pp. 114, 127.

71. *Sondages sur les opinions de la jeunesse*, No. 3 (May 1948).

72. *Jahrbuch der öffentlichen Meinung*, p. 127. An excellent study of the German state of mind at this time was published by the French magazine *Esprit*, No. 6 (July 1947), 890–1076. The magazine's impartiality so impressed the Germans that it was published in the French zone with the title *Anthologie der deutschen Meinung: Deutsche Antworten auf eine französische Umfrage* (Konstanz, 1948). Section six deals with the opinions of young people and their teachers.

73. Raymond Schmittlein, "Briser les chaînes de la jeunesse allemande," *France-Illustration*, September 17, 1949, p. 18.

74. Interview with Raymond Schmittlein, June 1960. According to Clark Delbert, who was in Germany on an assignment for the *New York Times*, "The French were the only ones who approached this problem of democratization from the right end. They thought of the Germans as people who knew little or nothing, even in theory, of the principles by which free men live, and who must be taught carefully and patiently from the beginning." Clark Delbert, *Again the Goose Step: The Lost Fruits of Victory* (New York, 1949), pp. 93–96.

75. "L'éducation publique en zone française d'occupation," *Notes documentaires*, No. 1, 163, p .3.

76. Germany (Territory under allied occupation, 1945———, French zone), Commandement en chef français en Allemagne, Direction de l'éducation publique, *L'Œuvre culturelle française en Allemagne* (Baden-Baden, 1947), p. 9.

77. *Ibid.*, p. 11.

78. Robert J. Havighurst, *Report on Germany* (New York, 1947), p. 104; Botrot, *Allemagne toute neuve*, p. 112.

79. *Notes documentaires*, No. 1, 163, p. 3; *France en Allemagne*, No. 3 (October-November-December 1946), 54.

80. *France en Allemagne*, No. 7 (November 1947), 66–68.

81. *Ibid.*

82. *Die Freiheit*, July 18, 1947; *Trierische Volkszeitung*, July 26, 1947; *Rhein-Zeitung*, July 26, 1947; *Rheinischer Merkur*, July 26, 1947.

83. Germany, Rheinland-Pfalz, Landtag, *Verhandlung*, August 29, 1947, pp. 80–86. See also Germany (Territory under allied occupation, 1945——, French zone, Baden), Ministerium des Kultus und Unterrichts, *Die Soziale Gestaltung der Schule: Denkschrift über die Schulreform als Grundlage zur Diskussion* (Freiburg im Breisgau, 1948).

84. Helen Liddell, "Education in occupied Germany: a field survey," in Liddell, *Education in Occupied Germany*, p. 116. See also Edmond Vermeil, "Les destins de l'Église évangélique luthérienne en Allemagne," in Edmond Vermeil et al., *Les Églises en Allemagne: The Churches in Germany* (Paris, 1949), pp. 58–60.

85. *Schwäbisches Tagblatt*, March 25, 1947.

86. Adolf Süsterhenn, who played a large part in the writing of the constitution of Rheinland-Pfalz, and who is now president of the constitutional court of Rheinland-Pfalz, discusses these clauses at length in his book, written with Hans Schäfer, *Kommentar der Verfassung für Rheinland-Pfalz mit Berücksichtigung des Grundgesetzes für die Bundesrepublik Deutschland* (Koblenz, 1950), pp. 146–85.

87. *Badener Tagblatt*, December 14, 1948.

88. The parliamentary committee of inquiry found that many professors, although hostile to Nazism, upheld extreme nationalist views and insisted that the Western powers would soon need Germany as a bulwark of Western civilization against Eastern barbarism. France, Assemblée constituante, *Annexes*, No. 923 (April 8, 1946), 912.

89. *Ibid.* Gerhard Ritter, speaking in 1958, described the almost impossible task of the French curator in attempting to supervise the teaching done in such courses as German history, especially where a professor wanted to speak without notes. Interview with Gerhard Ritter, August 1958. See for comparison Gerhard Ritter's article on the position of the university professor during the Nazi period, "Der deutsche Professor im 'Dritten Reich,' " *Die Gegenwart*, No. 1 (December 24, 1945), 23–26.

90. See the very revealing annual report on the state of the University of Tübingen: Germany (Territory under allied occupation, 1945——, French zone), Commandement en chef français en Allemagne, Direction de l'éducation publique, *Rapport annuel sur l'université de Tübingen, 1947* (Tübingen, 1947). Robert Havighurst also gives an account of the conditions in Tübingen in 1947 in his *Report on Germany*, pp. 54–57.

91. *Ibid.*, p. 69.

92. "L'université Jean Gutenberg à Mayence," *France en Allemagne*, No. 1 (July 1946), 11–15. Interview with Rechtsanwalt Fritz Eichholz, Curator of the University of Mainz, August 1960.

93. *Rheinischer Merkur*, May 21, 1946. The early success of the University was greatly aided by the work of the dean of the Theological-Philosophical Hochschule, Prälat Professor Dr. Reatz, and to the first rector, Professor Schmitt, who worked closely in cooperation with the Directorate of Public Education. See Dr. med. Kurt Voit, "Die Johannes Gutenberg–Universität in Mainz," *Vaterland Europa*, July 1960, p. 49.

94. Interview with Mme Giron, June 1960.

95. *Notes documentaires*, No. 1, 164, p. 4; *France en Allemagne*, No. 5 (March-April-May 1947), 17–20.

96. Germany (Territory under allied occupation, 1945——, French zone, Württemberg-Hohenzollern), Landtag, *Verhandlung des Landtags für Württemberg-Hohenzollern* (Bebenhausen/Tübingen, 1947——), July 30, 1949, p. 1281. A further proof of this German appreciation of the work that was done by the French in the Directorate of Public Education was given in 1960. The Institute of European History in Mainz, which had been founded in 1950 largely at the instigation of Schmittlein, invited Schmittlein himself to be the main speaker at its tenth anniversary celebration. See *Staats-Zeitung: Staatsanzeiger für Rheinland-Pfalz*, July 10, 1960.

97. *L'Œuvre culturelle française en Allemagne*, pp. 30–31.

98. "Les rencontres de jeunesse en zone française," *France en Allemagne*, No. 9 (June 1948), 45–48.

99. German pleasure at renewal of international contacts, and surprise at the good reception abroad of German participants, was expressed by *Rheinischer Merkur*, which found especially newsworthy the visit of German students to Chartres and German participation with equal status in the meeting in 1949 of the Nouvelles Equipes Internationales. *Rheinischer Merkur*, June 5, 1948; July 23, 1949.

100. Grosser, *L'Allemagne de l'Occident*, pp. 119–20, 294–301; *L'Œuvre culturelle française en Allemagne*, pp. 30–31, 37–42; *Notes documentaires*, No. 1, 163, p. 9.

101. Dr. Kamm, "Deutsch-französische Vereinigung Ludwigshafen," *Vaterland Europa*, July 1960, p. 63. This whole issue of the magazine, which is under the editorship of the director of the Europa-Haus in Marienberg, is devoted to the union of friendship between the French province of Burgundy and the German Land of Rheinland-Pfalz. A good description of pairing of towns in the two countries is given by Flora Lewis in "Franco-German 'Twins'—A Startling Fact," *New York Times*, May 29, 1960, Magazine Section.

102. Grosser, *L'Allemagne de l'Occident*, pp. 298–99. A further illustration of the desire for better understanding between the two peoples was the meeting in 1951 of teachers of history from the two countries. These teachers agreed upon a basic interpretation of recent Franco-German history, with the aim of avoiding chauvinistic interpretations which, they believed, had done much to lead their

countries into the three wars of the past century. See *Deutschland-Frankreich*, I, 51–80, for the text of the agreement.

103. An appreciative account of the French educational program is given by Percy W. Bidwell in his article "Reëducation in Germany: Emphasis on Culture in the French Zone," *Foreign Affairs*, XXVII (October 1948), 78–85.

CHAPTER IX

1. R.I.I.A., *Documents on Germany*, p. 44.

2. Padover, *Psychologist in Germany*, pp. 65–66, 115, 132.

3. Snell, *Dilemma over Germany*, p. 5; Heinrich Fraenkel, *Help Us Germans to Beat the Nazis* (London, 1941). The anti-Fascist groups, or *Antifas*, which sprang up throughout Germany and which were treated with great reticence by the military governments, are described in Manuel Gottlieb's *The German Peace Settlement and the Berlin Crisis* (New York, 1960), p. 213, n. 10.

4. Hans Rothfels, *The German Opposition to Hitler* (Hinsdale, Ill., 1948), pp. 20–22, 40–46.

5. *Ibid.*, p. 10, citing a British Admiralty press release of July 20, 1947; Alan Bullock, *Hitler: A Study in Tyranny* (London, 1952), pp. 674–89.

6. Churchill, *Second World War*, VI, 252.

7. Commandement en chef, *Journal officiel*, No. 35 (August 30, 1946), 291–92.

8. *Revue de la zone française*, No. 3 (January 1946), 22–24. A good short description of the revival of local government in Germany is given in Roger H. Wells, "Local Government," in Edward H. Litchfield *et al.*, *Governing Postwar Germany* (Ithaca, N.Y., 1953), pp. 64–83.

9. *Badener Tagblatt*, April 10, 1946.

10. Interview with Dr. Paul Binder, August 1960. The provisional constitution was given in the *Amtsblatt* of Württemberg-Hohenzollern on September 2, 1945. *Deutschland Jahrbuch, 1949*, p. 26.

11. Württemberg-Hohenzollern, Beratende Landesversammlung, *Verhandlung*, November 22, 1946, p. 17.

12. Commandement en chef, *Journal officiel*, No. 2 (September 17, 1945), 8–9; No. 9 (December 21, 1945), 54; "Le syndicalisme en zone française," *Revue de la zone française*, No. 6-7 (April–May 1946), 37–39, 42; Wells, "Local Government," in Litchfield, *Governing Postwar Germany*, pp. 64–66, 72; Vera Franke Eliasberg, "Political Party Developments," in Almond, *Struggle for Democracy*, p. 231. Three useful articles throw light on the revival of German government: Leonard Krieger, "The Inter-Regnum in Germany: March–August 1945," *Political Science Quarterly*, LXIV (December 1949), 507–32; J. W. F. Hill, "Local Government in Western Germany," *Political Quarterly*, XX (July–September 1949), 256–64; Robert G. Neumann, "The New Political Parties of Germany," *American Political Science Review*, XL (August 1946), 749–59.

13. *France en Allemagne*, No. 5 (March-April-May 1947), 106. The organizations which the French finally permitted to extend in competence over the

whole zone (e.g., Comité allemand du ravitaillement, Office de la chasse et de la pêche), are described in Walter Vogel, *Westdeutschland 1945–1950: Der Aufbau von Verfassungs- und Verwaltungseinrichtungen über den Ländern der drei westlichen Besatzungszonen*, Teil I: *Geschichtlicher Überblick; oberste beratende Stellen und Einrichtungen für Gesetzgebung, Verwaltung und Rechtsprechung; einzelne Verwaltungszweige; Ernährung, Landwirtschaft und Forsten* (Schriften des Bundesarchivs, 2., Koblenz, 1956), pp. 81–85, 120–25.

14. *France en Allemagne*, No. 8 (March 1948), 15; *Notes documentaires*, No. 467, pp. 11–12.

15. Richard M. Scammon, "Political Parties," in Litchfield, *Governing Postwar Germany*, p. 478. A prominent German Socialist told me that no Socialist was called upon for service in the local government of his area for the first five months of the occupation, whereupon he stormed into the local military government office and asked, "Where does one sign up for the Nazi party? I see that one has to be a Nazi to get attention here."

16. *Notes documentaires*, No. 467, pp. 5–8.

17. The Pfalz separatists first formed a party called Friends of France (*Amis de la France*), which later fused with the Committee for an Autonomous Rhineland (*Komitee für ein Eigenstaatliches Rheinland*), which worked in cooperation with a similar organization in the British zone called the Rhenish Popular Party (*Rheinische Volkspartei*). The Rhenish Popular Party, although not authorized by the French, was also strong in Rheinland–Hessen-Nassau. However, the growing strength of the other parties quickly reduced the importance of these groups. *Notes documentaires*, No. 467, p. 12. Interview with Franz Bögler, Oberregierungspräsident of the Pfalz, August 1960.

18. *France en Allemagne*, No. 8 (March 1948), 15; *Notes documentaires*, No. 467, pp. 11–12.

19. *France en Allemagne*, No. 8 (March 1948), 19–20.

20. *Schwäbisches Tagblatt*, October 5, 1946.

21. *Badener Tagblatt*, March 23, 1946.

22. *Rheinpfalz*, January 16, 1946.

23. *Schwäbisches Tagblatt*, December 11, 1945.

24. Wells, "Local Government," in Litchfield, *Governing Postwar Germany*, pp. 72–73. Wells points out that the Germans themselves reorganized the Gemeinde form of administration, in Württemberg on March 14, 1947, in Baden on March 25, 1947, and in Rheinland-Pfalz on September 29, 1948.

25. Commandement en chef, *Journal officiel*, No. 26 (June 15, 1946), 206–8.

26. "Les Élections de l'automne de 1946 dans la zone française d'occupation," *France en Allemagne*, No. 3 (October-November-December 1946), 9–13.

27. Compiled from *Notes documentaires*, No. 467, p. 18, and *France en Allemagne*, No. 6 (September 1947), 81.

28. *France en Allemagne*, No. 8 (March 1948), 24.

29. *Ibid.*

30. Württemberg-Hohenzollern, Beratende Landesversammlung, *Verhandlung*, November 22, 1946, pp. 6–17.

31. *France en Allemagne*, No. 3 (October-November-December 1946), 52.

32. Interview with Dr Adolf Süsterhenn, former minister of justice and public worship, Rheinland-Pfalz, August 1960.

33. *Rheinischer Merkur*, September 24, 1946; October 8, 1946; October 15, 1946; October 22, 1946; November 26, 1946.

34. *France en Allemagne*, No. 8 (March 1948), 31–35.

35. Süsterhenn and Schäfer, *Kommentar der Verfassung*, pp. 27–61, gives full text of the constitution.

36. *Rheinzeitung*, May 3, 1947; *Rheinischer Merkur*, May 10, 1947.

37. *Neuer Mainzer Anzeiger*, April 18, 1947.

38. *Ibid.*, April 25, 1947.

39. *Rheinischer Merkur*, May 17, 1947.

40. *France en Allemagne*, No. 6 (September 1947), 80–81.

41. *Rheinischer Merkur*, May 24, 1947.

42. *France en Allemagne*, No. 8 (March 1948), 25–28.

43. Germany (Territory under allied occupation, 1945——, French zone, Baden), Beratende Landesversammlung, *Verhandlung der Beratenden Versammlung des Landes Baden* (Freiburg im Breisgau, 1946–47), April 10, 1947, pp. 1–11; April 11, 1947, pp. 1–14; April 14, 1947, pp. 1–32.

44. *Badener Tagblatt*, May 20, 1947.

45. *France en Allemagne*, No. 6 (September 1947), 81.

46. *Ibid.*, No. 8 (March 1948), 28–31.

47. *Schwäbisches Tagblatt*, November 29, 1946.

48. Württemberg-Hohenzollern, Beratende Landesversammlung, *Verhandlung*, December 2, 1946, p. 19.

49. *Ibid.*, December 3, 1946, pp. 1–7.

50. *Schwäbisches Tagblatt*, March 7, 1947; March 11, 1947; March 14, 1947.

51. *Ibid.*, March 25, 1947.

52. Württemberg-Hohenzollern, Beratende Landesversammlung, *Verhandlung*, April 21, 1947, pp. 1–58.

53. *France en Allemagne*, No. 6 (September 1947), 81.

54. *Ibid.*

CHAPTER X

1. Commandement en chef, *Journal officiel*, No. 78 (June 13, 1947), 783–84; No. 79 (June 17, 1947), 796. For the opening session of the Landtag of Rheinland-Pfalz, in which Koenig's message was read out, see Rheinland-Pfalz, Landtag, *Verhandlung*, June 12, 1947, pp. 10–11.

2. *Die Freiheit*, September 5, 1947.

3. *France en Allemagne*, No. 6 (September 1947), 82.

4. Rheinland-Pfalz, Landtag, *Verhandlung*, July 9, 1947, pp. 29–30.

5. *France en Allemagne*, No. 7 (November 1947), 92.

6. *Die Freiheit*, April 9, 1948; *Neues Leben*, April 9, 1948.

7. *Südwestdeutsche Volkszeitung*, May 20, 1947.

8. Germany (Territory under allied occupation, 1945——, French zone, Baden), Landtag, *Verhandlung des Badischen Landtags* (Freiburg im Breisgau, 1947——), August 5, 1947, pp. 2–6.

9. *France en Allemagne*, No. 9 (June 1948), 100–101.

10. *Ibid.*, No. 7 (November 1947), 90.

11. Württemberg-Hohenzollern, Landtag, *Verhandlung*, July 22, 1947, pp. 21–28.

12. "La Réforme agraire en zone française d'occupation (état au 30 avril, 1949)," *Réalités allemandes*, No. 4 (April 1949), 22. Koenig's announcement was generally well received by the Germans. Some papers regretted that the Germans had been so dilatory as to need French prompting. *Allgemeine Zeitung*, October 24, 1947.

13. *France en Allemagne*, No. 8 (March 1948), 46.

14. *Réalités allemandes*, No. 4 (April 1949), 22.

15. Rheinland-Pfalz, Landtag, *Verhandlung*, February 25, 1947, pp. 494–507; March 2, 1947, pp. 527–38; March 3, 1947, pp. 539–42; *Die Freiheit*, February 27, 1948, for the speech of Otto Schmidt; *Neues Leben*, March 5, 1948.

16. Baden, Landtag, *Verhandlung*, February 4, 1948, pp. 6–27; February 5, 1948, pp. 1–60; *Réalités allemandes*, No. 4 (April 1949), 22.

17. Württemberg-Hohenzollern, Landtag, *Verhandlung*, February 4, 1948, pp. 219–23, 233; February 5, 1948, pp. 262. For the second reading of the law, see *ibid.*, March 3, 1948, pp. 270–85; March 4, 1948, pp. 289–300. For the third reading, see *ibid.*, March 23, 1948, pp. 319–23.

18. *Réalités allemandes*, No. 4 (April 1949), 23.

19. Baden, Landtag, *Verhandlung*, August 5, 1947, p. 2.

20. *Die Freiheit*, April 23, 1948; May 14, 1948.

21. Rheinland-Pfalz, Landtag, *Verhandlung*, June 16, 1948, pp. 696–97; *Die Freiheit*, June 18, 1948.

22. *Die Freiheit*, June 16, 1948. The report to the Landtag on the food strikes was made by Bockenkruger and Stübinger. See Rheinland-Pfalz, Landtag, *Verhandlung*, June 16, 1948, pp. 680–84.

23. *Rheinpfalz*, October 22, 1947; *Rheinischer Merkur*, October 18, 1947; *Schwabenecho*, October 21, 1947; *Die Freiheit*, October 17, 1947.

24. *Südkurier*, May 23, 1947.

25. Baden, Landtag, *Verhandlung*, November 7, 1948, pp. 1–40.

26. *Ibid.*, May 12, 1948, pp. 7–22.

27. *Ibid.*, June 16, 1948, pp. 1–2.

28. *Ibid.*, August 26, 1948, p. 7.

29. *Ibid.*, pp. 8–12.

30. *Ibid.*, pp. 12–13.

31. *Ibid.*, p. 14.

32. *Réalités allemandes*, No. 1 (January 1949), 99.

33. Baden, Landtag, *Verhandlung*, November 23, 1948, pp. 34–36. The speech caused a similar burst of indignation in Rheinland-Pfalz. See *Die Freiheit*, November 26, 1948, and the Landtag debate of November 24, 1948.

34. *France en Allemagne*, No. 8 (March 1948), 138–39.

35. *Das Volk*, November 15, 1947.

36. *Schwabenecho*, November 14, 1947.

37. Württemberg-Hohenzollern, Landtag, *Verhandlung*, April 29, 1948, p. 346.

38. *Ibid.*, June 22, 1948, pp. 364–65.

39. *Ibid.*, June 23, 1948, pp. 372–77.

40. *Ibid.*, August 6, 1948, p. 564.

41. *Ibid.*, p. 559.

42. *Ibid.*, p. 564.

43. *Ibid.*, August 13, 1948, p. 568.

44. *Ibid.*, May 12, 1949, p. 1087.

45. *Rheinischer Merkur*, October 16, 1948.

46. *Réalités allemandes*, No. 1 (January 1949), 94.

47. Kehl had been cleared of its German inhabitants by the retreating Nazis. However, the French refused for the first three years of the occupation to allow the Germans to return to their homes in the city, thereby raising fears among the Germans that they intended to annex the city permanently to France.

48. *Rheinischer Merkur*, July 5, 1947.

49. Rheinland-Pfalz, Landtag, *Verhandlung*, April 7, 1948, pp. 546–80.

50. *Rheinisch-Pfälzische Rundschau*, October 5, 1948; October 7, 1948; October 9, 1948; October 12, 1948.

51. *Neues Leben*, April 9, 1948.

52. Rheinland-Pfalz, Landtag, *Verhandlung*, June 16, 1948, pp. 684–96.

53. *France en Allemagne*, No. 10 (October 1948), 79.

54. *Das Volk*, November 8, 1947.

55. Baden, Landtag, *Verhandlung*, July 5, 1948, p. 7.

56. *Ibid.*, July 6, 1948, pp. 1–2.

57. *Rheinischer Merkur*, October 25, 1947.

58. *Die Freiheit*, January 23, 1948.

59. Rheinland-Pfalz, Landtag, *Verhandlung*, January 21, 1948, pp. 388–89.

60. *Neues Leben*, December 23, 1947.

61. *Ibid.*, January 13, 1948.

62. *Ibid.*, January 23, 1948.

63. John Ford Golay, *The Founding of the Federal Republic of Germany* (Chicago, 1958), p. 177. Fritz R. Alleman discusses the part of Schmid and Süsterhenn in the Parliamentary Council in *Bonn ist nicht Weimar* (Cologne, 1956), pp. 69–73, 89.

64. Golay, *Founding of the Federal Republic*, p. 178.

65. *Rheinischer Merkur*, July 23, 1946.

66. *Ibid.*, June 18, 1946; June 21, 1946; June 25, 1946; June 28, 1946.

67. *Die Freiheit*, August 29, 1947.

68. *Rheinischer Merkur*, February 21, 1948.

69. *Die Freiheit*, February 27, 1948; March 1, 1948.

70. *Rheinischer Merkur*, March 13, 1948.

71. *Neues Leben*, March 5, 1948.

72. *Réalités allemandes*, No. 1 (January 1949), 96–97. *Die Freiheit*, July 10, 1948; July 14, 1948.

73. *Allgemeine Zeitung*, July 17, 1948.

74. *Réalités allemandes*, No. 1 (January 1949), 95–96.

75. Württemberg-Hohenzollern, Landtag, *Verhandlung*, October 7, 1948, pp. 586–93.

76. Baden, Landtag, *Verhandlung*, September 7, 1948, p. 2.

77. Hermann Haeberlin, *Das Land Baden-Württemberg* (shortened ed., Darmstadt, 1956), p. 3.

78. *Rheinischer Merkur*, February 19, 1949. The article was called, "The State Against the Parents?"

79. *Die Welt*, March 17, 1949, cited in Golay, *Founding of the Federal Republic*, p. 93.

80. *Ibid.*, pp. 96–107.

81. *Der Tag*, June 4, 1949, cited in Golay, *Founding of the Federal Republic*, p. 146.

82. Rheinland-Pfalz, Landtag, *Verhandlung*, May 18, 1949, pp. 1528–32.

83. Baden, Landtag, *Verhandlung*, May 18, 1949, pp. 2–18.

84. Württemberg-Hohenzollern, Landtag, *Verhandlung*, May 21, 1949, pp. 1112–25.

85. *Réalités allemandes*, No. 1 (January 1949), 15.

86. Litchfield, *Governing Postwar Germany*, Appendix O, pp. 640, 647, 650.

87. *Die Freiheit*, August 16, 1949; *Rheinischer Merkur*, August 20, 1949.

88. Alfred Grosser, in *La Démocratie de Bonn* (Paris, 1958), pp. 47–48, shows that "perhaps the most striking phenomenon of regional political life is the permanence in office since the end of the war of the politicians, especially when one considers that the majority have been put in office by the authority of the occupying power."

CHAPTER XI

1. De Gaulle, *Mémoires*, III, 152–53.

2. *Fait du jour*, No. 14 (July 16, 1946).

3. Rovan, "L'Allemagne," *Esprit*, No. 11 (October 1, 1945), 531–32.

Bibliographical Note

ALTHOUGH the policies applied in the British and American zones of occupation in Germany are abundantly documented, the facts about the French zone remain relatively obscure. The greatest lack is of personal testimony, from German and especially from French sources; no military government officer has recounted his experiences in the French zone, and no high official has given an over-all account of his part in the occupation. Reconstructing the French policies in Germany is largely a matter of testing certain critical appraisals against official documents and facts gleaned from a wide variety of sources.

The most useful documentation of policy in the French zone is to be found in the official publications of the French military government in Baden-Baden. All laws, ordinances, and so on were printed in the *Journal officiel du commandement en chef français en Allemagne*. Each division of the military government published frequent reports on its activities; the most useful of these are the three economic bulletins of the Direction générale de l'économie et des finances: the *Bulletin statistique, Statistique industrielle*, and *Statistique industrielle mensuelle*. The Direction de l'éducation publique summarized its activities in an excellent short pamphlet entitled *L'Œuvre culturelle française en Allemagne*. The activities of the army in the zone were reviewed in the monthly *Revue d'information des troupes françaises d'occupation en Allemagne*, a magazine whose literary caliber speaks most highly for the intelligence of the average French soldier. Most valuable of all is the series of magazines issued by the Division d'information: the *Revue de la zone française, La France en Allemagne*, and *Réalités allemandes*. These reviews, which were in fact the same magazine under different names and formats, contain studies of all aspects of policy in the zone, including explanatory articles on the machinery of government in Baden-Baden, reports on the progress of economic revival or of denazification, and reports of important speeches and press conferences. Together they give the most detailed, authoritative account of events in the zone from 1945 to 1949.

Another important source of information on the internal history of the zone may be found in the contemporary press. Coverage was sparse, however, even in French newspapers. *Le Monde, Le Figaro,* and *Le Populaire* devoted occasional short articles to events of outstanding importance, such as the resignation of Laffon. The pro-Communist weekly *France d'abord* and the Communist *L'Humanité* provided the most regular commentary on the zone, but their evidence, which was consistently anti-German and continually critical of the military government, was sharply slanted toward extreme Left Wing views. The *New York Times* provided occasional evidence, usually of French misdeeds. The London *Times* on November 30, 1945, and December 20, 1946, published two of the best newspaper articles on the zone, which combined factual evidence with an objective approach. A number of French journals devoted complete issues to the German problem, although they rarely dealt at length with the French zone itself. These special issues include "La 'question allemande,' " in *Fontaine* for November 1945; "Allemagne" in *Les Temps Modernes,* No. 46–47, August-September 1949; "Les Allemands parlent de l'Allemagne," in *Esprit,* VI (July 1947), 890–1076; "L'Allemagne vue par les Allemands," in *L'Age nouveau,* June 1949; and "Le Problème allemand" in *La Nef,* Cahier No. 1, December 1952. *France-Illustration* published a series of articles on the four zones of occupation in May 1947, with coverage of the French zone in the issue for May 10, 1947, pp. 457–60; the same paper devoted its whole issue of September 17, 1949, to a study of the French zone of occupation, with articles written by all the major figures of the military government. Much detailed information is given in the magazine *Documents,* which was published beginning in September 1946 by the Bureau international de Liaison et de Documentation in Offenburg.

A series of studies published by the Direction de la Documentation in Paris, called *Notes documentaires et études,* is of special value. Among some fifty studies in this series devoted to the German question, the most valuable are "La Zone d'occupation française en Allemagne" (No. 255), a study of the zone in March 1946, and "Esquisse d'une géographie politique de la zone française d'occupation en Allemagne" (No. 467), a detailed analysis of the electoral geography of the zone. The *Cahiers français,* also published by the Direction de la Documentation, contained occasional news bulletins of the zone, and issue No. 77 of February 1, 1947, was devoted entirely to the zone.

Debates in the French Consultative Assembly in 1945 (June 28), in the Constituent Assembly in 1945–46 (December 21 and 30–31, January 16, March 29, and April 3), and in the National Assembly in 1948 (June 11–15), provide a rich source of evidence. The report of the committee of inquiry sent by the Constituent Assembly into the zone in December 1945 was printed in the *Annexes* of the assembly on April 8, 1946; it emphasized the infiltration of Vichy supporters into the military government.

Statistics on the economic development of the zone were also provided by various United Nations studies. In 1948 the United Nations published its *Economic Survey of Europe since the War,* and in the following year issued an *Economic Survey of Europe in 1948.* The annual *Reports* of the Inter-Allied Reparation Agency provided detailed accountings of the state of dismantling in the zone. In 1948 and 1949, a thorough review of economic developments in the zone was made to provide justification for requests of allocation of Marshall aid funds. The OEEC published reports in 1948 and 1949 describing economic development planned for the zone in the following year. The Economic Cooperation Administration itself published a study of the western German economy in 1948 entitled *Western Germany: Country Study.* The publicity occasioned by the Marshall Plan had the result of forcing a review of the effects of French administration on the zone's economy. For the period before 1948, however, the major economic sources remain the publications of the French military government itself, the accuracy of which has been contested by Germans.

Two German statistical sourcebooks, the *Deutschland Jahrbuch, 1949,* and "Wirtschaftsstatistik der deutschen Besatzungszonen, 1945–1948" in the *Europa-Archiv* of Wilhelm Cornides, are convenient for reference. Of very great value is the series of publications by the Institut für Besatzungsfragen in Tübingen. From the time of its founding in 1948, the institute played a semi-official function in collecting all available documentation of the occupation and in giving advice through its "Gutachten" to private and public bodies on the legal aspects of the occupation. Through its close contacts with the Land governments, especially with that of Württemberg-Hohenzollern, the institute was able to make use of the best documentation available to Germans. The publications of the institute include two major studies on occupation costs, *Besatzungskosten—ein Verteidigungsbeitrag?* and *Sechs Jahre Besatzungslasten*; a study of the economic effects of the policy of the occupying powers, *Einwirkungen der Besatzungsmächte auf die westdeutsche Wirtschaft*; a study of the displaced persons question, *Das DP-Problem*; and several works on the legal aspects of the occupation.

The revival of political life in the French zone is best recorded in the debates of the assemblies in the Länder of the zone, first in the records of the Consultative Assemblies and then of the Landtage. No better evidence is available of the German attitude to the French occupation than in these outspoken, highly informed debates. Several Bundestag debates also afforded a retrospective glance at the French occupation. Most important were the debates on occupation costs, which took place on January 18, 1951, and April 26, 1951, and the debate of July 2, 1953.

The newspapers of the zone give full coverage of the political life of the Länder and provide a remarkably free expression of German opinion on French policy in action. Most useful in their coverage are the federalist *Rheinischer Merkur* of Koblenz, the *Badener Tagblatt* of Baden-Baden, and the *Schwäbisches Tagblatt* of Tübingen. After 1947 the political parties in each Land had their own party newspaper, of which the most lively and informative were the Communist *Neues Leben* and the Socialist *Die Freiheit* in Rheinland-Pfalz. The French zone also possessed one of Germany's best periodicals, *Die Gegenwart*, founded in Freiburg in 1945, which gave well-informed editorial comments on German developments.

The diplomatic bargaining that finally led to the grant of a zone to France and its final demarcation is still somewhat unclear. De Gaulle's *Mémoires de guerre* give an indispensable account of his relations with the British and American governments during the war, his attempts to gain acceptance of the French thesis on Germany, and his determination to gain for France a zone of occupation in Germany. Churchill, in *The Second World War* (Vol. VI), has described the reasoning that led him to champion the grant of a zone to France. The accounts of Sherwood, Byrnes, Stettinius, and Leahy throw some light on Roosevelt's attitude toward France at the Yalta Conference, but the full effect of the President's antipathy for de Gaulle remains to be explained. The discussions in the European Advisory Commission on the boundaries of the French zone are also unclear, although Philip E. Mosely's article, "The Occupation of Germany," in *Foreign Affairs,* Vol. XXVIII (July 1950), shows the part played by the United States War Department in causing the division of Baden and Württemberg along the Karlsruhe-Munich *Autobahn.* General de Lattre's *History of the French First Army* gives convincing proof of the determination of de Gaulle to use the French army to win for France the largest possible zone in Germany. The interlude of de Lattre's control of the zone as French commander-in-chief has been described briefly by his biographers, Chaigne, Croidys, and Thomasset. But the decision by the French government in Paris to recall him remains unexplained. General de Gaulle, in the third volume of his memoirs, gives a clear account of the action he took to ensure that France would be given a zone of occupation that would satisfy the demands of the French thesis on Germany, but he throws little light on the promotion of de Lattre.

The conflict between the civilians and the army officers in the military government still requires much greater documentation, as does the denazification process in the zone. Here the problems of writing about a period only recently past are brought out into the open. Documentation of individual cases is all too often lacking, so that discussions of motivation must remain largely speculative. Personal interviews, of course, can fill parts of this lacuna; and a host of persons connected with the French zone of occupation, both Frenchmen and Germans, have been exceptionally generous in helping to clarify the more confused issues of the occupation. These include the following (interviewed at the times indicated):

M. P. Arnal, former head of the Oficomex. June 1960.

Dr. Paul Binder, former minister of finance in State Secretariat of Württemberg-Hohenzollern. August 1960.

M. Franz Bögler, Oberregierungspräsident z. D. of the Pfalz, president of the Socialist party of the Pfalz. August 1960.

Rechtsanwalt Fritz Eichholz, curator of the University of Mainz. August 1960.

Dr. B. Dietrich, former Bürgermeister of Singen, Baden. August 1958.

M. Donnedieu de Vabres, former adjoint to the commissioner general for German and Austrian affairs. June 1960.

Ministerialdirektor Fritz Duppré, head of the Staatskanzlei of Rhein-land-Pfalz. August 1960.

M. Jean Filippi, former director general of economy and finance, 1945–47. June 1960.

M. André François-Poncet, French ambassador in Berlin, 1931–38; French high commissioner in West Germany, 1949–55. August 1958.

President Charles J. Furby, former director general of justice. June 1960.

Mme Germaine Giron, former adjoint to the director of public education. June 1960.

M. Gilbert Grandval, former délégué supérieur in the Saar, 1945–48; high commissioner in the Saar, 1948–52; and ambassador to the Saar, 1952–55. September 1960.

Dr. Martin Goehring, professor of European history at the Institute for European History, Mainz. July 1960.

Professor Alfred Grosser, author of *L'Allemagne de l'Occident,* etc. September 1958.

M. Hans Kern, Landrat of Reutlingen, Württemberg. August 1960.

M. Otto Künzel, former state commissioner for political cleansing, Württemberg-Hohenzollern; Bürgermeister of Reutlingen. August 1960.

M. Roger Lenoan, former head of the Division of French Justice at the Allied Control Council in Berlin, 1945–46. June 1960.

M. Paul Leroy-Beaulieu, former director general of economy and finance, 1947–52. June 1960.

M. René Mayer, former commissioner general for German and Austrian affairs. September 1960.

M. Jules Marx, foreign affairs counselor. June 1960.

M. M. Mitzakis, former director of the Exchange Office in the General Directorate of Economy and Finance. June 1960.

M. René Monnier, former director of external commerce in the General Directorate of Economy and Finance, 1945–54. June 1960.

Dr. Gebhard Müller, former minister-president of Württemberg-Hohenzollern, 1949–52; minister-president of Baden-Württemberg, 1953. August 1960.

Dr. Gerhard Ritter, professor of history at the University of Freiburg. August 1958.

Dr. Karl Schmidt-Lüders, former business executive in Reutlingen and Baden-Baden; vice-president, Robert Bosch & Co., September 1958–May 1959. August 1960.

Dr. Raymond Schmittlein, former director of public education, 1945–51. June 1960.

M. René Sergent, former head of the Economics Directorate at the Allied Control Council in Berlin. June 1960.

Dr. Adolf Süsterhenn, former minister of justice and public worship in Rheinland-Pfalz, 1946–51, and member of the Parliamentary Council, 1948–49. August 1960.

M. Guillaume Widmer, former délégué supérieur in Württemberg, 1945–52; director of the study mission to the High Commission, 1952–54. June 1960.

I have mentioned only those titles of these people which relate to the history of the French zone. It would be impossible to describe their many activities, since most still occupy important positions in the political, legal, and commercial life of their countries. The help they have given me has been invaluable in enabling me to complete my research for this history of the French zone of occupation. But as every writer on this period acknowledges, the time for a definitive history has not yet come; the present work, therefore, can only sketch out the lines for future investigation.

Index

71; policy in French zone, 73–76; recalled, 77; methods of discipline, 263 n.25; de Gaulle's opinion of, 263 n.35

Law for Liberation from National Socialism and Militarism, 154, 157–58

Leahy, William D., 3f, 6, 12

Leather industry, 104, 138 (Table 3)

Leibbrandt, Friedrich, 188, 213

Level of Industry Plan, 111–14

Lichter, Gerhard, 186

Liddell, Helen, 172

Livry-Level, Philippe, 91

London Conference (February–June, 1948), 51–52, 54; French attitudes toward, 55–60; significance of, 60–61; German attitude, 230–33; and Land boundary disputes, 236; *see also* Foreign Ministers' Conferences

Ludwig, Adolf, 194

Maier, Friedrich, 188, 235, 240

Maier, Reinhold, 238

Mainz, 98, 267; University founded, 175–76, 282 n.92, 283 n.93, n.96

Malburg, F., 165

Malraux, André, 70

Markscheffel, Gunther, 162

Marshall, George C., 49f, 227f

Marshall Plan, 28, 137; significance for France, 46, 48–53, 55; and dismantling, 114, 220–23, and economy of French zone, 140–45 *passim*; German attitudes toward, 212, 225, 227–33

Massigli, René, 11, 15, 23, 48

Mauser works, 113

Mayer, René, 80, 88

Metallurgy, 104 (Table 3), 137

Michelet, Édouard, 85

Middleton, Drew, 71

Military government, of French zone: recruitment of, 17f, 262 n.18; and decree No. 2, 80, 82; organization of, 81–83; charges of Vichyism, 86; charges of extravagance and inefficiency, 88–89; reorganized (1948), 90, 266 n.76; economic policy, 109; and restitution, 111–12; irregular requisitioning, 123; restoration of transportation, 128; reduction in personnel, 133; electricity exploitation, 136; denazification, 148f, 155, 158–60; and Resistance officers, 149–50; and Tillessen trial, 162; and re-education policies, 167–72, 179; and revival of universities, 173–76; and international youth program, 177; and city twinning, 178; and German self-government, 181; and zonal administrative framework, 183–

84; nominates German administrators, 186–90; and CDU, 191; and separatism, 191, 193; and election of Landtage, 207–8; restricts powers of Länder, 209–10; and Toleration Agreement, 212; and work of Landtage, 215; and agrarian reform, 215–18; promises end of dismantling, 226; and federal electoral law, 239–40; legal position of, 272 n.25

Minder, Robert, *Germanies and Germans*, 94

Mitzakis, M., 144, 296

Mitzakis plan, and currency reform, 144

Molotov, Vyacheslav, 11, 35, 40, 42ff, 50

Monde, Le, 90

Monnet Plan, 127

Monsabert, Goislard de, 79

Montabaur, Regierungsbezirk, 98, 185, 187

Montgomery, Field-Marshal the Viscount, of Alamein, 148

Morgenthau Plan, 23

Moscow conference, *see* Foreign Ministers' Conferences

Mounier, Emmanuel, 179

MRP, *see* Popular Republic Movement

Müller, Gebhard, 224–25, 238–39, 240

Müller, Herbert, 212, 230

Muller, Charles, 168

Murphy, Robert, 3

Nation, La, 38

Nazi party: and Potsdam agreement, 152–53; membership as evidence of guilt, 157; distinction between *Will-* and *Muss-Nazis*, 160; and youth, 164–66; and war guilt, 180; and German administration, 183; success because of German apathy, 194. *See also* Denazification

Neubronner, Karl, 219

Neuer Mainzer Anzeiger, 201

Neues Leben: on denazification, 162; criticizes agrarian reform, 217; opposes Marshall Plan, 230; and trizonal fusion, 234; and federalism, 237

Neumayer, Fritz, 187, 211f

New German party, 191

New York Times, 71, 161

Niemöller, Pastor Martin, 162

North Atlantic Pact, 46, 64

Nuremberg trials, 152, 161

Occupation costs, 117–25; in French zone, 118 (Table 6); comparison in three zones, 121 (Table 8)

Occupation currency, 130